Alfred Watkins was born in Hereford in 1855. On leaving school, he was employed by his father as outrider or brewer's representative, a position which brought him an intimate knowledge of the local countryside and local customs and legends. Watkins was an enthusiastic early photographer, the inventor of much apparatus, including the pinhole camera and the Watkins exposure meter, which he manufactured through his own company in Hereford.

Watkins's revelation took place when he was sixty-five years old. While riding across the hills near Bredwardine, he perceived the existence of the ley system in a single flash. When his theory was published first in *Early British Trackways* in 1922 and then in *The Old Straight Track* in 1925, it caused violent controversy in archaeological circles. Watkins invites his readers to prove the ley system for themselves both with map and ruler and through investigation in the field.

ALFRED WATKINS

THE OLD STRAIGHT TRACK

Its Mounds, Beacons, Moats, Sites and Mark Stones

ABACUS edition published in 1974
by Sphere Books Ltd
30/32 Gray's Inn Road, London WC1X 8JL

First published in Great Britain
by Methuen & Co. Ltd 1925
Reprinted by Garnstone Press Ltd 1970

ISBN 0 349 13704 8

Set in Linotype Baskerville

Printed in Great Britain by Hazell Watson & Viney Ltd
Aylesbury, Bucks

PREFACE TO THE ORIGINAL EDITION

THE pleasant land which has been my field of work is bordered by a broken ring of heights looking inward over lesser wooded hills and undulations.

The Black Mountains, Radnor Forest, Longmynds, and Clee Hills; the Malvern Hills, "for mountains counted" loom a-row on the horizon, and round by May Hill, the Forest of Dean heights, to the Graig, and Skirrid Mountain, complete the circuit.

I know now that in fully half a century's familiar contact with this region my other self had, quite unknown to me, worked at one subject.

The "Spirit of the British Country-side"—the dedication to which ("GENIO TERRÆ BRITANNICÆ") Mr. Collingwood found inscribed on a Roman altar in North Britain—had surely been hovering near, and some four years ago there stood revealed the original sighting pegs used by the earliest track makers in marking out their travel ways.

Like Jim Hawkins in "Treasure Island," I held in my hand the key plan of a long-lost fact.

A previous booklet ("Early British Trackways"), in which I outlined this plan, was a somewhat breathless production, an amplified report of a lecture, with many constructional faults, and a few crude speculations on place-names. It was sent to press only five months after I had the first clue. That five months had been filled with strenuous field work; and now, when forty more months' work has been added, there is nothing in the main outline of that pioneer sketch to withdraw, but much—especially in the matter of beacons—to add. To make a legal comparison, I then opened the case, with little more evidence than what is usually put before a grand jury. The time has now come to put what I hope is a sufficiently complete logical case, with necessary evidence to prove it. And just as an assize case is often tedious on account of the necessity for routine evidence, I must ask indulgence towards a mass of detail.

As the time for an outline sketch is not yet, I should suggest to those who wish for one that after reading the introductory chapter they then take the final one before tackling—with discreet skipping—the bulk. But—this an aside for critics—I did not write the said last chapter until last.

What really matters in this book is whether it is a humanly designed fact, an accidental coincidence, or a "mare's nest," that mounds, moats, beacons, and mark stones fall into straight lines throughout Britain, with fragmentary evidence of trackways on the alignments.

A. W.

HEREFORD
August 1925

CONTENTS

LIST OF ILLUSTRATIONS

Figures preceded by an asterisk * appear within text pages

(*Photographs by Alfred Watkins. Diagrams and Sketches by W. H. McKaig*)

Note from the Publishers

Garnstone Press, who publish *The Old Straight Track, The View Over Atlantis, City of Revelation, Mysterious Britain, The Black Horsemen*, etc., would like to hear from anyone preparing a serious, well-researched contribution to the subject of leys, prehistoric sites, solar instruments, dowsing, standing stones, and 'nearly lost' knowledge in general. They are most welcome to send a synopsis or typescript, enclosing a stamped addressed envelope, to Michael Balfour, Garnstone Press Ltd., 59 Brompton Road, London, SW3 1DS. Catalogue available.

ALFRED WATKINS

A Note by John Michell

ANYONE living in Hereford during the early part of this century would have recognized Mr. Alfred Watkins, the distinguished local merchant, amateur archaeologist, inventor, photographer and naturalist, notorious in academic circles as the author of a heretical work, *The Old Straight Track.* Alfred Watkins was born in Hereford in 1855. For several generations his family had farmed land in the southern part of the county until about 1820, when his father moved to the city and started up in business as a miller, corn dealer and brewer. On leaving school, Alfred Watkins was employed by his father as outrider or brewer's representative, a position which brought him into close contact with the surrounding countryside and its inhabitants. In this way he gained an intimate knowledge of local topography and of the legends and customs embedded in a way of life which had undergone little change in the course of centuries.

Watkins was an enthusiastic early photographer, the inventor of much apparatus, including the pinhole camera and the Watkins exposure meter, which he manufactured through his own company in Hereford. Examples are preserved in the city's museum, together with a large collection of his photographic plates, illustrating many aspects of the Herefordshire landscape and the social order of the time. There also are kept the records of the Old Straight Track Club, a society, now moribund, founded to promote interest in Watkin's great archaeological discovery, the prehistoric 'ley' system of aligned sites.

In his Preface (page v) to *The Old Straight Track* Watkins wrote, "some four years ago there stood revealed the original sighting pegs used by the earliest track makers in marking out their travel ways." The revelation took place when Watkins was 65 years old. Riding across the hills near Bredwardine in his native county, he pulled up his horse to look out over the landscape below. At that moment he became aware of a network of lines, standing out like glowing wires all over the surface of the country, intersecting at the sites of churches, old stones and other spots of traditional sanctity. The vision is not recorded in *The Old Straight Track*, but throughout his life Watkins privately maintained that he had perceived the existence of the ley system in a single flash and, for all his subsequent study, he added nothing to his conviction, save only the realization of the particular significance of beacon hills as terminal points in the alignments.

Since Watkin's day our knowledge of prehistoric life and civilization has expanded to an extent which may be considered revolutionary. The implications of the work of Sir Norman Lockyer and, recently, of Professor Thom, relating to the mathematical and astronomical skill of the builders of Stonehenge and other stone circles, are so fundamental, that our whole concept of society in Britain 4,000 years ago should now be altogether different from that which obtained at the time when Watkins announced his discovery of leys. Fifty years ago the possibility of accurately surveyed alignments set out across the landscape was considered utterly remote, far beyond the capacity of the handful of painted savages who peopled the imaginary prehistoric Britain of orthodox archaeology. Today we know that stone and mound alignments were indeed set out over considerable distances, often directed towards mountain peaks, cairns, and notches, just as Watkins described. The expansion in antiquarian thought, now taking place, is due in no small measure to the insight, scholarship and determination of a provincial visionary, a true gnostic in that he preferred the evidence of his own senses and the voice of his own intuition to the unsupported assertions of authority.

The publication in 1922 of Watkin's address to the Woolhope Club of Hereford, *Early British Trackways*, followed in 1925 by *The Old Straight Track*, provoked a violent controversy, characterised on the part of Watkin's opponents by much ill natured abuse. Yet for many others *The Old Straight Track* awoke as it were the memory of a half familiar truth. Watkins invites his readers to prove the ley system for themselves both with map and ruler and through investigation in the field. Few who take him at his word fail to benefit from the experiment. Even those with no particular interest in antiquities and ancient history have enjoyed *The Old Straight Track* for the delightful account of a quest, which led Watkins through many curious byways both in his native landscape and in the realm of scholarship. The clear, modest style of *The Old Straight Track* has reminded some of Watkins's fellow countryman of the Welsh border, Parson Kilvert, for both invoked the same *genius terrae britannicae* from the red Herefordshire earth that inspired their mystic predecessors, Traherne and Henry Vaughan. There would be no poetry without heretics.

London, 1970 *John Michell*

INTRODUCTION BY ALFRED WATKINS

And felt the hillside thronged by souls unseen,
Who knew the interest in me, and were keen
That man alive should understand man dead.
—JOHN MASEFIELD: "Biography"

"WE sometimes feel" (wrote W. H. Hudson in "Hampshire Days") "a kinship with, and are strangely drawn to the dead, the long long dead, the men who knew not life in towns, and felt no strangeness in sun and wind and rain. In such a mood on that evening I went to one of those lonely barrows."

In such mood we crave to know more of the life and doings of the people who lived in Britain before the Romans came. The knowledge is not attained by the same type of evidence which builds up the history of the period after written language commenced in this land. No learned student poring over old records, on stone, vellum or paper, can give help from such source, for the guesses of old writers who lived after the period are worthless, unless based on archæological evidence which they specify.

Knowledge is only to be gleaned from three types of evidence. Firstly and chiefly from what exists or is recorded on or in the earth of the work or remains of man of that period. Secondly, from what can be gleaned and surmised in place-names and words, for it is often forgotten that words were spoken in Britain for more centuries before they were written down than there have been centuries of written record, and there are indications that many word elements come down through both periods. Thirdly, from folk-lore legends; lingering fragments of fact disguised by an overlay of generations of imaginings.

Logical deductions from the above three types of evidence have at least a sound basis, and although subject to human error, ought not to be dismissed by the mere facile use of the much overworked word "theory." It is, however, necessary to base such deductions on a considerable and widespread number of examples.

My main theme is the alignment across miles of country of a great number of objects, or sites of objects, of prehistoric antiquity. And this not in one or a few instances, but in scores and hundreds. Such alignments are either facts beyond the possibility of accidental coincidence or they are not. These lines of necessity include, and mix up in the first place, human efforts and place-names of widely different periods of time; it is the task of other branches of archæology to work out the full chronology of the matter, and I only attempt those few obvious deductions as regards periods which the mechanism of the sighted track reveals.

The title reveals the logical deduction arrived at—straight trackways in prehistoric times in Britain. Surprise has been expressed at the difference between this conclusion and that arrived at by a number of competent observers who have explored and written on such as the Pilgrims' Way, Stane Street, the Foss Way, and the Green and Ridge Ways. But a continuous change and alteration in roads and paths takes place every century, and scores of centuries have elapsed since the earliest prehistoric roads were made. It is a hopelessly impossible task to build up from an examination of our present ways, and of those fragments of old ones which can be traced, an outline of the first tracks which either preceded them, or from which they have evolved. The changes down the ages are too frequent and too many.

The most skilful observer, working only on tracks now traceable, and surmising what civilized man would do under certain circumstances, might, and I think really does, roughly reconstruct the tracks of mediaeval England, say, five or six centuries ago.

But this is not prehistoric England occupied by uncivilized man certainly ten times as long ago, and both the subject-matter and the starting point of this investigation are entirely different from those of the observers I refer to.

The old straight track decided the site of almost every branch of human communal activity, and brings the investigator into contact with many of the -ologys, for he must follow where the line leads, and, like the ball of thread in the legend of Queen Eleanor and Fair Rosamund, it leads to all kinds of spots. It therefore possibly reveals new facts in other branches of knowledge outside his ken. I try to avoid following these up, especially as regards religion. But human knowledge is not built into water-tight compartments, and it does not help real advance for an investigator to be "warned off" any reference to the several -ologys with which his subject makes contact.

Now to face the task set before the observer of to-day.

The outdoor man, away on a cross-country tramp, taking in the uplands, lingering over his midday sandwich on the earthwork of some hill-top camp, will look all round "to get the lay of the land." He will first pick out the hill points: this one bare to the top, another marked by a clump of trees, or less frequently by a single one. Sometimes one or more mounds or tumuli will stand out as pimples on a hill ridge against the skyline and he will remember similar ones which he has passed in his valley route, perhaps belted by a water moat, built for a purpose so obscure that no one had yet explained it. He will not fail also to look for any entrenched hill-top camp he may know, sometimes with blunt notches on the sky outline where the earthworks run, but only too often quite smothered by trees.

Those authors who have written most feelingly on these outdoor footprints of a long-past people, and have dwelt most upon the topography of three results of human effort —camps, mounds, and tracks—have hesitated the most to dogmatize about their origin. Mr. R. Hippisley Cox, in his inspiring book "The Green Roads of England," rightly links up all three as being part of the same investigation. Perhaps the fact that most of the mounds or barrows are found when excavated to be burial mounds has tended to obscure what this book is written to prove. Yet Mr. Hippisley Cox over and over again connects them with the trackways, and (as other observers have noticed) describes them as "occupying for the most part the skyline of the different ridges," how they might have served from Stonehenge "as eight lines for observing the stars," in other positions, "on the conspicuous point of a hill, as if to serve as a guide or direction post"; and again two conspicuous barrows are described as "useful landmarks, for there is hardly any part of the plain from which one or the other cannot be seen by mounting the nearest ridge. To the earliest inhabitants they must have been of assistance in finding the trackways across the downs."

Mr. Jowitt, one of the earlier writers on mounds, also points out that " Formed on the tops of the highest hills, or on lower but equally imposing positions, the grave-mounds commanded a glorious prospect—of many miles in extent—while they themselves could be seen from afar off in every direction by the tribes who had raised them."

The basis of this book, and of the plan and system which it demonstrates, lies in the early artificial mounds, and these, therefore—not the tracks—form the logical starting point. To start in this way is to work forward from primitive facts. To start from tracks now to be traced is not only to work backward, but from recent facts which are the result of complicated evolutions, and now show little trace of their origin.

One definition seems to be needed. A trackway is a path across country for man and horse, often with no more structure than made by the users' feet, but perhaps stoned or " pitched " in soft places.

Also an explanation. My subject is not that of Roman roads.

THE OLD STRAIGHT TRACK

CHAPTER I

MOUNDS

> Which mounds seem to have been originally intended as places of sepulture, but in many instances were afterwards used as strongholds, bonhills or beacon-heights, or as places on which adoration was paid to the host of heaven.
>
> —GEORGE BORROW: "Wild Wales"

UNLIKE tracks, mounds remain unaltered in site down the ages; in many cases practically unchanged in form. Their antiquity is undoubted, as for the past half-century a concentration of archæological energy devoted to exploring their burial contents has proved most of them to be pre-Roman. The word "mound" in this investigation does not mean a continuous ridge or embankment, but infers a separate heap of earth—or earth and stones, usually circular in form, but sometimes of a longer shape. The word is also used to infer an artificial structure, not a natural knowl, although such a natural high point was often emphasized by slight artificial addition, and then becomes included in the designation.

Lasting through scores of centuries of unwritten and written language, it is natural that many different names have become attached to such structures, and they are accordingly known by the names—Barrow, Burf, Butt, Cairn, Cruc, Garn, How, Knapp, Low, Mary, Moat, Moot, Mound, Mount, Toot, Tump, Tumulus, Twt. Also less distinctively as Burgh, Bury, Castle, Knowl; these last names being also used in other senses.

As regards size, Mr. Mortimer points out that Yorkshire

examples "range at the present time from 15 to 125 feet in diameter, and from a few inches to 22 feet in height." But he mentions one "flat-topped mound (mainly artificial) at the bottom of Garrowby Hill, 250 feet in diameter, and 50 feet high." Those in the district explored round Herefordshire have much the same range of size, and Silbury Hill, a famous Wiltshire mound, is said to be 130 feet high and to cover five acres.

Mounds cannot be erected without a supply of earth and stones, and a certain amount of this, quite sufficient in fact for a small mound, is provided by cutting a circular trench and throwing the contents inwards. A ditch is therefore usually round a mound, and in the case of a larger one it is often of considerable depth, and often fills with water. In some cases no such trench can be seen, but excavation shows that it existed once. In some, earth was brought from a distance, perhaps in hods, skippets, barrows, or other form of appliance, which may survive in some place-names. Near a river, gravel from its bed was often used. The Castle Hill at Hereford—a lofty mound on Wye bank—has completely vanished, and the reason is disclosed in a Quarter Sessions order late in the eighteenth century that "the gravel from the Castle Hill be sold." The mount in the marsh on the Edw at Hundred House, Radnor, is built of gravel.

As regards shape, the "long barrow" (few in number) is one type; the remainder are circular or slightly oval. In Herefordshire and surrounding counties the circular ones seem to be of two types—round-top and flat-top, the last by far the most numerous. A small ring earthwork, 15 yards diameter, at Chilston, Madley, is an exceptional form. The type mentioned by Wiltshire and Hampshire observers as disc-barrows are unknown here, with two exceptions on the Longmynd Hills.

In flat-topped mounds there seems to be every degree of transition, from the lofty structure in which the height of the mound seemed to be a primary object and the surrounding moat or ditch an incident, to the comparatively large area scarcely higher than the surrounding land, encircled by a moat. In this final stage (as it seems to me) the defensive ditch is the motive, and the slightly raised platform within a mere consequent result.

To make a homely present-day comparison between the varieties, they might be called the inverted flower-pot, the inverted baking-dish, the sponge round, and the pancake types. It is not easy to state a dividing line between mounds and moats, the last having evolved from the first.

The topographical position of many of these mounds has been touched upon in the Introduction, and is a fact which lies at the basis of my investigations and conclusions. Writer after writer notes how the mounds crown the heights, and are placed in such positions that they command views for long distances. Two grave-mounds between Deal and Dover, for example, one mile from the sea, are described ("Arch. Camb.," 1872) as "on the ridge of a high down and form conspicuous objects from great distances."

Our earliest epic, Beowulf, relates how a barrow was built "upon the cliff that was high and broad, by wave-farers widely seen." Observation shows that in such positions the mounds seen from lower places show as points against the skyline.

As a result of this skyline position mounds often cluster along the watershed or ridge of a mountain group. Ancient ridgeways also often run along and near the watershed, and, as many observers have noted, have mounds in close proximity to them. But these old ridge tracks are not there because they can be seen from below, but for the totally different reason that they provide easy travelling, and are often carefully arranged (as is noted by Messrs. Hubbard in regard to tracks on the Malvern ridge), so that travellers on them are hidden by the ridge from observers below. It will be noted in another chapter that most of the alignments through mounds are across the ridges, and not (as might at first be anticipated) along them.

Mr. E. S. Cobbold, in Vol. III of a valuable survey book on "Church Stretton" (1904), makes about a dozen references to the special position of the various Longmynd mounds as he describes them, thus: "Nearly on the summit of the hill"; "to be seen against the skyline from the side of the Boiling Well"; "situation a commanding one on the watershed"; "visible against the skyline when viewed from the north"; "position very striking, for the summit of the mound dominates a very wide stretch of country, and stands higher than the tops of any forest trees that would be likely to occupy any ground in the vicinity." This last observation is important as indicating a reason for the widely varying height of mounds, and the next writer I quote notices it a century earlier.

Thomas Stackhouse, in his book published in 1806 termed "Illustration of the Tumuli" (chiefly of Dorset), calling attention to their "systematic arrangement," notes that they are in positions of visual communication from one to another, "between the castles and the beacons, or between the temples and the nearest castle." He also remarks that "the magnitude and position of each barrow is determined by the point to which its visual line is directed, and not according to the dignity of the person interred in it. A barrow is never found larger than its station (that is, the point to which its visual line is assigned) requires."

There has been very little excavation of mounds in the Herefordshire district, and most of those done (Llanigon and St. Weonards excepted) appear to have been under unskilled supervision and not recorded. In these cases it is doubtful whether the explorers went below the natural ground surface and really tested if a primary burial existed. But in other parts of Britain the exploration of mounds has been extensive and skilled. There seems no doubt of a general conclusion that the very great majority of such mounds—even on the hill crests—were built, in the first place, over a human burial, and that other interments were added afterwards, often in succeeding ages.

Mr. J. R. Mortimer, who spent a long life in these investigations, does not appear to refer to any mound excavated which did not contain evidence of burial. But, on the other hand, Mr. R. Hippisley Cox says, "There are round barrows in which there are no signs of primary burials, and these are often the single barrows placed on conspicuous points along the trackways, where it is astonishing how well they are seen from many parts of the landscape." Mr. Hadrian Allcroft ("Arch. Journal," 1920, p. 248) also states that many ancient mounds have been built for some purpose other than burial.

In Herefordshire (the centre of the personal investigation recorded here) it is only as yet possible to name one mound which is on an alignment and has had its contents exhaustively explored. This is at St. Weonards, in a commanding position on a bank, and Mr. Thomas Wright in 1855 made such a careful examination and report that, although there is no intention to here treat fully on mound burial contents, this illustrates more fully than usual the probable procedure in the erection of a mound:

"The summit of the present mound is a circular platform about 76 feet in diameter" (a recent measurement made it a rough oval, as are most flat-topped mounds, about 60 by 75 feet, the axis north and south). A cutting was made through it. Two interments were found, both alike in character, one a central one. "It appeared evident that the whole of the ashes of the funeral pile had been placed on the ground at this spot, and that a small mound of fine earth had been raised over them, upon which had been built a wide roof or vault of large rough stones." (Then followed a careful description and illustration of different layers of earth.) "It is evident therefore that when the small mounds roofed with stones had been raised over the deposits of ashes, a circular embankment was next formed round the whole; and from this embankment the workmen filled up the interior mounds towards the centre." This description should only be taken as applying to flat-top mounds of large diameter; the sections of round mounds given by other investigators do not show the same structure.

Three mounds I have found with their flat top enclosed by a low bank or rim of earth, or earth and stones. At Orcop mound, about 18 feet high (its top 20 by 17 yards), the broken rim or parapet is now only about 1 foot high. The taller mound at Llancillo—quite near the church—is about 25 feet high, the top 16 by 13 yards, with remains of the parapet up to 5 feet high; in places there are gaps in it; the top is rather hollow, with a full-grown oak in its centre. Both these are valley mounds close to a stream from which a leat has fed the deep moat (at Orcop still water filled) round the mounds. But at the most perfect of the rimmed mounds—Caple Tump (Fig. 1) adjoining King's Caple Church—the situation is on a bank, and no trench or moat remains. This one has an almost complete ring bank enclosing its flat top (Fig. 2), 2 feet high, with five elms growing in the bank encircling the flat circular dancing floor of 24 yards across from parapet to parapet; and here, as explained elsewhere, the village fête round the mound, with dancing on its top, is still kept up in Whitsun week. It is about 10 feet high and the parapet has three gaps.

There is a good deal of evidence (see Chapters VI and XVII) that many large mounds are often enlargements of a small primary mound, and that this enlargement did not always take the primary mound as a centre, but enlarged to one side, so that the whole of the first moat need not be filled up. I found indications of actual tracks to one side of the two barrows (Figs. 58 and 60) at Eardisland, and Lingen Castle Mound suggests enlargement on one side. In Homer's "Iliad" (Book XXIII), Achilles gives detailed instructions for the burning of the body of Patroclus and the collection of the bones:

> Let these, between a double layer of fat
> Enclosed, and in a golden urn remain
> Till I myself shall in the tomb be laid;
> And o'er them build a mound, not over-large
> But of proportions meet; in days to come,
> Ye Greeks, who after me shall here remain,
> Complete the work, and build it broad and high.

Note that here a subsequent burial and an after-enlargement of the mound is part of the plan.

The approximate date of a mound is important. Unfortunately, of our Herefordshire mounds only one (St. Weonards) has been efficiently explored and reported upon. The round-top type are usually set down by experts to belong to the Bronze Age.

Most of the Herefordshire mounds are of the flat-top variety, as at Chanston, near a stream which fed the moat by a leat still traceable, and at Buttas, Canon Pyon, on a bank with no trace of a moat.

While mounds are the first basis of this matter, my main theme is that of alignments, and these, as applied to mounds, are treated in the next chapter.

CHAPTER II

ALIGNMENT OF MOUNDS

Forth the earls proceeded through a great wood, and marked a way that over a mount lay.

—LAYAMON'S "Brut"

IN the district under investigation the mounds, or "tumps" as they are called on the Welsh border, are, as a rule, few and far between. But they do align with each other and their fellow-structures—moats—and also with other sites of antiquity.

To take a first example, stretching east and west across the border-line of South Radnorshire and West Herefordshire. It is a border-line of change; geological, between the Silurian and Old Red formations; physical, between rugged but not barren mountainous ranges, and the fertile undulations of Herefordshire; political, between the Celts and Mercians. Two alignments, chiefly of earthworks, cross on a ring mound at an acute angle, and both lines (A and B) are shown in Fig. 3. Taking A from its eastern (Welsh) end, it has an initial point in the lofty hill point Wylfre, a name meaning beacon (1,346 feet), and passing in succession through Cregrina Church and adjacent mountains Glascwm Hill and Black Hill (both over 1,700 feet), and through three of the scattered homesteads, it hits the first and the grandest of the mounds. Very appropriate seems its name, Turret Tump (Fig. 8), when first seen from the deep valley, so close beneath. The local informant, who referred to it as a "twt" (pronounced *toot*), also indicated its obvious purpose as a look out station. About 25 feet high, it has no trench at its foot; its slightly hollow top—suggesting a low earthen wall—is oval (17 by 12 yards), and the trees occupying it include three Scotch firs. To the east the eye is carried to the next ridge, two miles away, and exactly at the point which the map shows the alignment to cross is a solitary Scotch fir amongst other trees.

" The Camp," so called on the map, is the next on the line. But although high up overlooking the broad elbow of the Wye Valley, where it bends round the distant heights of Merbach, it is now little more than a circular moat (65 yards across), faintly to be seen in the pasture. Within, the ground rises a little, but with only the suggestion of a tump in the south-east corner. Yet it is the crossing point of two alignments. There comes up towards it, leaving the village of Eardisley near the Lower House, a third track, which the old people call the Corpse Road. The nearest farm is the Cross Farm—probably a crossing point of trackways, not, as I once supposed, the site of a wayside cross.

Descending to the plain, now comes a conical flat-top mound locally called the Batch Twt (Fig. 9), and although

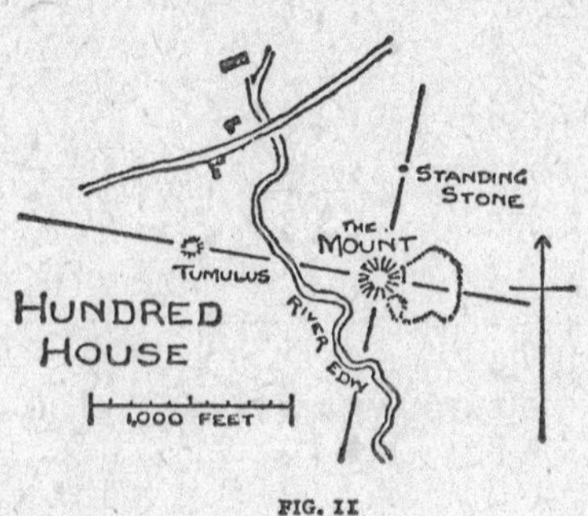

FIG. 11

it is in a hollow dingle—the Batch—it is seen across the level plain. Very different is the last to be shown on this alignment. Hell Moat, in Sarnesfield Coppice, is a strange irregular leaf-shaped moated enclosure, about 100 yards by 65 yards. The ground within is not higher than that without, and the earth from the moat on the western side is thrown outwards to form an embankment. Yet it aligns with the others, and might once have contained a mound.

Going back to alignment B on the same plan, the first on the east is in the heart of the Radnorshire Hills near Hundred House. There are two mounds near the hamlet, only 330 yards apart (Fig. 11), and the alignment passes through both. The first is the smaller one, described (433) in the Report for Radnorshire of the Ancient Monuments

Commission. It has been twice opened, and proved to be a burial mound, with cist not later than the Bronze Age, and with subsequent interments.

Just across the little River Edw, in a flat marsh, is The Mount (Fig. 7), a fine gravel mound fully 25 feet high, and with an oval top about 10 by 20 yards, its axis being north-west. Alongside it to the east is a camp enclosure or bailey, but the mound, like almost every one of its type, is a distinct structure, its ditch encircling it, and not even bridged by the earthwork of the bailey. It is not mentioned in the above report, although one of the largest and most complete in Radnorshire. A standing stone 170 yards distant (now inexplicably blown into several pieces by a quarryman's charge) indicates the direction of a cross ley. The alignment then passes over the heights (about 1,574 feet) of Little Hill, and through a small camp earthwork above Glascwm village, through the lonely mountain church of Colva, and on—most of this being at the twelve or thirteen hundred feet level—to "The Camp," previously described, above Eardisley. Then quickly descending to levels of 500 and 400 feet, it strikes the "Moat" at Lemore. This is a low mound, alike in structure and diameter, but differing only in height to the twts and tumps. The trench has been used for water, but is dry now. The alignment next goes through the fine moated mound adjoining Almeley Church. In dimensions this stands about 25 feet above the moat, which is 8 feet deep. The top, almost circular, is 12 by 13 yards, fairly flat, with no signs of edge walling of earth. The natives call it Ameley Twt to distinguish it from the Batch Twt, but in the maps it is labelled "castle." Adjoining are slight earthworks, suggesting occupation, and, as usual with these moated mounds, the brook is near by, although at much lower level. Across country again the invisible line goes, straight as a gun barrel throughout, and hits the final item in this present record, Sarnesfield Church, where, close to the tower and porch, there lies buried John Abel, builder of famous timber houses and town halls, and master carpenter to King Charles I. Up aloft nesting holes for pigeons line the walls of the bell chamber. Need it be pointed out that "sarn" is Celtic (and Welsh) for causeway or road? There is a Little Sarnesfield a mile away, where several tracks cross.

Every mound marked on the one-inch Ordnance map within the area of these two alignments is marked on this outline map, and it will be seen that there are only four surplus ones which do not align, while nine earthworks or mounds come into alignment.

The right-hand part of this map is reproduced in Fig. 12, on larger scale from the one-inch map, to show how exact the alignment is; and in this area it will be noted that all mounds align; there is no surplus which do not.

Another clear example is to be found in a Radnorshire valley of the Lugg near Pilleth. Unlike the last series, which stretched across mountain, hill, and vale, this one keeps along a river valley. It again happens that two alignments at an angle cross at a mound, and both can be shown conveniently in one illustration (Fig. 4). The mound first on the east in alignment A is Bleddfa Mount, moated and with a court, then two unnamed mounds in the valley, and Whitton Church, the alignment being sighted on Hell Peak, a thousand feet point 3 miles farther on. Alignment B passes through three unnamed valley mounds and Castel Foelaltt. This last is a moated and tree-clad mound about 20 feet high from the ditch, its top about 10 yards in diameter; there is an earthwork enclosure or bailey attached. Some 10 miles to the west this alignment passes through one of the three or four Radnorshire spots known as Bailey-bedw, or the "enclosure of the graves." To the east it exactly aligns with the mount of Lingen Castle, and then to a terminal in the north edge of the great camp of Croft Ambury, these being 7 and 12 miles from Pilleth.

The Radnorshire Commissioners of the Ancient Monuments Survey, speaking of the four unnamed valley mounds (which are ranged in the field of battle between Owen Glendwr's forces and Edward Mortimer in 1402), and noting their disturbed appearance (two of them are "long" mounds), say that "they have none of the characteristics of early tumuli" and think that the popular opinion that they are the burial mounds of those who fell in the battle is true. Their alignment is against this supposition.

Mr. E. S. Cobbold throws a possible light on this matter. He surmises that Dr. Dee (astrologer to Queen Elizabeth) probably excavated many of the tumuli in the Longmynds,

ALFRED WATKINS

TRACK SIGHTED ON NOTCH, LLANTHONY

CAPLE TUMP

FIG. I. MOUND ADJOINING KING'S CAPLE CHURCH

FIG. 2. ITS FLAT TOP, WITH EARTH WALLING, USED FOR DANCING

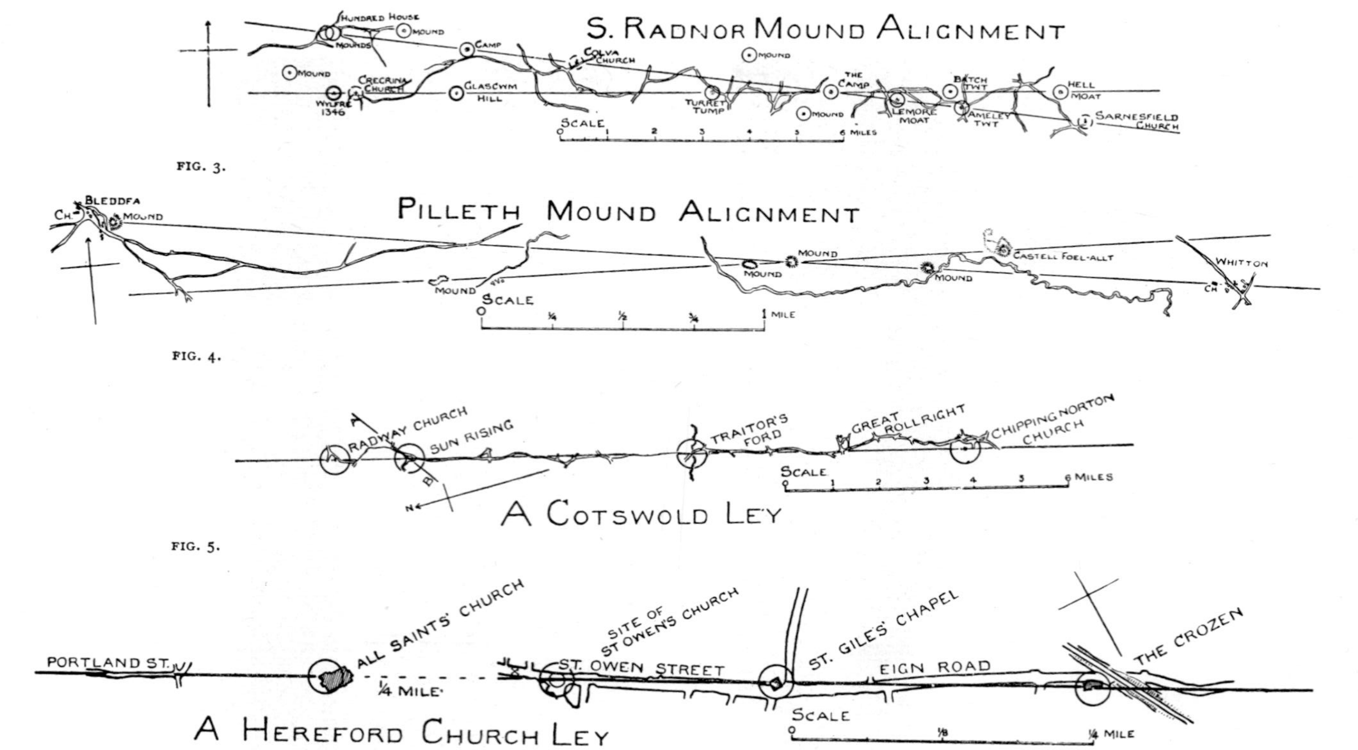

FIG. 3.

FIG. 4.

FIG. 5.

FIG. 6.

MOUNDS.

FIG. 7. HUNDRED HOUSE MOUNT, MOAT AND CAMP VALLUM

FIG. 8. TURRET TUMP, MICHAELCHURCH-ON-ARROW

MOUNDS

FIG. 9. THE BATCH TWT, AMELEY

FIG. 10. CAPLER CAMP, AT EASTERN ENTRANCE

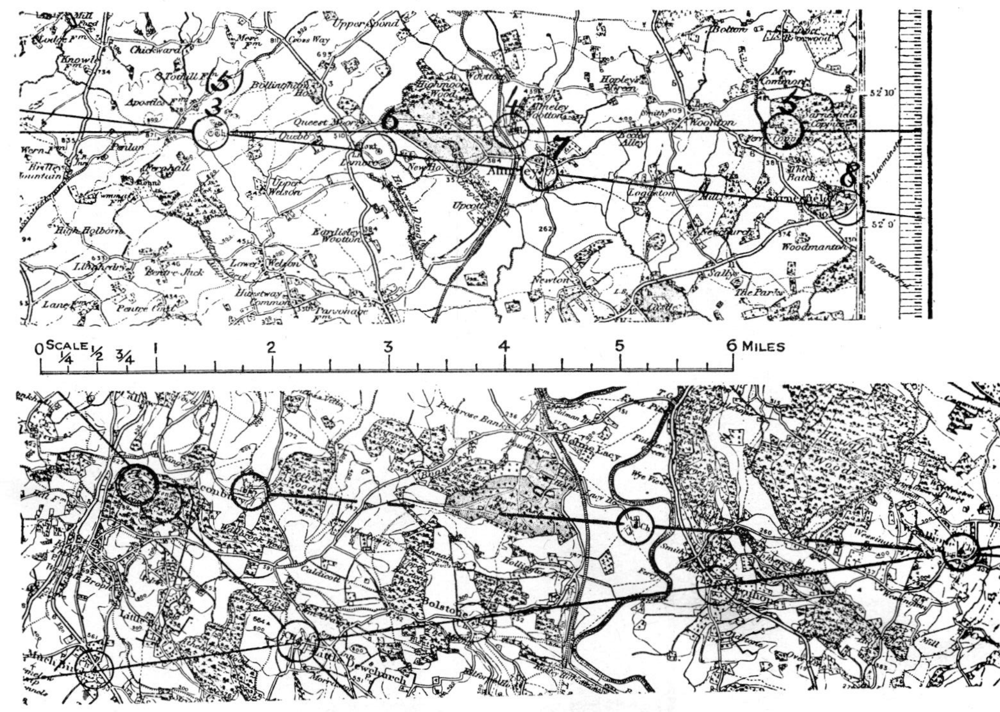

FIG. 12. PART OF SOUTH RADNOR MOUND ALIGNMENT

FIG. 13. CHURCH LEYS, WOOLHOPE AND ACONBURY

ARTHUR'S STONE, DORSTON

FIG. 14. GREEN WAY SIGHTED TO AND BEYOND THE MOUND   FIG. 15. NEAR VIEW FROM THE SOUTH

as he certainly presented a petition to Lord Burleigh for a grant of such hidden treasure as he might find. Now, Dr. Dee lived at Nant-y-Groes, from which the disturbed mounds are only about a mile distant. In the area included in this plan there is no mound which does not come into these alignments.

In the four examples of mound alignment just given there are several lessons from the facts which carry us a stage on towards a logical conclusion. Almost all the mounds marked on the Ordnance maps in the areas included line up. Accidental coincidence requires a surplus. Secondly, four other types of sites decided by man also come into alignment, namely, camps, churches, castles, and ancient homesteads. Thirdly, there are instances of the alignments going to lofty natural hill points.

Other observers have noted similar mound alignments. Mr. Allcroft speaks of three ring earthworks at Thornborough (Ripon), in a straight line. Between two of them, also in line, is a large barrow "Centre Hill." Mr. Lukis, who excavated it, found it to contain one interment (p. 571).

In the Avenbury map of Mr. Hippisley Cox's book, which embodies a plan of the barrows in the district, about ten separate alignments, each of not less than four barrows, can be found, but not along the ridgeways. The author also points out and illustrates (p. 53) that at Knowlton three mounds align, and point to the ruined church in the centre of a circular earthwork. Other cases of three mounds aligning near camps can be found in the plans of Oldbury, Whitesheet, Badbury, and Chanctonbury.

Admiral Boyle Somerville ("Archæologia," Vol. LXXIII, p. 216), makes it clear that two barrows in the Isle of South Uist, namely, Barp Frobost and North Frobost Barp, lie "on the exact Meridian line (north and south) which passes through the conspicuous (and cairned) summits of two hills, Reineval and Askervein."

Long barrows being very rare in my district, I have but little data concerning them. But the Long Barrow 1½ miles south-east of Stonehenge aligns with (and is oriented to all the points mentioned) Long Barrow Cross Roads (adjacent to it), two of the smallest tumuli in the "Winterbourne Stoke Group," two other small tumuli, and Fargo Down Barn, all shown on the six-inch map containing Stonehenge.

And the long barrow in the Pilleth map is oriented to the adjacent Litton Hill.

The next example—Arthur's Stone (Figs. 14 and 15)—seems at first sight out of place in this chapter. It is of that type of megalithic monument, the only one in Herefordshire, which used to be called a cromlech, but now (to be in conformity with Continental authorities) a dolmen, a huge altar-like stone, poised on upright pillar stones. It is now known that dolmens were the central chambers of one type of mound, not frequent in England; and it is as a mound, aligning with other objects and with trackways, it is here treated.

Approaching it along its striking upland green way (it stands on a broad hill ridge at 900 feet altitude), it seems strange that the fact of its being partly on and originally within a mound has not been described, for much of the earth of the mound and its base outline is still there, and the floor of the monument is well above the natural soil level. The spiked iron railings which now outline the mound are deplorable. The outline is round, for it was not a "long" barrow.

It can be approached by trackways from three directions, and in each the last 200 yards of the way is sighted precisely on the mound, as is well illustrated in Fig. 14, where the backbone of the track, its diversion to go round the mound, and its getting back in alignment on the other side, as seen by the skyline gap formed by the hedges lining the broad green way, is, I think, entirely convincing. The straight track in this picture, if extended on the map, goes through Newton Tump, 1¾ miles away to the west (the only mound marked on this quarter sheet of the six-inch map), and Bodcott Barn, half a mile to the east. The other present-day track, through a gate and along a hedge to the south, aligns through Dorston Church, a mile away, and northward in a full mile to The Knapp, a well-known point of 700 feet elevation above Bredwardine.

A third ley goes through ancient homesteads, Eardisley Castle moat and Snodhill Castle. Another ley from the Cefn Hill goes through the Golden Well, the Gold Post, and Bredwardine Castle. This (being at Midsummer sunrise angle) is detailed in Chapter XIV.

It requires no strained logic to show that man must have

made these alignments. Many of them are for long distances across country, and no actual line could have been stretched over such a distance. There is only one method, and it is one highly developed in primitive people—by sighting; and the practical way is to start such a sighted line by going to the top of the highest available hill; hence the natural hill peak in the alignment. Trained sight (in air not polluted by smoke) easily picks out a distant hill peak 60 miles away, and dropping the eye in the line it falls upon many intermediate hill ridges; hence the mounds or marking points in alignment on these ridges.

Subsequent chapters will provide data indicating why and how such work was carried out.

It should be noted that these and other alignments are, and must be, exact and precise through the mark-points; "close to" must never be accepted. The sighting method is just as exact as the aiming of a gun, bringing the two sights and the object into line.

For the rest of this book, an alignment—and each one is as distinct an organism from another as is one tree from another—will be called a "ley." Reasons for the name will be found in the place-name chapter; but even if the name is a mistaken one, this in no way weakens the fact of the thing named. The difficulties in tracing or proving mound alignments in those districts in which burial mounds are thick on the ground are referred to in Chapter XXVII.

CHAPTER III

LEYS IN RADNOR VALE

> I am told that there are people who do not care for maps, and find it hard to believe. The names, the shapes of the woodlands, the courses of the roads and rivers, the prehistoric footsteps of man still distinctly traceable up hill and down dale, the mills and the ruins, the ponds and the ferries, perhaps the *Standing Stone* or the *Druidic Circle* on the heath ; here is an inexhaustible fund of interest for any man with eyes to see, or tuppence worth of imagination to understand with.
>
> —R. L. STEVENSON : Note concerning " Treasure Island "

TO give selected examples of leys in different districts might possibly be less convincing than to take one compact district, mark on its map all the ley sighting points, and then illustrate and describe all—or the greater part—of the ley system in the area.

I attempt this as regards the eastern end of Radnor Vale.

The Vale of Radnor, or Radnor Bottom as natives call it, is something between a plain and a valley. Of a rough oval, 4½ miles in length, and about 2½ miles across, its gravel soil indicates a laıge spread of inland waters hereabouts. There is some 200 feet difference in level between the bottle-neck valley where the Summergill Brook enters it near New Radnor and where it flows out at Ditch Yeld Bridge—the " ditch " is Offa's Dyke—which crosses here. Owing to this gravel bed, the Summergill (an English name in a Welsh country) has a trick of disappearing underground for pieces of its course, a fact referred to in the Welsh name for New Radnor, Maesyfed.

Few hill groups are so striking as that which breaks the skyline in the Herefordshire side of the Vale. It is the edge of the Old Red Sandstone beds. A push up from molten matter below has made a sharp-pointed jumble of different formations, two or three of the hills being solid igneous rock, folds of limestone between, and beyond are the older Silurian beds in the huge mountain mass of Radnor Forest.

To see this border group, which range from 1,000 to 1,300 feet, it is well to walk out of Kington town on to Hergest Ridge, and from this height one can tell off the individual hills. And what splendid names they bear! Beginning with Hanter (the hill jutting out of Hergest Ridge) come Old Radnor Hill, Worsell, close under one's feet, Stanner with its jagged outline and Devil's Chair and Garden on the top, and Radnor Forest in the distance. Then a peep of Burfa, with its camp, the pointed Herrock, Knill Garraway, working round to Bradnor. The same group shows to almost equal advantage from within the Vale, as will be seen in Fig. 16.

The air—playing down from the Forest—is like wine all over Radnor Bottom, and folk from the more relaxing plains of Herefordshire come for a brace-up to such quarters as the " Eagle " or " King's Arms " at New Radnor, or to one of the roomy farm-houses which abut on the plain at Walton, Burfa, The Bage, and other spots.

The area is rich in two types of marking points—mounds in the first place; these not so thick together (as in some of the southern counties) but that they are all easily proved to be sighting points on leys. The other class is that of standing stones, or mark stones, and the examples given will serve to introduce to the reader this type of way-mark, and the facts demonstrated regarding them will, it is claimed, afford proof of their early purpose.

Dominating the Vale to the north, but out of our map, is the huge mass of Radnor Forest—a treeless sheep walk. Shaped like a starfish, it rises to well over 2,000 feet, and a deep and beautiful mountain glen—the Harley Valley—runs up into the heart of it from a spot beyond New Radnor. Its lofty skyline, as seen from the vale (Fig. 17), is a simple one, with only a conical rounded hill—the Whimble—as a natural mark-point for the traveller afar off. But close examination will show six mounds, to be seen from every part of the Vale as pimples. One only, that most to the right, is named on the Ordnance map—Stanlow Tump—a stony " low " with fir trees. The Ordnance map indicates no more, but they are there, and a personal examination proved four of the others to be tumuli (Fig. 18 illustrates two of them). One is on the 2,000 feet ridge marked as The Bach Hill (pronounced " bage "), another near it to the right, then nearer to the Whimble two more, the larger one, known as the Black Mixen, although the Ordnance map marks that name quite incorrectly for a ridge $1\frac{1}{2}$ miles away in the heart of the Forest. " Mixen " is an old word meaning scrap-heap or dung-heap, and " black " a generic title dealt with in the Ley Man chapter. There is a hill point called the Black Dunghill in Western Dartmoor.

These mounds lie in a serpentine line along the ridge, and not only is there no ridge track at present, but there probably never was, for the topographical position makes a ridge track here lead nowhere. It is an example which tells against the supposition that skyline mounds were guides for the ridgeways. It is also an example of another fact peculiar to skyline mounds. A mountain ridge is not —here or elsewhere—a knife edge, but barrel shaped, and a mound on the highest part cannot be seen (unless very lofty) from a fairly low point, such as a ford in the valley. To be so seen it must be slightly down the slope. Now these six or seven Radnor Forest tumuli are to be seen from almost all parts of the Vale ; but it was noted that on ascending a height (Smatcher) on the other side, two of them were no longer on the skyline, but could just be discerned on the flank of the mountain. It is scarcely noticeable in walking along the mountain that they are not on the highest part, but they are not. Yet they are so cleverly placed that most of them can be seen from the Forest uplands on the north. The men who placed these mounds were experts at very special work. There is some record of the cairn (it is not a tumulus) on Whimble being of recent piling, but it is on a peak which most certainly was in itself a sighting point.

There are at least five unworked stones in New Radnor town which marked the prehistoric tracks. The largest, at the corner of the Bank House, another at the blacksmith's shop near The Cross. A third at a corner of the King's Arms Inn, and this, with a fourth in the paddock behind, mark a track lying on the Station-Smatcher road and through the church. A fifth—all are of a rounded, not pointed, shape—now decorates the " Old Vicarage " wall.

The townlet of New Radnor, nestling under the steep slope of Radnor Forest is, and always has been, dominated by its Castle Tump, which almost overhangs its chief street. It is an artificial mound, notwithstanding a statement to the contrary, and is perched on a spur of the hill plateau. The author of "Radnorshire" in the Cambridge Series of County Geographies is right when he refers to the Castle as "originally built by Harold Godwin on Radnor Tump in 1064." Its lining up shows that it was there long before Norman times, and Fig. 20, photographed from a high slope behind it, shows its artificial character.

Standing on its apex, Old Radnor Church can be seen nearly three miles away on its granite hill, with an avenue of trees precisely in the sight line leading to it. This ley is K on the ley map. It passes through Harpton Court, and through the Broad Leasow Wood it lies precisely on a present-day broad drive through the woodland. The word leasow (pronounced *lezzow*) frequently occurs as a name for fields or enclosures in many counties. Then up a wide avenue of ash trees (Fig. 19) to Old Radnor Church, which local tradition says was a beacon church. The moat or camp behind the church is not on this ley, which lies on an ancient lane and over the middle of Old Radnor Hill. The ley could not have been used without a sighting point on this hill, and two exploratory visits discovered the remains of two small tumuli, one in about the right position. They stand, much eaten up by rabbit burrows, on each side of the present track, about 35 yards apart, now only about 20 inches high, and a few yards in diameter. Then the ley lies precisely on Gore Barn, a crossing point with another ley; then, out of the map, down the valley until it reaches the neck on which Kington town now stands. Here it passes over a mound which is the reputed site of Kington Castle. It passes in succession through a cross-road called Woonton Ash, a moat close to the high road at Little Sarnesfield, and the mound of Weobley Castle.

Although the description so far chiefly applies to the western (New Radnor) end of the Vale, the folding ley map (Fig. 22) is of the eastern end only. Of the several prehistoric stones in this area, the Four Stones group (Fig. 23), not far from Harpton Court, is the most interesting. As mentioned in my earlier book, I found indications that these stones are arranged as sighting stones for several tracks crossing at the point. They are the right height and shape for this, and it is theoretically possible to arrange them for indicating five crossing tracks. I outlined two, the most important (a piece of it on the ley map is marked D) being from Bach Hill (tumulus), through the " Stones," exactly on the road through Walton village, and other bits of main road at Eccles Green and Upperton, Kenchester Court, bordering Magna Camp on the south-west (see Fig. 83), and deciding its outline; then on a straight bit of road, and over the Wye through Breinton Church.

The tallest stones in the group are man-high; the shortest one was evidently arranged as a pointer. The suitability of the tops of these stones for indicating the direction of trackways is evidence of highly skilled work in their erection. One pair points out ley S in the folding map, but a full survey of the use of these signposts must be postponed.

Local legend tells that four kings are buried at the Four Stones, and if you stamp on the ground between them it sounds hollow. Fifty years ago I was told at the " Crown " at Walton, " They do say as how when the Four Stones hear the sound of Old Radnor bells they go down to Hindwell Pool to drink." There's the same yarn told about the Whetstone on Hergest Ridge, a mark stone you can see with a glass from the high road at the Gore Chapel, but the cock has to crow, and it is down at the brook the stone takes its drink.

In the folding ley map an attempt is made to show the full detail over a limited area, and it comprises two quarter sheets of a six-inch Ordnance map. There are great difficulties in adequately illustrating leys, as anything to show their full length is a mere diagram; and yet in the limited area as attempted, only such a small section of each ley (there are nineteen shown lettered A to S) that it cannot amount to full proof. All undoubted sighting points (mounds and stones) given on the map are ringed, whether a ley is found through them or not; one important mound which is not marked on the Ordnance map—that at Barland which has a complete bailey locally called Bandy Green—is ringed. The mounds number twelve, and there is also one mound site ringed, which is now occupied by a group of Scotch firs (illustrated in Fig. 21). Of the ten stones ringed, only three were marked on the Ordnance map, the others being found by personal survey.

About half the mounds are round-top, and the rest more

or less flat-top. The one behind Old Radnor Church is more like a moated enclosure than a mound, but is yet a raised platform. The fine one at Womaston, too smothered with trees to make illustration possible, has a complete moat, about 10 feet wide, filled with water; its flat top has a diameter of 21 by 19 yards, and it is about 14 feet high. Castle Nimble is given in the survey of the Ancient Monuments Commission as a Norman motte and bailey, but the "bailey" is the enclosure of a cottage homestead and garden which has "gone down" only a few score years ago, and I picked up on the mound (which is quite of a usual burial type) a piece of flaked chert which I feel sure indicates prehistoric occupation. Two of the mounds near Hindwell (both marked on the Ordnance map) are almost obliterated by cultivation. Six of them have a homestead (or the remains of one) nestling close up against them.

An interesting feature of the investigation of the stones was that the line of their sharpest point or top edge (none of them are worked) usually indicated the principal ley.

Thus, finding a stone in a meadow near a cart track, beyond Barland, and walking round it to get the sharpest outline, the compass direction of this was taken. I had no idea of what ley it was on, but afterwards applying the observed angle to the six-inch map, it went exactly through the two nearest mounds and formed ley B, which, being short, can be given complete between its two initial points as follows: Bach Hill (tumulus; Fig. 18), Kinnerton mound, Evenjobb (school) mound, mark stone near Barlands, 858 hill point north of Titley.

Another interesting observation regarding the above point was made at the fine standing stone in ley C, illustrated in Fig. 24.

Its sharpest outline was in the direction of the sharp outlined Burfa Camp, which, as is seen in the photograph, it seems to match in shape—two knobs. Not only does this line pass precisely through the tumulus at "The Bogs" (hidden in the photograph) but through a cottage, shown in the picture with a tree. And the name of this cottage is Knobley! It is a lesson in place-name derivation. This ley (the knob-ley), after going over Burfa Point, passes through Titley Church and Eardisland Moat (Fig. 60).

A similar stone—the one on ley A—is shown in Fig. 25,

in comparison with the similar shape of the Whimble hill point on Radnor Forest, but the ley on the map is not in that direction.

Ley M was discovered by noticing that Old Radnor Church aligned in the distance with a piece of the road up to Barlands, and after this observation it was found that the ley passed through Womaston moated mound, Walton cross-roads, a length of road, and a mark stone at the gate of Stockwell Farm (where there is an ancient spring), before getting to the church. This ley passes through Presteign Church, and is at a midsummer sunrise angle (49° E. of N.), as is also ley I (50° E. of N.).

An extremely interesting rock outcrop (not a mark stone) on ley L, shown in Fig. 26 and marked on the map as " boulder," was found to align with two mounds and a mark stone by the roadside in Walton village; also to pass through the homestead of Burfa Farm. This was marked on the map before visiting the farm. Then Lt.-Col. Symonds Taylor (agent for the estate) reported a fine mark stone at Burfa, and on visiting it I found that the line which (on other evidence) I had marked on the six-inch map went precisely through it. The rock outcrop must have been a primary point (I have marked it as such), and was presumably a station for assembly or Druidical practices. The terminal at the north-east end is Cole's Hill, and at the other end it precisely strikes the camp above Glascwm.

S is another ley over this rock, through Castle Nimble tumulus, the Four Stones, and confirmed by about 1½ miles of present road on or approximating to it. Off the map to the south it is sighted on Hanter as its initial point.

Leys D, F, H, J, K, M, and P lie on pieces of present road or cart track.

One of the most important features of this map is that two straight line portions of Offa's Dyke appear to be decided by leys O and Q. The first aligns through Castle Ditches, Evenjobb mound, Hindwell Pool, and the mark stone at Stockwell Farm; the second through Barlands Mound, over Burfa Camp (Fig. 22), the White House, and lies on a short piece of the county boundary. It would be perfectly natural, however much the dyke took up its own course, that here and there, if it came on a pre-existing track, this would border it as long as it suited its purpose. Another comparatively straight bit of the dyke—that pointed towards Burfa Farm and camp—although it has no convincing alignment in this small area map, does align with moats at Sarnesfield Coppice and Mansel Lacy.

Further proof that Offa's Dyke does for certain follow pre-existing sighted tracks on bits of its course is to be found in Mr. J. H. Hewlett's book on Offa's Dyke. Here it is asked, " What is the explanation of that remarkable feature the conical mound which stands on the dyke near Mellington Hall, said by local tradition to be an old armoury ? " The mound is elsewhere described as about 30 feet in height, with a round and flat top, and now covered with trees. The explanation is that this is a sighting mound on an earlier track, which the dyke here follows. Mr. Hewlett also describes that in the Shropshire Hills north of Knighton " occurs the second of the dyke's two right-angled turns, and the turn, beyond which the front wall does not go, is marked by a conical mound some 6 feet high standing on that wall." This is a still more striking example ; two leys crossing at a sighting mound, and the dyke appropriating in its winding course fragments of both leys or tracks, and therefore turning on the mound.

Evenjobb Church is modern and not ringed in the map ; nor is Kinnerton Church, for although on a good ley (Bleddfa Mound, Ednol Church to Kinnerton Mound) only two mark points fall on this map.

As regards ponds, leys pass through six (Hindwell Pool is on three tracks), and there are three cases of leys bordering ponds.

In summing up the results on this map it must be kept in mind that the area is not large enough for conclusive results. The average length of a ley in it is 3¼ miles, and as surviving mark points on leys barely average one to a mile (often much less), not many of the leys in it would be likely to have " four point " evidence, below which number coincidence might creep in.

There is a chance, therefore, of two or three of those marked being " mare's nests " ; and on the other hand I know of several good long-distance leys omitted because chance has not left three mark points within this area map. I have indicated outside confirmation to several of the leys, and could quote more for leys E, N, and Q. Leys D, K, and R have not much evidence on this map, but have been inserted because the outside marking points for them are numerous, and they are quoted in this and other chapters.

The main object of this chapter is to illustrate, firstly, how thick the "old straight tracks" were on the ground; secondly, how few and far between are the fragments remaining of present-day roads or tracks on the leys, but how they do occur convincingly; thirdly, the important part played by stones marking the way on the track.

CHAPTER IV

MARK STONES

> Through the mist the light glides away. Nearer comes the formless shadow, and the visible earth grows smaller. The path has faded, and there is no means on the open downs of knowing whether the direction pursued is right or wrong, till a boulder which is a landmark is perceived.
>
> —RICHARD JEFFRIES: "Open Air"

NO one can investigate leys in the field for long without being convinced that the way was planted at intervals with stones, which by their size, shape, or appearance, different from stray local ones, made assurance to the wayfarer that he was on the track. This has been partially expounded in the chapter on Radnor Vale. The usual characteristic of a prehistoric mark stone is that it is unworked, although of selected shape. Naturally they are placed on, or alongside, the track. The smallest are only a foot or so high, either pudding shape or flat-topped. Figs. 28 and 30 show a couple discovered when tracing the exact line of a ley (partly lying on a visible ancient trench or track) from Hereford to Cascob. There was often one at a ford or ferry, as at Shrewsbury (Fig. 31), close to the city side of the English Bridge, and this sometimes developed into a ferry cross as at Wilton, Ross, and at Vowchurch (Fig. 35) into a churchyard cross.

In Herefordshire the mark stones remaining are almost all of the above shapes, there being a few surmised "long" stones lying prone, as at Bush Bank, and on the churchyard wall at Madley. One fine long stone (besides the Queen Stone) remains standing in the county near Wern Derries, Michaelchurch Escley (Fig. 37), this about 7 feet 6 inches in height. The usual folk-lore legend that "a great general is supposed to be buried there" is attached to it, and also a more recent record, made colourable by the leaning position of the stone, is that a farmer in ploughing the field found it in the way, so dug deeply all round it, and then hitched twelve horses to it in a vain effort to uproot. In many other districts—as Wales and Cornwall—the upright long stones seem to be the most frequent shape; they are called menhirs, and range up to the height of the three "Devil's Arrows" at Boroughbridge, Yorks. These three are 16½ to 22½ feet high, in a direct line north and south, from 200 to 300 feet apart. Their alignment (there were four aligning in Leland's time) indicates that they are on a ley.

In a few districts—on Dartmoor in particular—there are stone rows or avenues with the stones quite near together.

A striking peculiarity of many of these "rows" is—as Baring-Gould has pointed out—they usually align with a cairn or mound. Professor Windle puts this clearly in his "Prehistoric Age," p. 192: "In its typical and complete form the Dartmoor row begins with a circle and ends with a menhir. Within the circle is very commonly but not always a barrow or cistvaen." Major Tyler has found four of the Dartmoor rows to align on leys.

It seems probable, although not yet proved, that mark stones were often planted quite near to sighting mounds, to indicate the direction of a ley. Apparent examples of this are found at Hundred House Mount, 170 yards distant; near Harpton, 17 yards distant; and at Barlands, about 100 yards distant. In Herefordshire there are forty instances of mounds or moats adjoining the churchyard. It will be shown in the chapter on churches that on the introduction of Christianity these were almost invariably built on the site of ley marking points, chiefly mark stones. In these forty instances it was more probable that a mark stone was close to the mound than that a second mound adjoined, for in Herefordshire instances of two adjacent mounds are rare. The disposition of a group of stones to form indicating pointers is described in the Radnor Vale chapter, as is also the arrangement of a stone so that its sharpest edge or point indicates the direction of the ley. The chisel-shaped top of the long stones illustrated has probably the same purpose.

A mark stone was very frequently placed at the crossing point of two leys, and is therefore often to be found—as is its successor, a wayside cross—at a present-day cross-road. Fig. 28 illustrates such at Beggar's Bush. Mr. W. Dutt, a well-known East Anglian topographer, makes an interesting communication on this point: "In three instances already the tracing of leys has enabled a friend with whom I am working to discover boulders embedded at cross-roads where he concluded they ought to be, but where they had become almost entirely hidden in roadside banks."

Many of the mark stones, as that at Burfa, are of altar-like shape. Sir John Cotterill took me to see such an example on his estate at Mansel Gamage. It is in the midst of a compact tree grove, called the Clump, which standing on the shoulder of a hill, can be seen for a good many miles. Fig. 39 shows it as seen against the skyline from a mark stone at Yazor but not in the same ley; and the next illustration (Fig. 40) is from a near point. Fig. 41 shows the mark stone, and it is almost impossible to look at it without thinking of the Biblical description of the prophets of Baal, and of the groves. This, like many others, is probably a glacial boulder.

Most inexplicable of all the mark stones are those with clean-cut grooves running from the top to the bottom of an upright or "long" stone. The Queen Stone in the horseshoe bend of the Wye near Symond's Yat is a fine Herefordshire example (Figs. 43 and 44). It measures about 7 feet 6 inches in height, 6 feet broad, and 3 feet wide. The south-east face has five grooves as illustrated, the north-west face three grooves, the north-east end two grooves, and the south-west end one only. The grooves die out before reaching the ground, but appear to continue in an irregular way over the apex. They are all much alike in width—from 2 inches to 2½ inches, but vary in depth from 3 inches to 7 inches, being much deeper than they are wide. It seems quite impossible that they should result from any natural cause. The top of the stone is irregularly corroded, and the probability of this being caused by fire presents itself. I tried the insertion of broomsticks in these grooves, but the tops projecting on opposite sides were too irregular for such a method to have been used for sighting. There seems to be no legend attached to this stone, and it aligns with other points. Whether it is a sacrificial stone remains a surmise. Similar grooves in a far less perfect form are to be seen (Fig. 36) on one edge of a "longstone," close to Staunton in the Forest of Dean—not far away. The stone is close to the high road and alongside a straight "drive" through the woodland. A passing country-woman supplied this bit of local legend: "Do you know what they say about it?—that if you prick it with a pin at midnight it bleeds." Might this not be a glimmer of folk-lore memory of a blood sacrifice at the stone? It is much spauled and might be a fragment of one much larger. The three taller stones at Boroughbridge, Yorks, called the Devil's Arrows (Fig. 48), have similar grooves, and Lockyer thinks them to be part of a sun-worship avenue. An illustration of a stone with upright grooves in India, much like the Queen Stone, appeared in a recent periodical.

There is a hint of a possible purpose for these stones with upright grooves in Lockyer's remark ("Stonehenge," p. 473) with regard to sighting stones from circles—"some of the outstanding stones must have been illuminated at night"—and this fits in with the facts regarding beacon lights. A fire-cage possibility fits best with the facts I have observed at the Queen Stone.

The two stones in the district reputed to be sacrificial stones are in natural positions apparently, and can scarcely be classified as mark stones. The first is a stone a few yards from Buckstone, near Staunton, Forest of Dean. The Buckstone is a Logan or rocking stone, an obviously natural product. The adjacent stone, with a rock basin cut in the top of its flat surface, has also a notch the size of a man's neck cut in one edge of the basin, and there is a draining channel. I think that these basins might have been used for beacon purposes.

The reputed sacrificial stone (Fig. 101) on the Malvern Range, near the Herefordshire Beacon, appears to be either a natural outcrop or a fragment fallen from above. It is in a hollow under Clutter's Cave, otherwise the Giant's Cave.

All down the Middle Ages the word "mark" (sometimes spelt merke, merc, or merch) has signified a boundary or a landmark. As late as 1565 its use in the latter sense is proved by a quotation in the "New English Dictionary": "A little hill or marke called a barrow."

March stone and mark stone are also headings in the "New English Dictionary," the meaning "boundary or landmark," and two quotations as follows: Laing Charters, 1536, "To the merch steane with one croce on the heid theiron," and in Durham Rolls of 1364 a boundary stone is called "merkstan."

In Hampshire are place-names as follows: Four Marks, Lee Marks, Markwell Wood, West Mark, Markfield, and Marks Lane. In London Mark Lane is familiar, in it being the market for corn, and there is an ancient Mark Lane in Bristol. There is "the very ancient road called the Mark-way, which is now a drift road from Winchester to Weyhill," and Markyate has the same meaning. A place called Mark Cross again indicates the transition from mark stone to cross; our Herefordshire Marcle was earlier spelt Marclay, and from the village of Mark in Somersetshire runs a Mark Causeway toward the coast.

In charters of the Edwards, quoted in Markham's "Northamptonshire Crosses" (we cannot escape from the name even in surnames), market is spelt mercate.

Major Conder, R.E., in his "Syrian Stone-Lore," referring to the peasant paganism of that country in the second century, says, "The Markulim (or Mercury) was a menhir, before which a rude altar was erected, on which (and sometimes on the menhir itself) small offerings were laid."

Note how closely akin in verbal origin are the mark or march or merch stones, the market or mercate, the merchant or marchant, and the god Mercury, whose symbol was an upright stone.

Another chapter will treat of trade routes sighted over mound and stone.

The primary purpose of these stones was not to act as boundary- but as way-marks; it is obvious that prehistoric ways must have been in use before ownership of land existed, and that as this later phase evolved trackways would naturally form boundaries and their way-marks become boundary marks. Lockyer ("Stonehenge," p. 141) is of opinion that "Cromlechs and Standing Stones formed important points in the landscape long before ecclesiastical divisions were thought of, or any attempt was made to indicate the boundaries of private property."

Fortunately there exists a written record of the transitional period, when, although some of the mark stones had become boundary stones, and others stones for ceremonial use, there still remained some used as originally. This occurs in the Welsh Triads, traditional, but written later (" Ancient Laws of Wales," Owen, Vol. II, p. 523) : " There are three other stones, for which an action of theft lies against such as shall remove them ; a meer stone (maen tervyn) ; a white stone of session (maen gwyn gorsedd) ; and a guide stone (maen gobaith) ; and his life is forfeited who shall do so."

The Anglo-Saxon word " haran " applied to these stones (now surviving in " hoar stone ") seems to have had the meaning of " old, grey," which indicates the antiquity—even then—of the stones. The fact (presently to be proved) that they became points of trade also indicates a way-mark ; for the chapman and the merchant would not be as likely to travel along manor boundaries as along the stones marking a well-used track.

An Anglo-Saxon boundary given in Heming's " Cartulary," p. 348, is " on to the ' haran stan,' from the ' haran stan ' along the green way."

In the present six-inch Ordnance map there are three enclosed woods adjoining Ivington Camp, Herefordshire (Fig. 82), namely, Wallway Wood, Hoarstone Coppice, and Roundstone Coppice. The second name is Longstone Coppice, in the previous edition of the map. About three-quarters of a mile away is the Titterstone Plantation. All five names indicate tracks and mark stones in past times. The local keeper does not know of any large stones now in these woods.

Near Rishworth in Yorkshire, so Leyland records, is The Waystone, " occupying the ridge of Waystone Edge," at the foot of which is a lonely pool called The Way Pit. What clearer indication of a stone marking the way can be imagined ?

The King Stone is a frequent name for mark stones. Gomme quotes three examples—at Rollright, Nine Ladies, Derbyshire, and King-standing Hill, Sussex ; the first two being connected with stone circles. That which gives its name to Kingston-on-Thames is famous as the coronation stone of Saxon Kings.

That open-air courts were held at exactly those types of sites which are sighting points on a ley is referred to in the other chapters, and they were so held at stones. Fortunately, there is the actual contemporary record of the proceedings, pleadings, and findings at such a court bound up in an Anglo-Saxon Gospel—a safe place for its deposit—in the Hereford Cathedral Library. The opening sentences are thus translated ("Woolhope Club Transactions," 1901, p. 109): "Note of a Shire-mote held at Aegelnoth's Stone in Herefordshire, in the reign of King Cnut, at which were present the Bishop Athelstan, the Sheriff Bruning, . . . and all the Thanes in Herefordshire."

The Court of Shepway, which is the ancient court of the Cinque Ports, presided over by its Warden, was held in 1923 with due ceremony at its reputed earliest meeting-place, Shepway Cross, where no cross or stone now exists. Whether it was the sheep-way or the ship-way may be in doubt, but that the cross—whether a structure or a cross of tracks—was upon an ancient way, and that it was probably at first marked by a stone, can be of little doubt. A previous meeting in 1861 under Lord Palmerston (Earl Beauchamp is the present Warden) was held, also in the open air, at Bredenstone Hill, Dover, on the site of a stone which had been called Braidenstone in the precept of Lord Sydney in 1693. Probably "braid" is "brade," the old form of "broad." There are many hill places called Broad Down, and the first element is a generic one, meaning a track broad enough for wheels, in scores of ley place-names.

The best known of all mark stones is the one enclosed in the coronation chair at Westminster Abbey, sitting on which every sovereign of England (except Queen Mary) has been crowned since Edward I brought the stone from Scone Abbey in 1296. It had a similar connexion with a long line of Scottish kings before that date, and is recorded as being at Iona in 503; and its still earlier but conflicting traditions of outdoor sacred associations, together with its shape (compare it with several here illustrated), show that it was originally a mark stone.

There are ancient cross socket stones (presumedly successors of mark stones) at both the Kingstone places in Herefordshire. Near Llanfilo, Breconshire, they speak of an important stone of the name; and two stones on the slope of Bredon Hill (whether natural or detached is not stated) are called the "King and Queen." The derivation of the word might come in several ways, for the "thing" or place of assembly has much the same origin, while in later days the chief stone of an avenue or circle would be so called for the same reason that the key timber in a roof principal is called a " king-post " by builders.

Kiftsgate Stone, in the North Cotswolds, which gave a name to a Doomsday Hundred (there " Cheftesihat "), provides triple information, for in the first place the latter part of its name shows that it was on a road or track ; its being the same name as the hundred is indication that it was the meeting place of the hundred court ; and finally in Mr. Gissing's delightful " Footpathway in Gloucestershire " is given direct personal evidence that up to the coronation of George III newly crowned kings were proclaimed at this stone.

In Mr. H. A. Evans's " Cotswolds," in the Highways and Byways Series, he speaks of " an ancient road, a well-trodden highway of the people," which runs south from Edgehill, and that " here and there along the sides of this road may be observed isolated upright stones." Now, 10 miles of this road aligns on the one-inch map with very little variation between the churches of Radway and Chipping Norton, and it would be interesting to find whether these stones (which another reference assumes to be ancient) also align. In any case, it is an instance of mark stones on an old trackway, which for part of its course is the county boundary. Fig. 5 illustrates this track going through a number of cross-road points.

The " stone at the cross-roads " seems to have had a far-reaching effect on the history of religion, commerce and topography.

One of the most constant and curious experiences in mapping out leys is the way in which present-day cross-roads seem to be also the crossing points of ancient tracks, and that while these points remain constant and unchanged the tracks and roads have entirely altered. This persistence is reflected in folk-lore customs.

Two Herefordshire informants have related to me their personal experience that at funerals in the present century they have been surprised to find the bearers lay down the coffin at a cross-road and say a prayer, " because it always had been done." At Brilley, Herefordshire, the " Funeral Stone " was outside the churchyard gate, and a coffin was carried three times round this before entering. Mrs. Leather

(" Folk Lore of Herefordshire ") reproduces an old print illustrating this; but the stone is now broken up.

Wergin's Stone, Sutton, Hereford (Fig. 34), with a cup-like recess—probably for offerings—and traditions of having been moved by the Devil in the night, is clearly a pagan stone of a date when stones were just commencing to be " worked." Its forecast of the shape of the later cross is most interesting.

It is difficult to assign the rudely worked head of the stone (Fig. 29) on the highway between Clyro and Painscastle (Radnorshire) to a Christian period, and it reminds me of the stones associated with Hermes. There is a legend of a haunted horseman attached to it, and standing at the junction of an ancient lane it is certainly a mark stone.

Folk-lore supplies many echoes of the placing of mark stones into position by persons of skill and power. Several are given in the chapter on folk-lore. Here is one such example. A friend motoring past Teddington Cross, east of Tewkesbury, noticed a large, irregular stone where six roads meet. The map names it the " Tibble Stone," and an old man at the adjacent inn told this tale about it. " A long time ago a giant lived about these parts, and he went up the hill to fetch a large stone to destroy his enemy's house. When he was carrying it down his foot slipped, and his heel made a great furrow in the hill-side, and you can see it to this day, and he had to drop the stone just where you see it. It is quite true, because you can see for yourself the holes where the giant's fingers had hold of it."

The Bellstone is preserved in a bank in Bellstone Lane, Shrewsbury.

The following are a few names of single ancient stones, not including those in stone circles, a subject not included in this volume. Hell Stone, Hele Stone, Grimstone, Crick Stone, Tingle Stone, Whittle Stone, Hurl Stone, King Stone (a number of these), Pecket Stone, Copstone, Ludstone, Rudstone, Bambury Stone, Kenward Stone, Hangman's Stone, Huxter Stone, Pedlar's Stone, Golden Stone, Black Stone, White Stone, Giant's Throw, Giant's Staff, Hurler. The word " The " is used with all.

In more than half the towns I have visited in the past three years I have found an ancient mark stone in the streets, such instances being at Talgarth, Hay (in Heol

Dwr), Presteign (Hereford Street), Pembridge, Weobley, Shrewsbury, Leominster (South Street), New Radnor (several), Hereford, Grosmont. These are illustrated in Figs. 95, 31, 32, 42, and 96.

Almost all the wayside and churchyard crosses evolved from mark stones. There is a good deal of evidence for this in some names of the wayside crosses, which are usually at crossings of old tracks. The White Stone at Withington (Hereford) is part of the shaft of a cross, and that its name is prehistoric is confirmed by the White Stone Cross near Exeter, and the Hereford White Cross, neither being of stone which was ever white. Regarding a cross socket stone at Huntley (Glos.), a lad from the village told me, "We boys always called it the Black Stone." There is a Cole Cross, just as surely at a mark stone as is Coldstone Common. Then as regards the churchyard crosses, I have found two local instances where closely adjacent straight trackways are to be seen sighted directly on them; the Monks' Walk, an ancient avenue at Much Marcle, is the first, and at Kingstone (Herefordshire) a straight piece of ancient lane paved with cobble-stones aligns with the cross in the churchyard, which, although now "restored," is, to my personal knowledge, still on the ancient site.

At Bosbury (Herefordshire) the churchyard cross was moved from its old site in 1796, and the movers were so surprised to find embedded in the fabric a huge boulder of stone that they recorded the fact, and placed the stone under the tower, where it still is; but it is a local "pudding stone," not from a distance, as wrongly stated in the account.

At Vowchurch, Herefordshire (Fig. 35), the churchyard cross (which aligns with the ford over the little river) is clearly an unhewn mark stone; and above Llanigon, a longstone has been roughly shaped to give it some resemblance to a cross. I have given several examples and illustrations of this transition in "Early British Trackways."

There are instances in Cornwall and Brittany of a menhir having a cross cut upon it when Christianity came, and I have taken a rubbing of the Maltese cross cut on the wayside stone at Partricio in the Black Mountains, on which tradition tells that Archbishop Baldwin stood when preaching for the Crusade in 1188.

A vivid field observation, made just before going to press, shows the mark stone in the Clump (see p. 25) to be on a ley with three other mark stones. Passing Yazor Old Church on a day of clear distances, its ruined tower was seen in exact alignment through the Clump mark stone to the Black Mountain peak, Pen-y-Gader (2,624 feet). In preparing to photograph this an exclamation from my helper revealed an unmistakable mark stone (not that in Fig. 39) in the highway hedge three yards away.

The ley is as follows: Mark stone on highway at Yazor Church, tower of Yazor Old Church (in ruins), Monnington Court, mark stone on highway at Wilmarston turning Peterchurch, "Camp" (1,222 feet) near Whitehouse Farm, Churchyard Cross at Capel-y-Fin (illustrated as a mark stone in "Early British Trackways"), bridle pass over Taren-yr-Esgob, and Pen-y-Gader.

The three first points can actually be seen aligning to a fourth point (the mountain peak) from the highway at Yazor.

The churchyard, market, and wayside crosses were alike in form and origin. All sprang from the mark stone and were on its site.

But the evolution of the cross is too wide a subject for this chapter, and must be postponed.

CHAPTER V

THE SIGHTED TRACK

> Cador proceeded over wealds, and over wilderness, over dales and over downs, and over deep waters. Cador knew the way that towards his country lay, by the nearest he proceeded full surely right towards Totnes.
>
> —LAYAMON'S "Brut"

THE previous chapters have made out, and, it is claimed proved, a case for actual alignments across hill and dale by detailed evidence about the sighting points—mounds, moats, stones, etc. It would be an absurdity to assume that early man did this without some practical end in view. We should probably come to the conclusion by negative evidence that this end was the provision of clearly defined tracks or roads, for it is not easy to find another sufficiently good reason.

But there is sufficient positive evidence left of the actual trackways on the alignments to prove the case, and this chapter attempts to give some of it, in addition to that indicated in Chapter III.

The facts that a human trackway is an ever-changing thing, and that some thousands of years for such changes have gone by since the first alignments were made, make such evidence none too plentiful.

The first instance is a short track sighted between Hanter and Herrock, both in the hill group described in the early part of Chapter III. In June, 1914, the Woolhope Field Club visited this district, and, alighting at Stanner Station, climbed, on their way to Hergest Ridge, the very steep, wooded hill-side of Worsell. The recollection of this very uncompromising and direct track, and my picking up two ancient flint flakes on it, lingered. So eight years later an investigation walk resulted in the track being photographed in the line of its ley, as shown in Fig. 49, which shows it to be sighted on the hill point Hanter. The camera was then taken to the point marked X in the hill track on Worsell, and a photograph (Fig. 50) taken in exactly the opposite direction, looking down the cutting of the track (shown in the picture) towards the previous standpoint of the camera, again marked X. It will be seen that this end of the ley (and of a proved trackway) is sighted on the hill point Herrock, which is marked by a tree clump. The ley goes—beyond Hanter—through a near church, Gladestree.

Between Pandy and Llanvihangel is the Tre-Fedw mound (Fig. 51) on a bank, and the ley through it and the ford over the Honddu at Llanvihangel Mill lies on a piece of the present road, as shown in Fig. 52. The same ley also lies on another straight piece of present road passing Pandy Station, as shown in Fig. 53, and the ley then passes through the eastern vallum of Walterstone Camp.

A vivid instance of an actual straight sighted track being used to-day, almost in the old way—by sight points—is given in a letter from my son dated June 16, 1924, the track evidently being Stane Street: "A friend of mine—Lambert—was walking in Sussex last week. Wishing to get to Chichester he asked the way, and was told by a countryman, 'Well, it is some way round by road; but if you go to the top of that hill you will see Chichester Cathedral, and a path leading to it in a dead straight line.'" This ley is sighted on St. Catherine's Hill, the lofty coast headland in the Isle of Wight, which Mr. Belloc lays stress upon as being a sailing mark for seamen; to the north-east it goes towards Sevenoaks, through Pullborough and lies on several very convincing fragments of present road. It is a long way from being directed towards London, and probably there was not any London when it was first planned, nor a Chichester town or cathedral for that matter.

A most convincing instance at Eardisland of a present-day straight path aligning over a moated mound, its causeway, and an ancient ford with mark stone, is detailed in the next chapter, and the Green Way sighted on Arthur's Stone described and illustrated (Fig. 14) in Chapter II shows the track going round and returning to the ley.

Instances of tree avenues being on leys, confirmed by several sighting points, are numerous. Such are: Monnington-on-Wye (illustrated in the previous book); the ley through New Radnor Tump and Old Radnor Church

(Figs. 19 and 20) already described; the Scotch Fir Avenues at Llanvihangel Court and Trewyn, Abergavenny; the Duchess Walk in Oakley Park, Ludlow; that at Cotheridge Court, Worcester; at Madresfield Court, Malvern; at Catesby, Warwick, which aligns with two churches and Warwick Castle; and the well-known Stowe Avenue, Bucks, which, after passing through Stowe, Fleet Marston, and Little Kimble Churches, aligns with the Great Mound and Keep of Windsor Castle.

Queen Anne's Drive, with a straight length of 2¾ miles, is sighted precisely on the great mound of Windsor, and the fact that about a mile and a quarter of Windsor Town and outskirts lies between the Castle and the entrance to the Drive indicates the antiquity of the alignment.

Another instance of an ancient road sighted on a mound is best given by quoting a reference to Silbury (the largest artificial mound in Europe) given in the "Archæological Journal" for 1920, p. 340: "The most important evidence of its prehistoric date is perhaps to be found in the fact, proved, as it appears, by excavations undertaken by the Wilts Archæological Society in 1867, for that purpose alone, that the Roman road was deflected from its straight course to avoid the mound, passing thirty yards to the south of it instead of under it, as from its general direction it seems it should have done."

To give another instance of existing track to be seen on an ancient alignment or ley, there is a straight road through Stowe Park which, extended to the south-west, passes through the sites of six churches, Fringford, Caversfield, Weston, Yarnton, Longworth, and Ogbourne St. George.

In many cases a modern road or track swerves more or less from a straight ley, but comes back to it, and the points at which it comes back are almost always cross-roads of tracks or a meeting point of tracks; this is noticeable in all the plans.

Practically all the "Roman" roads, as the Foss Way, on the map will be found on examination to be built up, not of one line across country, but of a number of short lengths of different alignments, and in many cases each of these sections have the characteristics of a separate ley in its alignment with sighting points and with cross track points.

The piece of the Foss Way not far from Leamington is

dead on an alignment for 3 or 4 miles, through the middle of a square camp, past two Fosse Farms; then for about 6 miles in its north-easterly course it breaks away a little to the right of the ley, past the villages of Eathorpe, Princethorpe, and Stretton-on-Dunsmore, only to come back to the alignment to hit it exactly at two cross-roads a little east of Wolston. In this total length there are no less than six cross-roads of the Foss Way exactly on one ley, and reference to the chapter on mark stones will show that in all probability a mark stone for this ley once existed at each cross track, and this is the reason why these points do not change down the ages.

Vivid proof of two sighted tracks is to be found in the centre of old Hereford. Standing in the Cathedral Close (at the western iron post of a gate), and looking the whole length of the two lanes—Upper and Lower Church Street—traffic can be seen passing in the High Town 183 yards distant, although in some parts the lane is only 7 feet wide. The other instance is to stand at a point in East Street, where it begins to bend to get round to St. John Street, and look (westward) the whole length of the continuous East and West Streets. Here again traffic can be seen passing in Victoria Street, which is 430 yards distant, although the streets narrow down to 12 feet wide in places.

In these cases narrow, straight sighted tracks are still preserved between the houses of these narrow lanes (notwithstanding several obvious encroachments) for 183 yards and 430 yards respectively. The crossing point of these two tracks was the highest ground within the ancient city.

Another example, this time of footpaths and high-road on a ley, is in the Droitwich district. The ley is sighted through Doverdale and Salwarpe Churches, and comes down south-west to (and probably beyond) Low Hill, which name indicates a sighting mound. Five cross-roads are precisely on the ley.

Sometimes the record of a long-unused ancient track is to be seen in meadow land as a slightly sunken trench. There is one near the "Three Elms," Hereford. Examination showed that it was not a watercourse, and that it was continued on the other side of the main road in the same alignment; and as it also aligned with a back street (behind

Walmer Street) in Hereford, it was extended on the map and found to go to Cascob Church (Fig. 106), the tower of which is on a tumulus. The reality of this ley was confirmed by finding on it the two mark stones illustrated in Figs. 28 and 30, the straight earth cutting Fig. 57, and other confirmations.

Approaching Ivington Camp for the first time from the north (July, 1924), by a cart track over the fields, I found that this became an ancient hollow track climbing the hill. It appeared to be fairly straight, but trees interfered with long-distance visual test, and trials were therefore made by sighting compass at two points more than 100 yards apart. The direction of both tests was identical (23° W. of N. magnetic). It was therefore a straight track (Fig. 82), and two convincing mark stones were by its side near the foot of the bank. On the map it was found that this straight hollow road (unknown until actually seen), if extended, would pass exactly through Kingsland and Aymestree Churches, 4 and 6 miles distant, good proof, in conjunction with the mark stones, that it was an ancient sighted long-distance track.

It might naturally be asked whether there has been any confirmation by excavation of trackways indicated by alignment of sighting points, but with no other surface evidence. Although no organized spade research has been attempted, the reply is—Yes!

In the latter part of 1923 extensive sewer work was done in meadows on the south side of the Wye at Hereford. In three cases sections of buried trackways were discovered in the cut trenches, and in all three cases their position and direction was that of trackways which—assumed from alignment of points—had been mapped out. In the first instance, I was walking across the "Bishop's Meadow" and explaining to my companion that I surmised a track from the Palace Ford to the Bassam, or Bartonsham, Ford at the mark stone. In walking along this surmised line to the open trench, the section of a bit of cobbled trackway (shown in Fig. 54) was found within two yards of the surmised spot. Its surface is shown in Fig. 55, and it was at this spot probably crossing a streamlet, for on cutting a parallel trench a few yards away it was found to continue in the expected direction as a slight "dirt track," not cobbled. It was 2 feet under the present surface, and probably 6 or 7 feet wide.

A second instance, in another part of this sewer cutting (in the Hinton meadows), took the form of a thin layer of gravel, 7 inches below the surface, its terminations sharply defined, showing in sections on both sides of the trench, but with the terminations on one side some 5 feet more southward than on the other. The cutting was in clean stoneless loam, and the gravel was certainly not a natural deposit. Both the position and the direction (indicated by the diagonal terminations of the section) were identical with a ley already marked on the map which had been seen in winter sunlight as a broad track climbing the back of Aylestone Hill on the other side of the city. On plotting the section and the trench on the map the track width was found to be approximately 8 feet.

A third instance of a buried trackway in the same sewer work was first seen by Mr. J. Hoyle, a Woolhope Club member. I had previously told him of a surmised sighted track alongside the Wye towards the farm and hamlet of Hunderton, and that something might be expected when the sewer cutting came near that spot. At the expected position was found a layer of gravel 2 feet below the surface, and of considerable thickness (up to 12 inches) as the spot had a water trench near. It was clearly " foreign matter," not natural, and, as in the last, had definite terminations with the ends on one side 11 feet more to the east than on the other. On plotting the length of section (27 feet) at the indicated angle over the trench, the width of the track was made to be 7 feet, the crossing being at an acute angle.

The direction indicated was identical with the previously surmised ley on the map, which came from the Castle Hill, through the Wye Street mark stones (Fig. 41), and was sighted on Pen-y-Gader.

The width of the early trackway was as little as 4 feet, but usually 6 to 7 feet. This is not wide enough for wheel traffic, and the British people were certainly expert users of chariots when the Romans landed. The place-name elements " broad," " brad," or " brade," so frequently to be met with indicate the fact that the spot is on a broad track fit for wheel traffic. The fact of four " Broad " names on a ley is given in " Early British Trackways," and at one of these, formerly Broadford, now Broadward Bridge, the recent widening of the bridge has uncovered an ancient paved ford (seen and photographed July, 1924) which is certainly not narrow.

Mr. Alfred Pope saw in several places the section of an early hollow trackway cut into at Dorchester; it was 5 feet 4 inches deep, 8 feet 3 inches wide at the top, and 6 feet 6 inches at the bottom, evidently cut out of the chalk, not made deep by wear.

The narrow foot and pack-horse track seems to have persisted, and at Risbury, Herefordshire, the approach arches of a bridge over a stream for such a track are exactly 6 feet in width. They are probably of mediaeval date. Until the sewer-cutting discoveries just detailed there was no information as to the surface of the ancient tracks; it is possible that—except in soft places—many were not stoned. There is need for spade investigation in the matter.

It is not probable that the actual track usually went over the top of a mound on which it was sighted. Yet there are two instances at least where Ordnance maps show this to be the case at the present time. In the 1832 one-inch map of Exmoor a well-confirmed ley can be traced over Stoke Rivers Church to Two Barrows Down. To the right of the former is a circular earthwork on the ley, and a road (in the same direction) is shown passing through its centre. In the present six-inch map of Amesbury, Wilts, a path is also shown through the centre of a tumulus within "Vespasian's Camp."

The fact has to be faced that if a track is on a sighted ley it does not go along a selected route, but over whatever steep and seemingly improbable obstacles come in the way.

Objectors have said that man did not go up the steep side of a mountain if he had a chance to take an easier track; but anyone who has really studied a mountain district knows that to this day there are straight tracks which go right up a mountain-side, and that in many cases they are still in use, as in Fig. 49. Moreover, I deny the capacity of a twentieth century man to judge the travelling preferences of a prehistoric man, who lived by hunting down wild animals.

But early man was not quite a fool, and there are some indications that if, for example, a long sighted ley crossed several loops of a winding river, he did not make several crossings where one was enough, and his track diverged enough from the ley—perhaps aided by additional sighting points and mark stones—to go round the bends.

There are indications of the sighted track over mounds in the Welsh traditional legends—the Mabinogion. Pwyll at Narbeth goes " to the top of a mound that was above the palace and was called Gorsedd Arbeth," and from there sees a vision " coming along the highway that led from the mound." Peredwr in another legend came upon a youth sitting upon a mound: " And there were three roads leading from the mound, two of them were wide roads, and the third was more narrow."

Another interesting point in the Mabinogion is the reference to Sarn Helen, the causeway or sarn which traverses Wales. It relates how an Emperor of Rome, coming to Britain, wooed and won a British maiden, who in other traditions was daughter of King Coel. It is related that Helen asked to have three chief castles made for her in whatever places she might choose. " Then Helen bethought her to make highways from one castle to another throughout the island of Britain. And the roads were made. She was sprung from a native of this island, and the men of this Island of Britain would not have made these great roads for any save her." The point to note here is that these long-distance roads are attributed to native design and execution even in the time of Roman conquest, and also to the direction of one of Coel or Cole descent.

While the earliest long-distance tracks were probably as far as the keen sight of the outdoor man could spot a distant peak in a smoke-clear air, they seem to have been made much shorter in later days. At New Radnor, for example, there is clear evidence of a track sighted between the Mynd and Knowl Hill, passing through a cottage which used to be called Hunger Spot but now Sunnybank. And the mountain points are only 2½ miles apart.

CHAPTER VI

WATER SIGHT POINTS

At daybreak they came upon the ford that leads across the water to the mount. Looking towards the mount they beheld a burning fire up on the hill, that might be seen from very far. —WACE: "Arthurian Chronicle"

THERE gradually dawns upon the observer who does actual field work on the straight tracks which were projected across country with so much skill by the ley-men of old, two outstanding characteristics. These in addition to the provision of mark stones. The first, already dealt with, is the effective way in which the eye was caught by the planting on ridges, banks, and hills artificial marking points such as mounds and tree clumps. The second, now to be described, applies to lower ground, and has the same aim in supplying directing points on the ley to be seen from a distance.

The bold way in which the track plunges, not merely towards, but directly through, pieces of water, both natural and artificial, is at first a matter of perplexity until a study of the beacon fires begins to reveal its full significance.

First, take the approaches to ancient fords on rivers, natural water sighting points. It is soon found that these approaches are so cut that the traveller sees the water from afar, if on the right track. Even to this day in London, walking on the northern pavement of the Strand, the water of the Thames can be seen at high tide looking down Buckingham Street over the York Water Gate. And from the actual steps of Covent Garden Market, Thames water can be seen in like manner down Southampton Street and the narrow Carting Lane, the ley (for it certainly must be such) passing the corner house bearing the ancient name of Coal Hole.

In the examples now to be given it is probable that some of the stone pitching may be of a later date than prehistoric

FIG. 16. HILLS ROUND RADNOR VALE. EASTERN END FROM BARLAND BANK

FIG. 17. SKY-LINE OF RADNOR FOREST SHOWING MOUNDS

FIG. 18. THE BLACK MIXEN, NEAR VIEW

FIG. 19. OLD RADNOR CHURCH, ON LEY

FIG. 21. SCOTCH FIRS ON A BARROW SITE, RADNOR VALE

FIG. 20. NEW RADNOR CASTLE, LEY TO OLD RADNOR CHURCH

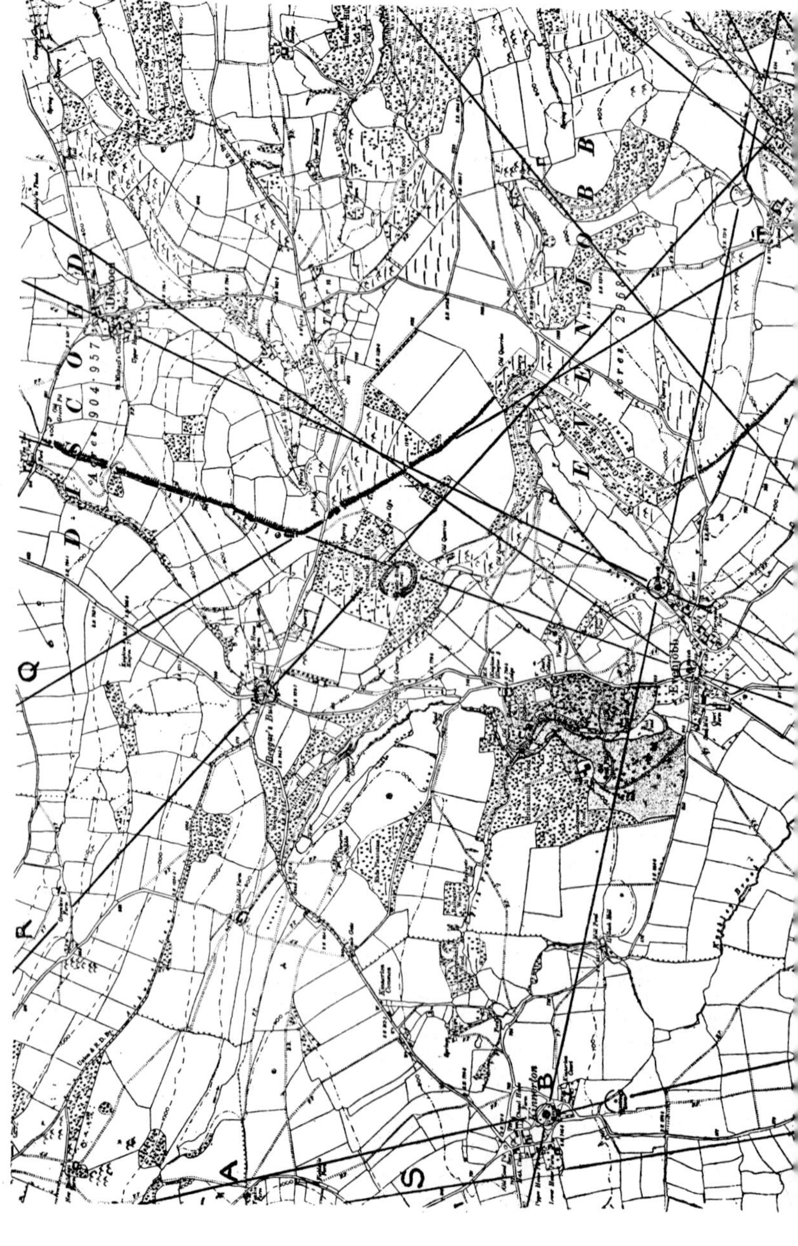

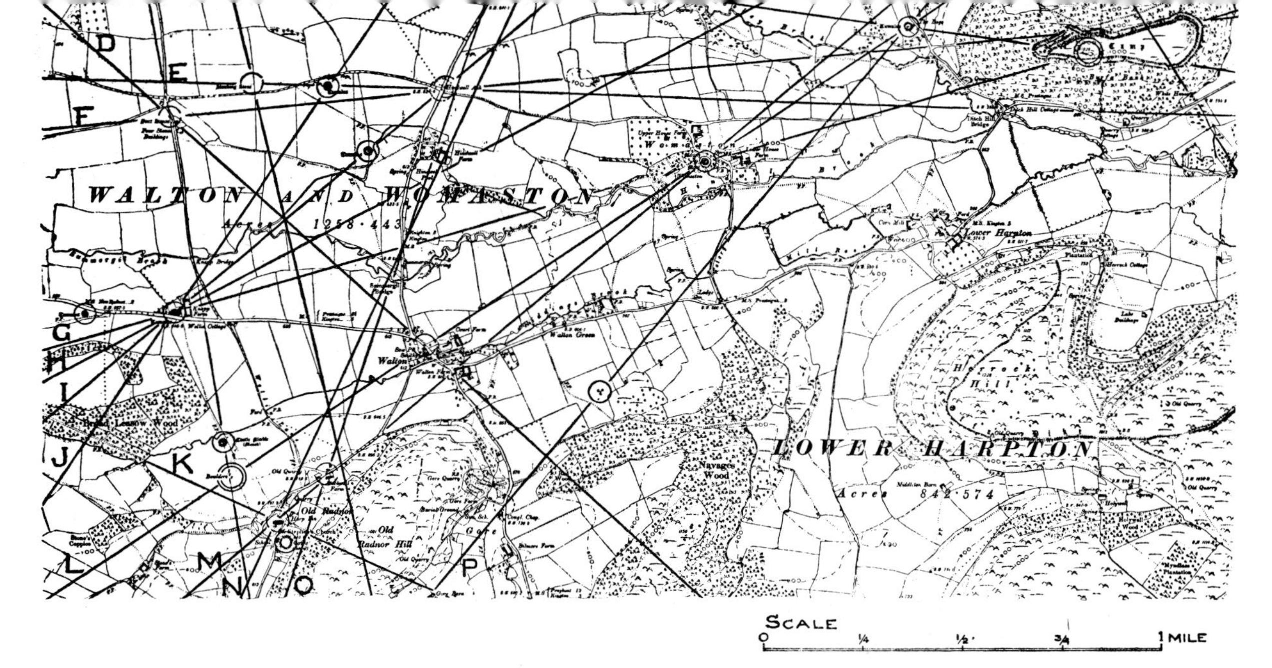

RADNOR VALE – EASTERN END

MOUND ○ STONE ○ CHURCH ○ CROSS ROAD ○ INITIAL POINT ○

FIG. 23. FOUR STONES, NEW RADNOR

FIG. 24. MARK STONE, KNOBLEY, BURFA

FIG. 25. MARK STONE, KINNERTON AND WHIMBLE

FIG. 26. NATURAL BOULDER, OLD RADNOR

FIG. 27. VALLUM, BURFA CAMP. RADNOR FOREST IN DISTANCE

MARK STONES

FIG. 28. BEGGAR'S BUSH, RADNOR

FIG. 29. CWM BWNT, CLYRO, RADNOR

times, but all the same they are the survival of a structural principle.

The hollow road down to the Monnow Ford, described in the next chapter, was constructed so that the water could be seen down the cutting when approaching, and it is so seen in Fig. 61.

At Much Fawley is a similar hollow road on a larger scale sighting down to a ford on the Wye, unused as such for centuries, although my old friend Edmund Bellamy (who farmed here, and now lives at the beautiful old house of the Kyrles, Fawley Court) tells me that in his younger days he kept the road in good order, and hauled down it many a load of wheat to be taken in a barge down the Wye. It is more like a watercourse now, but as straight as an arrow down to the river (Fig. 56), and at the V notch seen in the photograph is a sloping bit of paved ford going down under the water.

Other hollow roads to fords are described in the chapter on sighting notches.

The Tre-Fedw example (Fig. 52) shows how from a barrow on a bank there was a clear view down to the water at an organized ford. The help to a traveller of seeing reflected sky-light in the water from a distance when evening shades were falling can be imagined.

The second type of water sighting points—moats—are artificial. Evolved from the trenches out of which the mounds were thrown up, they were—in their earlier form—circular rings of water. At first, no doubt, a mere trench filled with water, then in most of our local examples the trench becomes of considerable width, and is fed by a leat connected to a stream, just as a mill is supplied. In such, as at Eardisland (Fig. 58), the flat-topped mound within the moat is of considerable height, from 15 to 30 feet. But there are also much flatter moated mounds, as the other one in the village of Eardisland, and at Lemore, in which the mound seems to disappear, and the ring of water becomes the main object.

Moated mounds required some communication—either stepping-stones or a causeway—over the ring of water, and traces of one or the other are to be found in most moats. It was not until I found the very plain causeway over the moat at Castle Farm, Madley (see Chapter XVIII), to be sighted on a ley, that I realized that the position of such a causeway probably indicates the direction of a ley. A causeway will be seen crossing the fine Eardisland moat in the photograph (Fig. 58), and on making a special visit I found that a previously noted existing straight path going past the school, and sighted on the moat, also sighted with absolute precision on the causeway, which is on the other side of the mound to the path. The observation was made by sighting rods, and the ley passes, not through the centre of the flat-topped mound (29 yards top diameter), but only

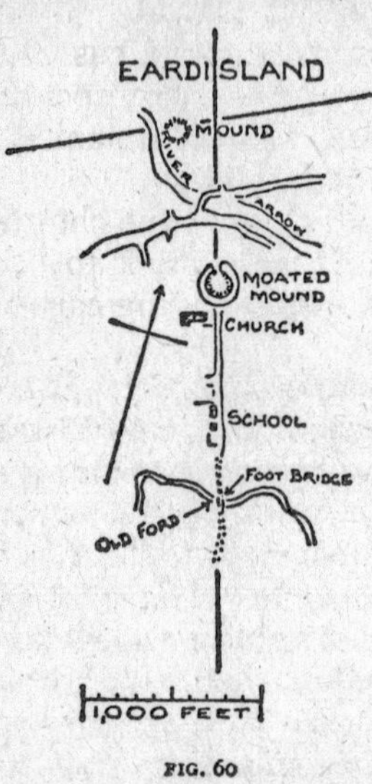

FIG. 60

6 yards from the top edge. This is one of several indications (cited in Chapter XVIII) that the original sighting mound was of a smaller size than the present, and that the enlargement was eccentric. This very perfect mound is about 15 feet high and its slopes 30 degrees.

The existing path (shown in the diagram Fig. 60) crosses by a bridge over the Southall brook, which the Lugg Drainage Board men were cleaning out at the time. At the exact spot, alongside the bridge, where the ley crosses, they found several cartloads of stones instead of the mud above and below. A convincing mark stone was also uncovered on the bank; it was an ancient ford.

The ley goes over the River Arrow, where it is open to the road on this, the prettiest of all our Herefordshire villages, and then through a little field called the Monks' Close, in one corner of which, near to a bend of the Arrow, is another mound, flat and shallow, with slight indications of a moat. This (also shown in Fig. 60) was found to have clear indications of a straight track slightly sunk in the grass sward (both in the same field and over the river, in an orchard), sighted through the mound. Here again the ley (exactly magnetic west) passes through one side of the mound, about 4 yards from its edge, not central.

In no case where a causeway has been found over the present trench of a moat has a corresponding one been found on the opposite side. One communication to the centre seems to have been sufficient.

A moat at Yarkhill, close to the church and to the River Froome, has a 15 feet wide track to be seen in the grass sighted on it, and a corresponding causeway also indicated in the moat bed.

The moated mounds and moats align with other points, as shown in a previous chapter, and the deduction now made is that the ring of water was a valuable sighting object, as it reflected light from the sky (and perhaps at times from a beacon on the ley) when seen from a distance and from higher ground. It may be only a coincidence that the word mote means a speck of light in the eye as well as the ring of water round a mound.

Another "coincidence" of word meanings goes far to indicate that the ring of water, as shown in Fig. 58, was intended to view from a distance. In the old English epic, Beowulf, the two words used for a barrow (such as the mound at Eardisland) are "hlaew" and "beorh." In present English there are two words used for the ring of light round the moon in our misty atmosphere. They are "halo" and "burr." Look at the photograph and judge whether it does not suggest a halo?

There are a large number of moats of a square, not round, shape, probably of later date, and it is a little doubtful whether these all have much to do with the ley system. Undoubtedly it was found that the early round moats formed desirable sites for defendable residences, not to mention castles; and it is quite probable that after the ley system had decayed the custom of digging a moat as defence to a dwelling still continued.

Lyonshall Castle is a flat moat of large extent, and the small mound on which the castle keep is built is not central but close to the ditch, and through this eccentric mound a well-authenticated ley passes. It here seems evident that the mound was prehistoric, and that the far more extensive moat was an addition in castle-building times.

An intermediate type of water sighting point became very evident in three years' ley hunting, namely, the pool or small lake with an island. One at Lyonshall in a field a third of a mile distant from the castle is typical. It is a fairly large artificial pool, the water held up by a slight embankment. In its centre is a small island with several trees, one being a Scotch pine, the only one—as is often the case—within sight. This pond and island are on a well-authenticated ley which starts at Croft Ambury, passes through Milton House, Court of Noke, Elsdon, Bollingham Chapel (or mound), Clyro Church, Llowes Church, Slwych Camp, near Brecon, and terminates at Y-Fan-Dringarth, a 2,410 feet height. And a cross ley appears to go through it and Lyonshall Castle.

There are many such pieces of water with islands, and many of them have leys through the islands. Some of them are queer, overgrown marshy swamps, but with very decided islands in their midst, and others orderly lakelets in the grounds of a mansion, each with a neat island. There are often ponds or lakelets or streams created by an obvious dam, and with no signs of their being made for a mill pond. These also might be made for sighting points, and the name Flash Dam (on the Matlock Moors) is significant; the probable meaning of "flash" is indicated in the chapter on The Beacon.

There are two instances at Holmer (1½ miles north of Hereford City) of perplexing narrow causeways between pairs of ponds. The one is somewhat muffled by trees, and careful observation on the spot showed it to be sighted on Cole's Tump about 10 miles distant.

As regards such a causeway being a road, there is the evidence of Mr. O. G. S. Crawford on pages 176–178 of "Man and His Past," who found several ponds "caused by the damming action of Roman roads." If such a road is a straight sighted one, the pond so formed might be a valuable sighting point from higher ground.

Most amazing of all experiences in ley hunting is the fact that not only do leys often go precisely through small ponds (without islands) in the fields, but the actual paved roads or causeways in the direction of the ley are sometimes found at the bottom of the ponds. This has been reported several times by farmers and labourers when cleaning a pond in dry seasons. The best example—at Holmer—is reproduced from the earlier book. It is 9 feet 6 inches wide and its direction as a causeway is unmistakable, being given in Fig. 59. It slopes into the pond at an angle of 15 degrees, and the criticism of a reviewer as to its being "modern-looking" is disproved by the fact that a bit of Anglo-Saxon pottery was picked out of the crevices of the stones. Another roadway through a pond is at Bridge Sollars, and the course of the road through it was not only obvious in the same orchard, but was confirmed on the other side of the highway by the farmer having come upon a stoned road surface when planting apple trees. Several other similar instances have been reported, the "horse ponds" in question being either at a farm homestead or (as in the Holmer example) in the fields, away from any building. Six examples of leys through ponds occur in the Walton map (Fig. 22.)

Most of these ponds seem to have one shelving edge, down which the causeway slopes, but the opposite end a perpendicular bank. Pitched causeways under water were certainly constructed in prehistoric times, and constructed for actual use, for Mr. Robert Munro in his book on "Scottish Lake Dwellings" gives a number of instances of a "paved ford" or "stone causeway" of narrow width, completely under water, connecting the island with the shore. Sir Laurence Gomme also mentions in his "Primitive Folk Moots" a record of suitors crossing a moat to the seat of justice on the island by stepping-stones.

A reason why water sighting points are of special value on a ley is given in The Beacon chapter, and the instance given from the "Pilgrim's Progress" in the Bible Record chapter is very striking. Here Bunyan not only describes a stone causeway through a "slough" or pond, but also shows clearly that it was on a straight sighted track which aligned to a beacon light. It is also curious—in the light of the example given by Gomme—that Bunyan describes the "steps" as being made "by direction of the lawgiver."

The men of the Lugg Drainage Board in cleaning out Southall's Brook, Eardisland, have just found a causeway of cobble-stones crossing it, and there are other instances of fords over a brook or river being artificially "pitched" with stones.

In the traditional Welsh Triads one of the "defences" (legitimate excuses) "against summons of a session of a court" is "floods in rivers without bridges without cobbles," this clearly inferring that where a cobbled ford was available you had to get through even if the water was high.

One of my critics expressed contempt of the idea that man could ever have walked through ponds. He overlooked the fact that prehistoric man had horses and rode on them. An elderly man told me that an old friend used to speak of the days when outside two entrances (Eign Gate and Barrs Court) of the City of Hereford were ponds, and that it was the custom of farmers when they came to town to bring their horses and wagons through the ponds. As regards primitive instincts, a few days ago I saw where a pool of water, a couple of yards across, had been formed in a walking way by the stopping of a drain. A girl of ten came up, inspected it with much interest, and with plenty of room to go round, she deliberately walked through, with the water over her boots.

CHAPTER VII

SIGHT NOTCHES

This bwlch, a hollow way, was a regular pass, which put me wonderfully in mind of the passes in Spain.
—George Borrow: "Wild Wales"

ON the map near Holme Lacy is marked Coldman's Hill. The place-name took me there to investigate. It is scarcely a hill, although perhaps a mound stood there once, but is high ground above the Wye. A straight, hollow track led down the bank to the river, and was afterwards found to continue on the map as a ley. Going down to the river bank at the point where this track anciently crossed as a ford, and looking up the hollow track, I found the section of the track to show against the skyline (see Fig. 71) as a notch. What an excellent guide on a dusky night this notch made when a traveller crossing the ford wanted the exact direction to take up the bank, but could see little but a skyline! This was not the first notch discovery, but serves as a first illustration.

At Wormsley (Herefordshire) I found on a previously proved ley the deep hollow road shown in Fig. 57, the camera being within this straight V-shaped cutting, which is perfectly dry and has never been a watercourse.

It will probably be said that the sunken roads are due to the wear and tear of centuries of traffic. This is so in some cases, and parallel sunk roads up the mountain-side, due to bringing down peat in sledges, are to be found in such districts as the Radnor Forest, it being evident that when one road was cut too deep another alongside it was formed. But in several cases there is a ridge or raised bank on one side of the hollow road. Such a bank against a climbing sunk road is found in the Navages Wood, Stanner Rocks. It is difficult to see how "wear and tear" piles up an embankment on one side. Some sunken roads, although having straight portions which would provide the "notch," often make a curve (still as a sunken road) above or below the straight part. This is probably due to subsequent use.

I have found several examples of the straight deeply cut hollow roads down to fords; two close to the Pontrilas-Pandy road, not now used, far too narrow (3 feet 6 inches to 4 feet) for wheels, and obviously not water worn, so cut that for the last 50 or 100 yards they give a glimpse of the water to a traveller coming down and a sky notch for the reverse direction.

On the Monnow, behind the Tan House at Longtown, is the fine causeway shown in Fig. 62. Probably of later than prehistoric date, for it is right for wheel traffic, it is splendidly engineered, with great stones set in concrete holding it up on the downstream edge. It will be noted how deep is the cutting which comes down to it. Fig. 61 shows how, looking down this cut road, the stones of the causeway and the water over them can be seen; and when so looking, if the eye be lifted to the ridge of the Black Mountain, close under which the Monnow flows, there (in a rock ridge called the Black Darren) is a clean-cut notch (Fig. 70) which serves as a sighting point for the traveller using this ford. Both the causeway and notch were illustrated in my earlier book before I knew that a hollow road sighted over both.

It is to cross mountain or hill ridges that the sighting notch finds its chief use; and as my examples are almost all from one compact mountain district, it will be well to give an outline sketch of its topography.

THE BLACK MOUNTAINS

This huge mountain group of Old Red Sandstone, bordering the three shires of Hereford, Monmouth, and Brecon, can be represented by the right hand laid down on a table, fingers and thumb slightly opened and pointing south-south-east. The fingers exactly represent the ridges of the group, closed at the knuckles end by a lofty cross ridge, and here the streams flowing out between the fingers have their rise. The thumb represents (but it is rather too long) the short outlying ridge, the Cat's Back or Black Hill, shown in end section in Fig. 64. Averaging 2,000 feet, and about 11 miles in length, many points of the mountains rise one, two, three, and up to six hundred feet higher. The reputed highest point is the 2,624 feet Pen-y-Gader-fawr (head of the great chair), which is the knuckle of the third finger in my comparison, and is seen as a wart on a long level ridge from all parts of Herefordshire. As a fact, however, there is a bit of the ridge (Waun Fach) 36 feet higher. The chief valley, that of the river Honddu, lies between the first and second fingers, its floor about 500 feet above the sea at its outlet. The Grwyne Fawr and the Grwyne Fechan come between the other fingers, and the Olchon between short thumb and finger. All these rivers die off to nothing in the great cross ridge, and give their names to their valleys. The Monnow, a larger river than either, runs outside the group, but alongside the first ridge from Herefordshire. The great cross ridge closing all these valleys drops 1,000 feet in splendid sheer escarpment to a plateau above the Wye at the Hay and Glasbury end. Outliers of the main group, the Sugar Loaf and Skirrid, form striking sighting points at the Abergavenny end (Fig. 80).

Many trackways cross these ridges with their 1,000 feet dip to the intervening valleys, and although there are a few sighting mounds on the ridges to mark the way (Garn Wen—" the white cairn "—is one) they are not nearly so plentiful as are sighting notches, although cairns of stones, of which some remain, were also used.

It was from the outside of the ridge, following the road (and the Monnow) from Pandy to Longtown, that I first noticed the notches, and in this stretch are at least half a dozen, some here illustrated (Figs. 67, 70, 72). That opposite to Pandy is now formed by the earthwork of a camp, but was probably on a ley before the camp was made. Fig. 67 shows it.

A pair of notches opposite Clodock (Fig. 72) can be seen from different angles, because the roads which form them are cut through a narrow rock ridge, and this pair of notches can also be seen (for the same reason) from within the mountain group, when fairly high up on the central ridge near Llanthony. This particular track is now called the Rhiw Cwrw or beer path, the chief track from Longtown coming through it for Llanthony, its use by the monks being inferred by tradition in its name. It is strange that notches often go in pairs close together. A notch illustrated from the Longtown series is that sharp V-shaped one through the Black Darren, illustrated separately and as a sighting point over the Tan House causeway (Fig. 70). This is of the type which can only be seen of full sharpness if standing in the ley, for seen from points only 100 yards right or left it is smaller and less sharp.

It is well here to visualize the two different types of notches. The first (as illustrated at Coldman's Hill) is where a rounded bank or mountain is crossed, and is made by cutting the road deeply for a distance over the breast, this type being only visible when on that side of the bank or mountain, and then only when in or very near the right line of sight, for the same reason that you cannot see the hole through a gun barrel unless you hold it aligned. The second type is made by cutting the track deep when passing through a fairly sharp ridge, and is like a notch in a paper knife, it can be seen at different angles, and if on the top of a mountain or hill can be seen from both sides.

There is a favoured spot—Llanthony—in the heart of the Black Mountains where primitive tracks and notches can well be studied. Its situation was well described by Giraldus after his tour with Baldwin in 1188: "In the deep vale of Ewias, which is about an arrow-shot broad, encircled on all sides by lofty mountains, stands the church. . . . Here the monks, sitting in their cloisters, enjoying the fresh air, when they happen to look up towards the horizon, behold the tops of the mountains as it were touching the heavens, and herds of wild deer feeding on their summits."

It is a sighting mound on the skyline as seen above the triforium of the ruined priory from the coffee-room window of the comfortable inn embedded in the ruins which now interests us. There is little else in sighting points to be seen from the Abbey (it is always so called and should not be confused with a structure built by Father Ignatius 4 miles away in a different parish). But go to the top of the beautiful meadow on the way to Sarpel, the site of the house which Walter Savage Landor (the ancestor of the well-known explorer of Tibet, who is still owner of the estate) began but left unfinished, and there is plenty to be seen.

A short length of hollow, grassy roadway sights up to a sharp notch on the northern ridge. Planting sighting rods for this alignment, and then sighting backward (both directions being shown in Figs. 75 and 76), the ley passes through the chancel of the original priory (for this is the second building), and then falls upon one of the three deep gullies or tracks which steeply climb the central ridge. It is a good four-point example—the notch, the fragment of old road in the valley, the church on the ley, the steep track up the mountain. It is true that the last is said to be (with the others) caused by sliding down from quarries the tiled stones for roofing the old priory, and it may be so ; but the two others (the central one the most complete) has each its own notch aligning with its direction. From near our standpoint several notches (on the northern ridge) can be seen. More to the right is another notch with a straight track climbing diagonally to it. From about here too can be seen southward (Fig. 77), spread out on the central ridge behind Llanthony, a most instructive series of trackways of four types :

Firstly, the three almost vertical primitive tracks on extreme left already described.

Secondly, a long, straight sunken track climbing the mountain diagonally, appearing to aim for Bal Mawr, and obviously forming a notch for those using it. It is called Rhiw'r-mwnt, the peat-track, the farm at its foot being Troed-rhiw'r-mwnt, the foot of the peat track. Above on the skyline can just be seen the worn outline of two sighting mounds.

Thirdly, a perfectly horizontal terrace track along the side of the ridge, in at the cwm, and out round the headland, and continuing for miles up the valley. This type seems a later evolution, made with a determination not to dip at a cwm (only to climb up again), and although sighted in a general sense, sighted on a horizontal rather than a vertical plane. The type wants careful investigation.

Fourthly, on the right, a far more recent utilitarian horse-track just going up the side of Cwm-Bwchel and following the contours of the hill-side in the way most convenient for a man with a horse in one valley wanting to get to the top to drop down to the next valley. No elements of a sighting system seem to be in this. Yet (more than half a century ago) I saw a schoolfellow pick up a " large brass " coin of Antonius on the shingle of the Honddu just where this newest track crossed. I think that it set going a mental train of inquiry as to the tracks of our ancestors of which these pages are a result.

Another instance of part at least of a track sighted on a notch—shown in the frontispiece—is quite close to Llanthony on the first part of the usual track for Longtown or Pandy.

Mr. Knight, of Llanthony Abbey, points out a notch a mile or two up the valley, which the natives simply call " The Notch," and give it as the point to aim at if you wish to cross over into the Grwyne Valley. This shows from Pen-y-Gader as a notch, and is marked on the map as Bwlch Bach.

More important is the Bwlch Effengyl (the Gospel Pass), which is not only the main track out of the valley at its closed end for Hay, but is so called as being traversed by Archbishop Baldwin when on his recruiting crusade in 1188; the local tradition being that " St. Paul came preaching over the mountains." From a point on the hill-side opposite Llanthony, and six miles distant, I saw this pass as a clean-cut notch, obviously not a natural configuration (Fig. 74). It happened that a few weeks later I was at Llowes, 5 miles beyond Bwlch Effengyl in an exactly straight line from my first standpoint, and, as anticipated, the pass also showed against the skyline as a clean-cut notch. These notches are sometimes called the crack, and there is a Crack-o'-hill farm near Much Dewchurch.

The philological evidence is convincing. " Bwlch " is frequent in maps of a Welsh mountain district, and I have always found it to mean a mountain " pass " over a high ridge or gap. In the glossary written by Mr. Ivor B. John for a recent edition of Lady Charlotte Guest's " Mabinogion " the word " Bwlch " is simply defined as " notch," and on tracing the reference in the text I found it to come through personal names so called from presence or absence or number of notches in the glaive or sword.

Two other languages provide in British place-names elements indicating hill-notch. The " Introduction to the Survey of British Place Names " (1924) gives " skard " as old Norse for " notch, cleft, mountain pass," with Scarcliff (Derby) as an example; Mr. G. B. Grundy in his " Saxon Land Charters of Wiltshire " quotes " Hwite Sceard " as " White Gap," and in Milne's " Gaelic Place Names of the

Lothians," Cat Nick Road is "notch in which there was a path"—"cat" being Scotch for path.

The early surveyors (whether called ley-men or dod-men or othor title) must have had some means of marking out the path of these straight deep-cut tracks, in their proper position of alignment between two distant hill peaks or other mark points. This method—that of the two sighting staves which the Long Man of Wilmington carries—is described in the Sighting Staff chapter.

An actual verification of sighting notch alignment is so convincing that I must give it in detail. From the bridge over the Honddu (its parapet shown in Fig. 52) at Llanvihangel Mill I had noted two sharp but tiny notches on the skyline of the lofty Bryn Arw. I also noted that they altered in sharpness and intensity with very little lateral change of standpoint, and that the maximum was in a Honddu-side meadow. So while I called on the miller to transact some business, I asked my very competent helper (Mr. W. H. McKaig) to plant a staff in the line of maximum intensity. When I came out he had not only done this, but had planted a second staff a dozen yards away, in alignment to the notch. These, of course, sighted to the notch, and in sighting backwards we found that the alignment passed through the Scotch firs in Llanvihangel Park, which are on a knowl close against the road junction for the Graig. Now, we could not locate the hill notches on the map, but we could locate these firs and the spot where we planted our sighting staves, and when I got home a pin was driven in at each of these points on the map and a line drawn through them. One end of this line rested on the Sugar Loaf Mountain (1,955 feet) and the other end rested on the apex of Garway Hill (1,203 feet). The ley passed through two corroborative points—Great Campstone Farm and the chief road junction not far above it. We could not see either of these mountain points from below, but the ancient surveyor on Bryn Arw who planted his deeply-cut road in exactly the right position could see both, and had used his primitive staves in the way described in Chapter XII for sighting to these—his two hill terminals.

The well-known carriage road cutting through the crest of the Malverns called the Wych shows as a skyline notch from Coddington. Although partly of modern excavation

I have no doubt from the evidence of ancient straight tracks climbing to it from both sides, and from its name, that it was a prehistoric notch, smaller than at present.

An illustration of a hollow road across a sand ridge in Palestine forming a sighting notch is illustrated in Fig. 66; and in this case my friend, who actually used it as a directing point, assured me that the road was only cut deep where it went over the ridge, that is, only at the place where a sighting notch would be effective.

Three very striking photographs of sight notches (at close range) in Yorkshire will be found illustrating Mr. Kitson Clark's paper on a Prehistoric Route ("Proc. Soc. of Antiquaries," 1911, Vol. XXIII, pp. 321–323); the purpose I assign to them is not there indicated, although Mr. Clark (and Dr. Miller whom he quotes) both note that where a route proved by evidence of barrows crosses a ridge there is often a deep indentation.

CHAPTER VIII

INITIAL POINTS

Whose height commands as subject all the vale.
—"Troilus and Cressida"

A SIGHTED line across country must have two initial points, but never more, for an observer must stand at the first and, aiming at the second for a mark, produce his line.

In the nature of things only one of four procedures can be taken when initialing a ley: (1) Sighting from one hill peak to another, this being the usual method. (2) Sighting from a hill peak to some objective on lower ground. (3) Sighting from (comparatively) low ground to a hill peak. (4) Sighting over or from a fixed point to a heavenly body (as the rising sun), which thus becomes one of the initials.

An initial point from which, or to which, a sighting line is directed might possibly be an object of rite or reverence, and there is a good deal of evidence found in ley mapping that such fixed objects as sacred wells and natural fixed rock outcrops of peculiar shape were often on leys; and if thus on leys it follows that each one must be one of the two initial points. A very little reflection will show that it is most unlikely that when a ley is sighted from one natural peak to another a *third* unmovable objective such as a natural well or spring should align.

It is a feature of all the sighting points (after the initials) whether mound, stone, earth cutting or tree, that they are artificially placed so as to be on the ley.

It is not an easy task (and usually left unaccomplished) to find the two initial points of a ley. A personal knowledge of the country is necessary for this.

It by no means follows that the two initials terminate the ley. When sighting staves were used (as they were) it was as easy to sight backwards from a hill point as forwards, still keeping to the ley. And, for example, although the ley sighted from Hanter to Herrock (Figs. 49 and 50) had their two peaks as initial points, it was continued to the south of Hanter for at least as far as some mark which decided ages later the position of Gladestree Church.

There is a good deal of evidence that certain natural rock structures used for early ritual or ceremony became initial points from which leys were started, and this type of site, being decided by nature, cannot come under the heading of mark stones. The natural boulder (Fig. 26) described in the New Radnor chapter is on the crossing of two leys, and in the whole of this district I know of no rock platform so exactly suited for the performance of religious rites in the presence of a large assembly.

Then there is the case of the Logan or Rocking Stones, the centre, all over the world, of superstitious interest. Even where they are "perched blocks" placed by glacial action they are not placed by man. The Buckstone near Staunton in the Forest of Dean is a rocking stone; it is on the edge of a steep escarpment, not perched above other rocks, but on a level with them, and clearly of the same structure and formation. It is certainly a natural feature due to the wear and tear of ages. It commands extensive views, and a ley passes through it, the Long Stone, and the Berry Hill cross-road. The remarkable thing about it is that adjoining, within 7 yards, there is an artificial stone basin cut in the top of one of the natural rocks, which are grouped around, the basin obviously made for some purpose or ritual. Any suggestion of "pot-hole" caused by water action is ruled out in this case. At first a "sacrificial" purpose suggests itself, and the curious notch in the side seems suitable for a man's neck. But I now think it quite as probable that this rock basin was a recess in which was burnt oil or fat for beacon use. There is the unexplored possibility that "burnt sacrifices," utilizing "the fat of rams," in some way was linked up with the beacon light, and that the two purposes are compatible. These matters are touched upon in other chapters; the point here concerned with us is that two objects of prehistoric use and reverence are together, that both are naturally placed rocks, that a ley goes through or to the spot, which is therefore an initial point.

As regards "sacred" wells, there can scarcely be a doubt. Repeated evidence in ley hunting shows tracks straight for them. One of the earliest, shown to members of the Woolhope Field Club in the early days of this investigation (to their almost unanimous disbelief), was a track in an orchard aiming straight for the Coldwell (Cole-well) at Holmer. Leys with abundant sighting point evidence make straight for such wells. They often seem to have been marked with a stone, as in the well at Michaelchurch-on-Arrow (Fig. 93), and there is an Oldstone Well near Symond's Yat. Dom Ethelbert Horne in his "Somerset Holy Wells" (p. 22) quotes a thirteenth-century document as giving the Priddy Fairwell as a boundary mark. "Thence to Cold Ovens, thence to a stone in Fairwell, in Priddy Minery." I show (Fig. 45) a Cornish Holy Well (photographed forty years ago with no note as to its locality) in which the mark stone appears to have been utilized as the apex of a pyramidical stone covering to the well, and a cross surmounts it. This seems to have an affinity to the idea of a steeple over the mark stone which settled the site of a church, and in earlier days with the apex stone of an Egyptian pyramid which was furnished with two look-out eyes. Might not all three be survivals of sighting points on leys?

Holy wells often had a church built over or alongside them. Marden Church, with a well in the western end, is our Herefordshire instance, and there are churchyard wells at Goodrich and Pilleth—the latter a holy well.

Winchester Cathedral has one under the high altar, and the one at Wells is famous. Dursley churchyard has a copious flowing spring.

Several ancient crosses, as Geddington and Rockingham in Northamptonshire, are built over flowing springs of water, and these, like the well churches, therefore combine what are usually secondary ley marking points with a ley initial point, exactly as the chapels on the summits of the St. Michael's Mounts (and there are a number of them) do with regard to hill peak initial points.

There are wells called by names which are peculiar to leys. Such are Blackwell, Whitewell, Colewell, and Dodwell. This fact is evidence that wells were on leys.

When a ley comes down to the coast it must have a terminal near—perhaps on the cliff—as Whitby Abbey on the headland; sometimes a point like Worm's Head, or Lantern Rock, Ilfracombe; sometimes a rock in the sea, as the Oar Stone, and Thatcher Stone off Torquay.

Where more than two leys cross at one point it is probable (and where more than three cross it is certain) that the point has become an initial point for originating all after the first two. Stonehenge, for example, first had its site decided by the crossing of leys, then a sun temple built on a mark stone, which then became the initial point from which other leys were sighted.

I have probably dwelt too much upon the exceptional initial points, and must point out that lofty hills or mountains are the most frequent.

In my own district these are seldom under 1,000 feet. As a type of such there are on the Black Mountains, Pen-y-Gader, Pen-y-beacon, and Bal-mawr. Then the Brecon Beacons, the Begwins, Gwaunceste, the Whimble on Radnor Forest (Fig. 17), the Shropshire Longmynds, Wrekin and Clee Hills, and the various points of the Malvern range, namely: North Hill, Worcester Beacon, Pinnacle Hill (Fig. 78), Herefordshire Beacon, and Midsummer Hill (Fig. 79). The Stroud district also provides initial points for leys crossing Herefordshire, some of which run right across to the Radnorshire mountains. Cole's Tump (Fig. 80) was, with its exceptional position, certainly an initial point.

CHAPTER IX

MARK TREES

> The close combination of sacred tree and sacred stone is frequent and significant.
>
> —GRANT ALLEN: "The Crouch Oak"

THERE is every reason to surmise that trees were planted in prehistoric times as sighting marks, although it is obvious that none so planted can now exist.

The frequent "One-Tree" hills, with those to this day marked with compact tree clumps, such as "The Clump" described in the Mark Stone chapter, indicate this. One of the meanings given in the "New English Dictionary" for the ancient word "folly" so frequent in place-names is "a clump of fir trees on the crest of a hill." Trees are joined up with stones, water (wells), mountain-tops, mounds, and fire as objects of ancient reverence and even worship; all these are found as sighting points on the ley.

The grove of Dodona was the chief place of oracles in ancient Greece, and the curious affinity between the Latin names for grove and light might be due to ley sighting. Although the prophets of the grove are named in the Bible side by side with the prophets of Baal, the word "grove" is said to be a mistranslation which should read "standard" (akin to our present May-pole), probably originating as a single tree.

As a matter of present-day observation the outstanding conclusion, after exploring hundreds of leys about Herefordshire, is that the Scotch fir is the typical tree of the ancient track, and that from some peculiarity in its habits it affords most evidence on the subject of this chapter. It is continually said that this tree is not indigenous to the southern parts of England, and was introduced from Scotland about the time of a Scotch king (James I) coming to the English throne. It may well be that it became fashionable to plant avenues or clumps of it about that time; but as regards the bulk of the Scotch firs in this district the assertion is sheer nonsense.

Nine-tenths are in such ancient or, at first sight, casual and out-of-the-way spots that they could not have been planted but must have seeded naturally.

Dr. Williams-Freeman points out that the remains of this tree (*Pinus Silvestris*) are to be found in peat bogs in the south, and a correspondent writes that it is also in fossil deposits in the Berkshire district.

It is not a theory, but an observation slowly built up that Scotch firs (in the district named) are almost certain signs either of the line of an ancient track, or more particularly its sighting points. They are to be seen in twos and threes about the very ancient homesteads, or a thin line of them running along a hill ridge or flank as (formerly) at Garway Hill, Shucknell Hill, Herefordshire, and Linley Hill, Salop. A group on a high ridge sighting point can be seen by Londoners in Constable's Firs at the top of Hampstead Heath. Richard Jeffries and Walter Johnston have remarked how frequently they are planted on a tumulus, and that also is the fact in this district. The strange thing is that where so found no others can usually be seen in the country round, except perhaps a solitary one in a field which also marks the same ley track.

Sometimes a clump (Fig. 21) (as described in the Radnor Vale chapter) denotes where an ancient barrow once stood.

In the wood called Homme Bank (a ridge in Stretton Grandison, Herefordshire) are two tumuli, much worn away with rabbit burrows. Both are packed with Scotch firs, and no other Scotch firs are near in either case. At the other end of the ridge an ancient (unused) hollow road climbs the hill, and this has its line of Scotch firs with no others near to it. A single Scotch fir now crowns the castle mound at Lingen. On Cole's Tump (Fig. 80) a well-proved sighting point, commanding views of other mountain points for twenty miles, half the trees are Scotch firs and half are beeches; this is typical of other hill points and tumuli, for other trees are also present on marking points. The Scotch fir is "a Carlyle among the trees," says Grant Allen, and its rugged beauty is well displayed in the noble avenues which I shall mention.

The oak was probably quite as much typical of the early track, but it does not afford such clear evidence as does *Pinus Silvestris*, for it is now the "weed of Herefordshire" (as Sir James Rankin once termed it), found everywhere. Yew trees are reputed to be marks of old tracks, but this investigation makes them appear to be more typical of early mediaeval tracks than of prehistoric ones; still the yew tree is an early British tree, and the mound at Capler Camp is packed with them and no others near.

Perhaps the most unexpected observation with regard to trees is the large number of the broad, stately avenues of our seats and parks which prove to be on leys. Details and illustration of that one called Monnington Walks is given in my pioneer book. This and the Duchess Walk in Oakley Park (significant name), Ludlow, apparently lead nowhere, but the remainder to be mentioned are sighted on the mansion itself, the first-named mansion being proved to have been built on a tumulus, the second reputed to be so. Trewyn (close to Pandy Station, Mon.) has its Scotch fir avenue directed straight to Alt-y-ynis (an ancient seat of the Sessyl or Cecil family), and a letter from Mrs. Gillespie, who lived at Trewyn seventeen years, and, having been a Whittaker (of the Yorkshire historian family), had a taste for investigation, tells me that in the absence of her husband she had the floor under one of the rooms of the house dug up, and they came to the burial cist of a tumulus reputed to be there. Llanvihangel Court, Mon., is the second instance, its fine Scotch fir avenue with the Skirrid in the distance. Other tree avenues are given in a previous chapter.

Catesby Avenue, Warwickshire, sighted through the mansion, is on a ley passing through Southam and Whitnash Churches (with other confirmations), and over the mound of Warwick Castle.

Stowe Avenue, Bucks., has an alignment which, passing through Stowe, Fleet Marston, and Little Kimble Churches, arrives in a course of about 45 miles to the Great Mound and Keep of Windsor Castle, to which also is sighted Queen Anne's Ride in Windsor Park.

Tree-crowned hill-tops may once more "come into their own." A Surrey correspondent tells of a conical hill, topped with Scotch firs which he purchased since the war. A timber merchant told him that many applications had been made to purchase this timber during the time of scarcity, but the Government refused to allow it to be cut down, as it was on the line of flight for aeroplanes to France, and was used as a sighting mark.

Single trees probably formed mark points on the early track, and the custom continued for boundaries and meetings. In Gomme's "Early Folk Moots," there are about twenty-five instances given of the names of Hundreds indicating that the Hundred Courts were held at a tree. Thus in Herefordshire we have Webtree, Greytree, and Brocash Hundreds.

Several ancient trees, and others with names, have been found in alignment with churches and other points. Gospel Oaks usually so align. In Hampshire are place-names Mark Oak and Mark Ash; and Broad Oak and Whitnash are other instances combining ley and tree names. Grove place-names are abundant and constantly found on a ley.

The road junction called Weobley Ash (formerly Webley) is, like Webtree, the tree on the track of the weaver or webbe. There is Cross Ash, Cross Elms, Cross Colloe (hazel), and Cross of the Tree, all at cross-roads, all indicating mark trees on the track, Taylor's 1757 map of Herefordshire actually depicting them in the last two spots exactly in the centre of the crossing roads.

Cold Ash and Cold Oak are places close together near Ivington Camp, and Cold Elm is at a cross-road near Forthampton, Worcs. These are on the track of the Cole-man.

On a high roadside point nearly 3 miles from Hereford is a spot called the "Yew and Ash," where on the law day the Herefordshire sheriff met with his javelin men the judge of assize, on his way from Shrewsbury, and the present yew and ash trees were planted in 1855 (as a stone records) to keep the spot marked.

The hawthorn or May-tree was a favourite mark tree, and many spots are named "The Thorn."

Two legends connecting this tree with a "holy" staff will be found in Chapter XXII.

CHAPTER X

CAMPS

War is a civilized institution, based as a rule on a desire to obtain some other nation's property. Prehistoric man had little temptation in this way.

—M. and C. H. B. QUENNELL

I HAVE to use the name "camp," but it infers all kinds of conclusions which may be hopelessly inaccurate. The word "wall," used in Sutton Walls and the two Wall Hills in Herefordshire, and in Walbury, conveys the more accurate impression. So what is here inferred is a space enclosed, usually on the top of a hill or high ground, by ancient earthen embankment. The early antiquarians who dragged in what a Roman military commander did in a hostile country, and the later topographers who introduce their own idea of where military defences for protection of this or that route or valley should be, have retarded the investigation of facts.

In plotting out the leys of a district it is found that every camp had at least one, and more often several leys either (as is most frequent) touching its boundaries, or going through its highest point. Either leys were planned as tracks to camps, or the positions of the camps were decided by existing tracks, just as, in later ages, the position of towns as trading centres were evolved. To find out which, a large number of examples must be examined.

There are several recurring features found in examining a number of camps which bear on the track question. It is constantly found that mounds form part of the embankment (or vallum), are adjacent to the entrance as guard mounts, or are contained within the camp enclosure. In Mr. Hippisley Cox's "The Green Roads of England" there are seven instances of mounds forming part of the embankment, and seventeen of their being within the camp.

In many cases the mound—or such a greater height of

the vallum as to indicate a mound—is at the knuckle or corner of the embankment. In our Herefordshire camps this seems to be the case at Hereford Castle Green, Longtown Castle, Dinedor, Ivington, Aconbury, Capler, and Credenhill. In the last three cases the mound appears to act as a " guard mound," the entrance coming into the camp round its base. It is a constant experience in the map plotting of leys to find them coming to these mounds.

It has been thought that the very frequent greater height of a camp vallum at a corner is due to the constructional feature that in digging a trench and throwing the earth inward more accumulates at an angle. Hogg's Mount, the corner of the Hereford Castle Green, shows more earth than can be accounted for by the above reasoning, and, moreover, this is a proved sighting mound on an important salt track.

The outline of a hill camp is usually decided for the most part by the contour of the hill. But it is a very frequent

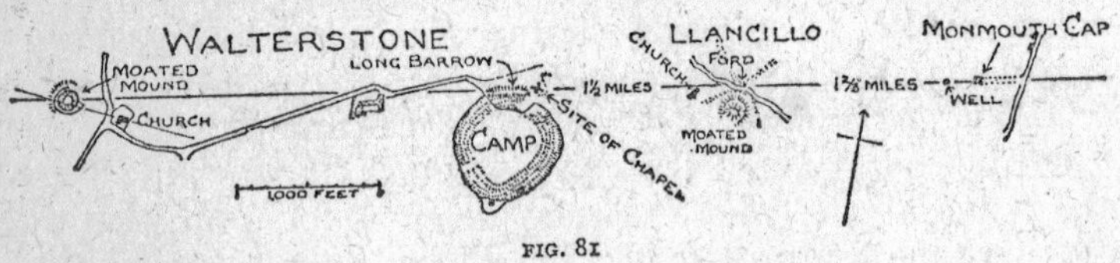

FIG. 81

feature (and this affects our present inquiry) to find straight line portions.

The general experience of the relation of camps to leys in plotting out the latter is that in the majority of cases the ley touches the boundary of the camp, sometimes coming to a mound, sometimes lying on a piece of straight vallum, sometimes doing both.

In other cases the ley comes to a mound within the camp, or to the highest point of the hill within the enclosure.

At Walterstone (Fig. 81) a ley first passes through Llancillo Church, over the site of a demolished chapel, which almost touches the embankment of a circular camp whose contour was decided by that of the hill, immediately afterwards over what appears to be a long barrow, then crossing a small valley, through a very fine moated mound near Walterstone Church. Beyond this point the Monnow Valley (lying alongside the ridge of the Black Mountains) has to be crossed, and standing at the Walterstone mound, a cairn or mound exactly on the ley can be seen on the mountain ridge, so placed that it is invisible from the valley. But a deep sunken road goes up from the ford exactly in the right position, and no doubt gave a notch indication. The ley continues through Oldcastle, and terminates in Pen Cerrig Calch, a 2,302 feet mountain peak.

To take examples where leys align on parts of the camp earthworks, with or without mounds. Ivington Camp, on a hill (Fig. 82), has two straight sides formerly with ("Woolhope Transactions," 1881) a mound at the corner junction. The north side alignment passes at either end through

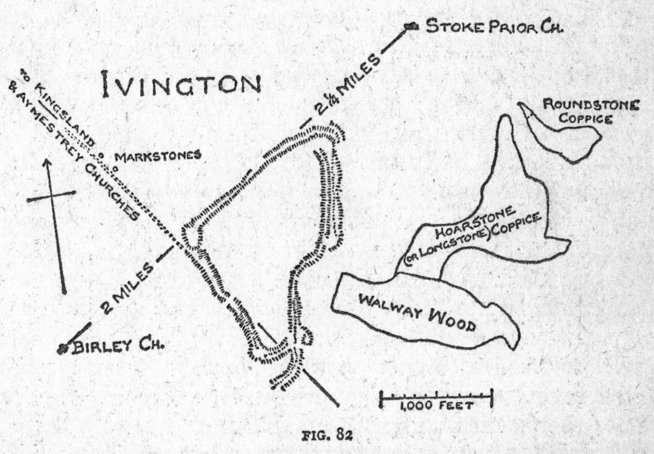

FIG. 82

Birley and Stoke Prior Churches, each about two miles distant, and, confirmed by road fragments, has a terminal in Abberley Hill, Worcestershire. Three adjacent coppices close under the camp, called respectively Longstone (or Hoarstone), Roundstone, and Wallway Coppices, give clear evidence of ancient tracks with mark stones to the camp. On the north side I found the actual straight track with two mark stones on it which I have detailed in Chapter V; it is shown in the diagram. This track does not outline the western edge of the camp, which is decided by contour.

Three camps—Credenhill, Kenchester or Magna, and Brinsop (Fig. 83)—lie near together. Credenhill is a lofty hill-top camp with magnificent earthworks, chiefly of a contour outline enclosing a large area of about 45 acres. It has, however, about three straight pieces of embankment. One of these (on the east) aligns with Credenhill Church, and another (on the north) aligns with Brinsop Church, which is also oriented on the same alignment. The guard mound might be a sighting mound, but there are no others now. The highest point is about the centre of the enclosure. Magna or Kenchester is a small Romano-British town with many foundations of buildings and streets below the surface. It has six sides, and these appear to be decided by sighted leys. The short west side, sighted on the Graig Hill, aligns with a ley passing through Brinsop Church. The north-east side with another passing through Kenchester churchyard. The south-west side is irregular on account of the contour of the ground, but it is decided by a ley thoroughly well authenticated by being sighted over two of the "Four Stones" group (see Fig. 23) near New Radnor, by lying on a bit of straight road in Fig. 83, and (outside this map) by passing through Breinton Church. The north-west line extended passes through Monnington Church, several miles distant. This is not a hill camp but on relatively high ground. The third of this trio, not on a hill, is Brinsop Camp enclosing the church; it is rectilinear, small, with rather confused outlines. But personal examination made it plain that a mound formed the junction of two earthworks at the north-west corner of the churchyard, and a ley aligned with the church running south, which ley exactly touches the eastern corner of Magna Camp.

This camp group deserves careful study to throw light upon the relation of Roman to earlier encampments.

No less than thirty of the camps illustrated in "Green Roads of England" have some part of their circumference in straight lines; and I find that in most cases if these lines are extended they touch the boundaries of other camps at a distance. In one case—Segsbury—a sarsen stone or "altar" was found on the entrenchment or vallum, and beneath it a cist and prehistoric burial, this appearing to indicate a mark stone on a trackway.

As regards mounds preceding camps, there are often strong indications in a greater height at the angle of a camp vallum or entrenchment that a mound was there to begin with, and this will be verified by examples which will be given on tracks sighted to such angles. Dr. J. Williams-Freeman in his "Field Archæology of Hampshire" describes the camp at Ellisfield. "At the north-west corner the bank is raised about five feet higher than at the sides, and at the other corners to a less degree, and not perhaps more than is necessarily the case at square corners." But the assumption made in the last part of the sentence is a doubtful one.

At Dinedor Camp, Hereford, there is considerable increase of height at the corner, and standing there the spire of All Saints' Church aligns exactly (see Fig. 47) with the tower of Hereford Cathedral, another track indication. Another mound in this camp (Fig. 84) is placed as a guard mound at the south-east entrance, and there is an indication that it

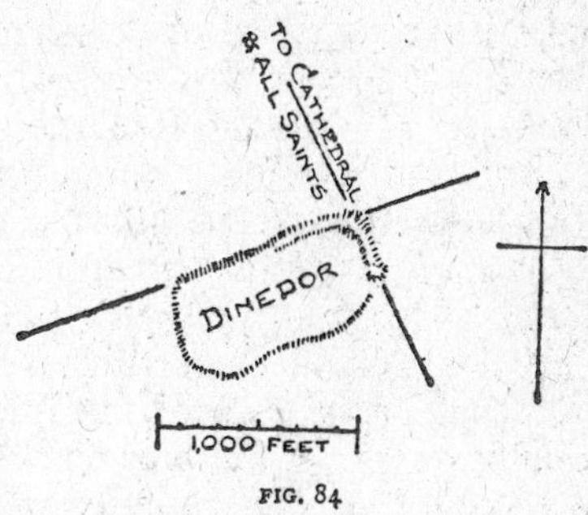

FIG. 84

is a tumulus in the persistent legend that a "general and his horse were buried there, and you can see the mark of the horseshoe on the turf."

A similar legend that "soldiers are buried here" is applied to the eastern mound at Capler Camp, presently to be described, and at Sutton Walls camp (Fig. 127), which has a pair of mounds with an entrance between them, both at the western and the eastern ends; an interment was found near the top of one of the eastern pair.

Mr. Hadrian Allcroft ("Earthwork of England," p. 592) gives an instance of Pitt-Rivers' excavation of Church Barrow, Cranbourne Chase. "The vallum, embedded within which were found Roman remains, was raised upon an ancient roadway of pre-Roman character, and showed also that the roadway had at this point made a curious bend, only to be explained by supposing that there had at a still earlier date been some obstacle on the spot. It is conceivable that the site was once occupied by a tumulus, which the British road would naturally avoid." Here, then, is evidence that a tumulus was the earliest work on the spot, that a British road sighted on it, came so straight for its mark that it had to bend to go round its base, and that in an after-age, when the mound and track were "of no account," the vallum of a contour camp was thrown up over both mound and roadway.

Aconbury Camp (Fig. 85) has a very perfect conical tumulus—higher than the earthwork which runs into its

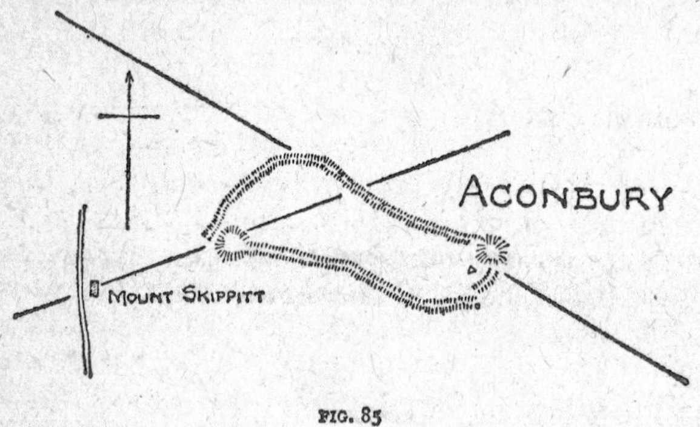

FIG. 85

flank—at the south-west corner. The camp entrance is cleverly designed to come round the base of this mound, which takes its place as part of a strong defence. That it is a sighting mound has been proved.

Capler Camp (Fig. 86) or Woldbury, as it used to be called, has also a large mound (Fig. 10), crowned in this case by a group of yew trees at its eastern end, and round this again the entrance curves. The character of the vallum of our Herefordshire camps is well shown in Fig. 87. Such camps, with their thickly wooded banks, bring the photographer to despair; as a rule, he simply cannot get a view of them. The winter, with its light of low elevation, and with an absence of leaves, is by far the best season, and the lovely December day on which this last photograph was taken gave an opportunity long hoped for. Sollers Hope church aligns and orients to the mound and decides the south vallum of Capler.

Whether the enclosure (Fig. 88) attached to Longtown Castle is to be treated as a "camp" or "bailey" is a moot question. But as the corner mound, which is undoubtedly prehistoric, and which carries the keep, has a ley to it which lies on the western limb of this rectilinear enclosure, a plan

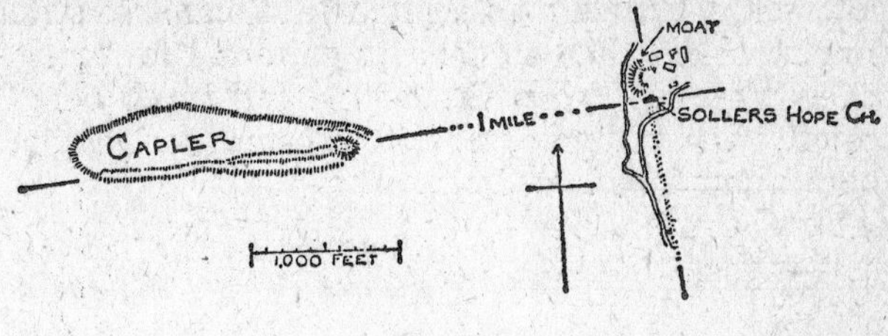

FIG. 86

is subjoined. The photograph (Fig. 63) shows how the mound is a separate structure to the camp "walls," and another photograph (Fig. 65), with the plan (Fig. 88) illustrates the way in which the embankment aligns with the keep, the ley going precisely to Llanthony Abbey. The gallows mound was on that part of this bank nearest to the

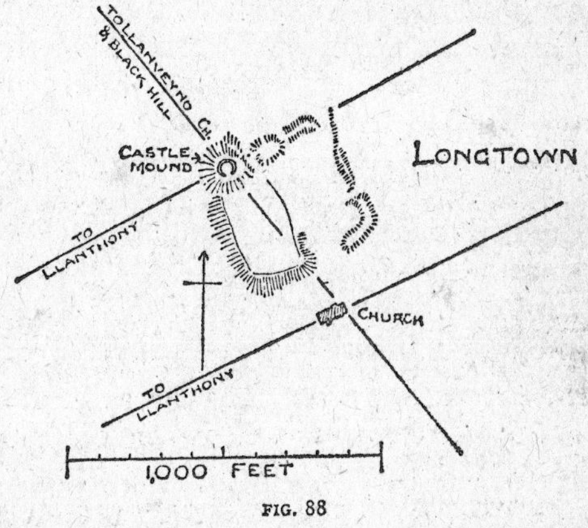

FIG. 88

Castle keep, and the memory of the last gibbeting (of a wife-poisoner, and there was "another lady in it") is still kept up, for all that summer no one on Abergavenny market would buy their butter from Longtown valley—on account of the flies! Fig. 64 shows how this castle tower (and mound) align with Llanveyno Church, the Great Black Hill, and the chancel of the church; and an ancient village well close to the church is exactly on the ley, which passes over a place called the Garn, which is Celtic for tumulus.

A still more striking instance of a mound attached to a camp (Fig. 11) being a separate and earlier structure, although obviously part of the enclosing scheme, is The Mount, Hundred House, Radnorshire, already described.

The camp is of considerable extent, but the earthen rampart does not cross at either side the very considerable moat, which completely encircles the mound. This is well shown in Fig. 7, where the rampart is to the left of the mound. Such an enclosure is very weak as a defence from armed attack, and rather indicates a peaceful purpose for the camp.

The index to "Earthwork of England" points out numerous instances of mounds in camp entrenchments. It is in Mr. J. R. Mortimer's "Burial Mounds of East Yorkshire" that the most definite information as to the relative age of mound and vallum is given; and this, after all, is the point which decides whether the camp came before the track, or if the track were the earlier. On p. 379 thus: "In fourteen instances (all of which are alluded to in the account of the opening of the barrows) where the two (earthwork and barrow) have come into collision, the barrows have always been more or less mutilated by the entrenchments in a manner which shows clearly that the latter are more recent. . . . When planning these earthworks, it would seem that in many instances, certain barrows had been chosen as points to mark the direction the entrenchments should take." Mr. Mortimer on the same page also quotes a good deal of evidence, including statements of Canon Greenwell and Dr. Thurnam, to much the same effect.

It will be noted that there is very strong evidence that the mounds were built at an earlier date than the camp entrenchments; and if my general framework is sound, the tracks were as early as the mounds, and therefore also preceded the camp. In other words, camps were made after the ground was covered with a network of tracks, often sighted over mounds on high ground, that in many cases the mounds were used as corners or as guard mounds in planning the camp, and that also in many cases part of the camp vallum was decided by a straight track. In some cases, as at Magna, the outline of the camp was decided almost entirely by existing trackways—and this often explains the polygonal shape of later camps, although the contour of the hill played a far greater part in the hill-top examples. Naturally the site (of the scores available with hill mounds and intersecting tracks) most favourably situated for defence or enclosure would be selected.

How thick the tracks were on the ground, and the large number of potential camp sites available, can be judged by the map of the Radnor Vale district. Burfa Camp, shown in that map, seems to have no tumulus in its earthworks or within its enclosure, its rocky ridge summit being natural; but although its outline is a contour one, it is evidently partly decided by the line of leys passing over the hill.

The British Camp (Fig. 79) competes with Maiden Castle, Dorset, for being the most imposing earthwork in our islands. Its summit was an initial point, and its entrenchments entirely contour ones.

Walled towns are really camps, and their walled outlines when in straight lines were often decided—like camps—by leys, with a prehistoric mound at one or more corners. The earlier the walls were built the more is this likely, and in addition to Magna already described, the Roman walls of London (Fig. 123) are an example. In other chapters it is shown that two straight line sections of London walls are sighted on the corner mound of the White Tower, and were therefore on prehistoric leys.

Some striking Breconshire proofs of camp alignments will be found in the Appendix.

CHAPTER XI

LEY-MEN

King Cole was King before the troubles came,
The land was happy while he held the helm.

. . . . .

Beneath the light arch of the heaven's span
He chose to wander earth, the friend of man.

. . . .

Men hear him on the downs, in lonely inns,
In valley woods, or up the Chiltern Wold.

—John Masefield: "King Cole"

THE planning and laying-out of the tracks, moats, mounds, and cuttings was not only skilled work demanding experienced qualifications, but employed considerable numbers of men, who had to work under such skilled direction. A class of men of knowledge must have existed, and probably other classes of men of skill working under them. Such types of men must have had class-names applied to them; and both in place-names and in other branches of the language there is such strong evidence of these names that they can be given with some certainty, although with no attempt as yet to deal with their chronology, or to which exact type of worker or directing head they applied.

The chief names here dealt with in succession are Cole, Dod, and Black, and a large volume of detail and widespread examples must be forgiven, as it is necessary to show that conclusions are not drawn from a few local facts. It is uncertain whether these same names might have applied in the same age or in succeeding ages. What is certain is that at some time or another a Coleman, a Dodman, and a Blackman did live, work, and give their names to a great variety of places

The line of deduction was first revealed by the way

MARK STONES

FIG. 30. THE LEYS, WEOBLEY
FIG. 31. ENGLISH BRIDGE, SHREWSBURY
FIG. 32. LEOMINSTER
FIG. 33. MICHAELCHURCH-ON-AVON
FIG. 34. WERGINS STONE, SUTTON
FIG. 35. VOWCHURCH

LONGSTONES

FIG. 36. STAUNTON, GLOS.

FIG. 37. WERN DERRIES, MICHAELCHURCH ESHLEY

THE CLUMP, MANSEL GAMAGE

FIG. 39. DISTANT VIEW FROM YAZOR

FIG. 40. NEAR VIEW, WITH LADY LIFT

FIG. 42. MARKSTONE FOR FORD, WYE ST., HEREFORD

FIG. 41. MARK STONE IN THE CLUMP

FIG. 43

FIG. 44

FIG. 45. HOLY WELL, CORNWALL

FIG. 46. CRESSET, LLANTHONY

FIG. 47. ALL SAINTS AND HEREFORD CATHEDRAL ALIGN TO CORNER OF CAMP. TELEPHOTO AT 4 MILES

FIG. 48. DEVIL'S ARROW, BOROUGHBRIDGE, YORKS.

HANTER-HERROCK LEY

FIG. 49. LOOKING S. TO HANTER, FROM X IN FIG. 50

FIG. 50. LOOKING N. TO HERROCK, FROM X IN FIG. 49

TRE-FEDW MOUND

FIG. 51. NEAR VIEW, SKIRRID IN DISTANCE

FIG. 52. SIGHTED ON ROAD TO SOUTH, OVER THE HONDDU AT LLANVIHANGEL MILL

FIG. 53. SIGHTED ON ROAD TO NORTH, PAST PANDY

STONED TRACKWAY, HEREFORD

FIG. 54. SECTION IN SEWER CUTTING

FIG. 55. SURFACE OF ABOVE

(detailed in the chapter on Traders' Tracks) in which the "White" places aligned to the place of salt production.

Cole occurs as a place-name element in hundreds of places. Map students should note how frequent are Cole Farm, Coles Farm, and Colman's Farm, and if inclined to derive them from an occupier's surname should reflect on the rarity of Jones, Smith, or Williams Farms. There are in Herefordshire two hills of the name; both are lofty and proved sighting points on leys. The first, Coles Tump, illustrated in Fig. 80, is crowned with a clump of trees (seven beech, and seven Scotch firs) enclosed in a rough circle 15 yards in diameter, and the clump is to be seen for many miles. The other, Cole's Hill, in the extreme north, was visited by the Woolhope Club in 1898, and the report records several pits on the summit, attributed to beacon fires. There are Coleshill names in other districts, as Warwickshire; one, Colleshyl, mentioned in a Saxon character of A.D. 799 (Gomme, "Folk Moots").

Near Cheltenham, a Coleman's Farm is on a ley through another homestead called Colways, a name used by Masefield in that monument to the beauty of English place-names, "Reynard the Fox." St. Nicholas Cole Abbey is a London Church; Colegate is a street in Norwich.

In the "Chronicon Scotorum," an Irish record, about a score of separate persons called Colman are recorded in the index, and they are bishops, archbishops, and the sons of kings.

The "New English Dictionary" gives a rare obscure word "Cole," as meaning a juggler. Also, as of more frequent usage, "cole-prophet," sometimes spelt "cold-prophet," a wizard, sorcerer, or diviner. Also the word "cole-staff" or "cowl-staff."

In Rowland's "Mona Antiqua Restaurata" the word "coel" is mentioned in connexion with tumuli and cairns, and it is said there are "grounds of probability that it really was some solemn appurtenance or religion, although now quite forgotten."

It appears to have a Celtic origin, for in Pugh's Welsh Dictionary will be found: *Coel*, an omen, belief; *Coel-bren*, a piece of wood used in choosing or balloting; *Coel y beirdd*, the alphabet of the bards; *Coelcerth*, omen of danger, beacon, bonfire; *Coelfain*, the stones of omen.

The above, which suggest early practices, are connected with cole by the fact that east of Colchester is an ancient earthwork marked as King Coel's Castle. Between Neath and Brecon is an early camp called Coelbren. And Old King Cole is not the only instance of the name being recorded in folk-lore, as will be seen by the legend of "Old Coles" in the chapter on that subject.

The following is a list of "cole" place-names, the "cold" ones being also added:

Cole (rivers, hamlets), Cole Abbey (St. Nicholas, London), Colebatch, Colebreen, Colebrook, Coleburn, Coleby, Colebury, Cole Church (St. Mary, London), Cole Cross, Coledale, Colefax, Coleford, Coleham, Cole Harbour, Colehill, Colehouse, Coleman's (Hatch, Farm, Town, Well), Colemere, Colemore, Colepike, Cole Pool, Coleraine, Coleridge, Colerne, Colethorpe, Colewell, Colewood, Coley.

Colesborne, Colesdon, Coles Farm, Coles Green, Coles Hall, Coles Hill, Coles Lake, Coles Park, Colestock, Colesty, Coles Tump, Coleswood, Colesworthy.

Colbury, Colchester, Coldrum, Colfin, Colford, Colgate, Colgrain, Colham, Colhugh, Colkirk, Colman, Colman's (Well, Street, Town), Colstey, Colway, Colwall, Colwell, Colwich, Colwick, Colwyn.

Cold Ash, Cold Ashby, Cold Ashton, Coldborough, Cold Brayfield, *Coldbrook, Coldcoats, Coldcotes, Cold Conniston, Cold Eaton, Cold East, Cold Elm, Cold Fair Green, Cold Fell, *Cold Green, Cold Hanworth, Cold Hatton, Cold Henley, Cold Higham, *Coldham, *Cold Harbour, Coldhayes, Coldheart, Coldhesledon, *Coldhill, Coldhurst, Cold Kirby, Cold Kitchen, Coldman's Hill, *Coldmore, Coldmeece, Coldnap, Cold Newton, Cold Norton, Cold Nose, Cold Oak, Coldon, Cold Overton, Coldrenick, Coldrey, Coldred, *Coldridge, Cold Rowley, Coldroast, Coldshiels, Coldside, *Colds Farm, Coldsmouth, Coldstead, Coldstone, Coldstream, Coldswaltham, *Coldswood, *Coldwell, Cold Weston.

The ten "cold" names marked with an asterisk (*) have, it will be seen, corresponding names in one (or sometimes two) of the other lists, but without the "d."

Colemanstrete of London city is mentioned in the "Libercustumarum," *temp.* Ed. I; and Lethaby in his book on pre-Conquest London, quotes a very early Saxon charter referring to this spot as "Coelmundingehaga not far from Westgelum," but I doubt whether this is the street. Mr. P. H. L'Estrange tells me of Chapel Coleman, a church in Cardiganshire, and how quite near it is an upright Coleman's Stone with an Ogam inscription and an incised emblem embodying two conjoined curves like a pair of eyes. In Herefordshire, Villa Colman was one of the churches of the Ergyng or Irchenfield district, although its identity is now lost.

In the "Chronicle of Roger of Hovenden" (twelfth century), Vol. I, page 45, Coldingham is spelt "Collingham," but with the "d" in other pages. In MSS. *temp*. Ed. I, St. Nicholas Cole Abbey is given as St. Nicholas "Coldabbay."

Alles in "Folk Lore of Worcestershire," in mentioning Cold Place, Lulsley, says: "Here we have a clear case that the name Colles was corrupted into Cold; Colles or Coles having been the name of its early owners."

The much talked about Cold Harbour is given as "Cole Harbour" in Ben Jonson's "Silent Woman," and in Healy's "Discovery of a New World"; and in London, on the Thames, was a Cole Harbour. Another Cole Harbour is marked on a 1597 plan of the Tower of London, within its precincts, adjoining the White Tower. A ley through this, lying on Great Tower Street (Fig. 123) goes to Primrose Hill, through the Mansion House (on site of ancient "Stocks Market") and St. Martin's le Grand to Primrose Hill.

When old John Lingen, of New Radnor, was quoting to me an ancient local jingle, he gave the opening lines as:

Silver John is dead and gone
And buried in Cole Harbour,

and when I asked him whether he did not mean "Cold" Harbour, he was very emphatic in his first version.

The supposed chilly meaning of "cold" is fairly probable when applied to -well, -brook, and -stream, just possible with -harbour, -hill, and -cot, but breaks down entirely when applied to -man, -ash, -oak, -elm, and other forms.

Cold was "cole," and the "d" was intruded in quite early times, the meaning of the word being obscure even then.

The general conclusion is that the Coleman, who gave his name to all kinds of points and places on the tracks, was a head-man in making them, and probably worked from the Colehills, using beacon fires for marking out the ley.

Three local experiences connect also the "cold" names with old tracks and their sighting points. (1) Visiting Coldstone Common on account of its name, a straight, slightly sunken track (not a watercourse) was found along its whole length. (2) At Coldman's Hill the deep sunken road illustrated in Fig. 71 was found. (3) Halting at a road junction on a highway because a long-distance track was marked as crossing; a cottage (unnamed on the map) stood on high ground at the spot. I remarked to my companion that it was obviously a sighting point, and might have an ancient place-name; would he knock at the door and ask? The reply was the name—Cold Nose.

"Dod" place-names and words yield much information, and lead to the conclusion that the early surveyor who used a pair of staves in the way described in the Sighting Staff chapter was the dod-man.

Didley Mound, illustrated in my earlier book, was Dodeley in "Domesday Book," just as the present Diddlebury in Shropshire was Dodylbury in the "Bishops' Register" of 1461. In these registers are found places then called Dod, Doditree, Doddington, Dodesley, Dodderhill (a church on a hill-top close to Droitwich Station), Dodelaye, Dodestone, and Dodmarston. The name element is added to -hill, -marsh, -green, -cot, -lee, etc., all over the Kingdom, and Dodman's Point is a cliff-castle on the Cornish coast. There are two indications in Mr. Hugh R. Watkins' fine book on Totnes that point to "dod" and "tot" or "toot" being akin. An old writer there quoted says that "Totneys should be Dodneys," and a place called Totefen had an alternate name Dodefen. It should be mentioned that the "Tot" or "Dod" at Totnes was the mound of the Castle keep; and it sights precisely down the main street of the town. The "New English Dictionary" gives us one of the meanings of the word dod: "In the North of England and South of Scotland a frequent term for a rounded eminence."

Mr. James G. Wood, F.S.A., in a paper read to the Woolhope Club in 1920 on the Scot or "scout" place-names (to be mentioned in another place) says, "As an alternative for 'Scotland' we find Deadman's (i.e. Dodman's) acre, furlong or green, adjacent to a Toothill, Totman's low and such like." There is a "Deadman's Hole" in Norwich, Hole being, as usual, Lane.

Another "New English Dictionary" meaning for "dod" is an old name for "a stalk, staff, club," and several water reeds or plants (the fox-tail, cats-tail, reed-mace) have been given that name. Here a staff is linked up with sighting points.

There is an old name for snail quoted by Dickens in "David Copperfield." "'I'm a regular Dodman, I am,' said Mr. Peggotty, by which he meant snail, being an allusion to his being slow to go." Generations of doting mothers and nurses, when telling off the identity and titles of babies' little pink toes, do it in the old jingle: "Peedy Weedy, Pally Ludy, Lady Whistle, Lody Wassel, and GREAT BIG Hoddyman Dod!"

The sight of a snail out for a walk one warm moist morning (Fig. 73) solved the problem. He carries on his head the dod-man's implements, the two sighting staves.

At Wilmington in Sussex, the Long Man, with his 240 feet length cut in the turf on the hill-side (Fig. 89), the largest and perhaps the earliest representation of prehistoric man in England, carries two staves. Now the soldier carries but one spear, the shepherd one crook, the pedestrian one staff, the farmer one pike. The surveyor alone carries two rods. The Long Man is the dod-man, the prehistoric surveyor. If any doubt is still felt, look up in the "New English Dictionary," the meaning of the word "dodge" as moving something "to and fro, or backwards and forwards, or up and down," and compare such action with the constant and alternate moving of the two sighting rods in work, as described in the next chapter.

Consider also the movement of a "doddering" old man, who feebly goes through the same action with his feet or sticks.

"Black" is one of the abundant place-name elements, and like those just dealt with occurs both in the "high places" and at all track points. It seems to apply to a man on the ley, for Blackmarstone in Hereford suburbs was Blakemanstone in 1400 ("blake" and "blache" were early variations), and there are also Blackmanstone places in Dorset and in Kent. It is a track name, for we have two Blackways and a Blakeway, also a Blacklains and a Black Yat (" gate " or road), this last high up under Gwaunceste Mountain. There are Black Holes (" heol " or road) in Herefordshire and Devon—two in the first county. Other examples are Blackwardine, Black Down, Black Bush, and Blakemere, in Derbyshire as well as Herefordshire. There are two Black Hills on a spur of the Black Mountains, and grouped near them no less than seven Black Hill Farms; also a Black Darren or rock escarpment, and not far off is a Black Wood and a Blackbrook, which has a Derbyshire counterpart in Blakebrook.

There are Blackstones for mark-points on the coast, and a native telling me about the remains of the village cross at Huntley (Glos.) said: " We always called it the Black Stone." At Iona are Black Stones which the recorder mentions are really grey.

The Black Mixen (Fig. 18) is both a tumulus and an initial sighting point on Radnor Forest, and there is a tumulus near Brighton called the Black Burgh. Black Hill is another sighting point close to the Wynds Point pass on the Malverns.

Bateman's " Ten Years Digging on Grave Hills," records four Blake Lows or tumuli.

Look up the word in the " New English Dictionary " and it is said to be a " word of difficult history," for (once again a track name is connected with light) it seems to come from blake and blac, which even in Anglo-Saxon days did not mean without light, but " shining, white, pale," and which root has in fact given us " bleach " and " bleak." There was a lane or " hole " in ancient Norwich called Blekesteres from the fullers or cloth bleachers who worked there.

Mr. Hugh R. Watkin, of Torquay, in an exhaustive paper read to his local Natural History Society, links up the " black " names with " blag," an element meaning in Slav languages blessed or light-given. He concludes—rightly—that most of these places were not so named from being what we now call black, but that the sites were of special or religious interest.

Mr. Watkin gives place-names which commence with Black and end with -borough, -pool, -stone, -grove, -well,

-slade, -ford, -cap, -tor, -heath, -lake, -brook, -burn, -moat, -end, -gate, -broom, -acre, -land, -hole, -way, and -ley.

In "Early British Trackways" I attributed the black places as being on the track of the ironworker or charcoal carrier to the forges. But evidence obtainable has not confirmed this, and I now think (since the information in the chapter on Beacons has accumulated) that the cole-man or beacon-minder would quite likely be the "black"-man as well; and as, no doubt, all forms of ley sighting points become objects of reverence, the "black" places would be so. The beacon tender, in days of greatest reverence or awe, would—whether a "blake" or "cole" man by name—be associated with gleaming light; but in later days the ashes of his occupation might well alter his name to another meaning.

Surnames show the transition of the name, as in Bleek, Bleak, Blake, and Black; they indicate derivation from a place-name on a track in Blakeway, Blakeley, Bleackley, and Blackley; and from a man's occupation or characteristic in Blachman, Bleakman, Blackmon, and Blackman.

If the foregoing conclusions are true the present meanings of the two leading words in "As black as a coal" come down from the occupation of the beacon-man, associated with light and help, but involving a grimy face and appearance. Note how an observer now to be quoted, quite independently, concludes with the "black" man lighting the beacon.

Mr. J. G. Wood, F.S.A. (Woolhope Club "Transactions," 1920, p. 198), finds that the place-name element Scot frequently occurring all over England in such names as Scot's Hole, Scot's Hill, Scotland Bank, etc., has nothing to do with the northern nation, but simply indicates the shelter on the look out place of the watcher or scout, and associates the name with the touts or beacons. He concludes thus: "If any doubt is felt as to the identity in origin or meaning of 'Scot' and 'Scout,' reference may be made to the arms of Sir Walter Scott, in which the sinister supporter is a black man holding a lighted torch in the position for lighting the beacon; and the motto is 'Watch Weel.' The closing chapters of Sir Walter's 'Antiquary' also seem to indicate a more than casual interest in the history and practice of signalling by beacon fires."

It is not completely clear in this if "Scot" refers to a man; the "New English Dictionary" shows no connexion between it and scout, but some connexion with a cutting, an incision, a score; and a rare obsolete meaning of scut is embankment.

One meaning of "scot" ("scot and lot") was a payment, contribution, or tax. "Cole" ("plank down the cole") had a similar meaning in slang.

I see considerable evidence connecting the place-name element "jack"—also a personal name element—with ley matters, and the same to a lesser degree with "grim."

Totman's Low and Laidman's Low among the Derbyshire tumuli, and Tutman's Hole on the Dodd in Cumberland, suggest other passing names for the ley-men. The tutti-man, indeed, survives to this day, for he parades the streets of Hungerford once a year, as presently to be described, and carries in his six-foot staff a relic of his predecessor's occupation. Near Clifton-on-Teme is a Weyman's Wood.

I cannot sort these names out as regards time sequence, racial derivation, or grade of occupation.

The Welsh Triads ("Ancient Institutes and Laws of Wales," Vol. II, p. 523) have muchinformation about bards, their privileges, and position in household and law court. I quote sufficient to show that their connexion with earlier mark stones continued down to Anglo-Saxon days, and that they were successors to the Druids, who must have derived their supervision of ancient stones from the ley-men. "It has been established for bards, qualified by the privilege and degree of session, specially to have the custody of kin and descent, and of territorial divisions, and in addition to that the memorial of fire-back stones, and meer stones and mounting stones, and rules as to those who should remove them without the authority of the court and judges."

The "three branches of the art of bardism" are: Firstly, the Primitive Bard, gaining his position by discipleship under an authorized teacher; on him depends records of territorial divisions. Secondly, the Ovate, authorized by a customary session of bards. Thirdly, the Druid or presiding bard. This classification of bards is much the same as that given by Cæsar for the Druids.

There are further indications in these Triads (which were

handed down by tradition) that the priest who carried a rod on which oaths were taken was a gorsedd priest, and officiated at these assemblies, being, in fact, a Druid.

The reputation and knowledge of the ley-man did not perish as the old sighted track decayed. In the Sighting Staff chapter are some indications of this.

But while I feel that ley-man, astronomer-priest, druid, bard, wizard, witch, palmer, and hermit, were all more or less linked by one thread of ancient knowledge and power, however degenerate it became in the end, I can attempt no genealogy.

CHAPTER XII

SIGHTING STAFF

And ten by ten under a quicken tree
The Druids chaunted, swaying in their hands
Tall wands of alder and white quicken wands.

—W. B. YEATS

TWO impressions come to my mind as illustrating this theme, and long ages separate them. They are the starting and the present-day phases. The first, the prehistoric outline of the Long Man (Fig. 89) cut through the turf to show the chalk on the steep slope of a grassy down at Wilmington in Sussex. No two writers have quite agreed on the meaning of this early drawing on a huge scale, for the height of this nude figure is about 240 feet, or as to the use of the two long staves he holds in either hand. But there is general agreement as to his age—that he was here before the Romans landed.

The second is the impression of to-day's county assize court on the law day. The under-sheriff, walking in front of the judge's carriage, his wand of office—a white rod—in his hand. And then in the court the usher in charge of the jury, he too with his long wand. They are carried as the Long Man carries his, are about the same length, and are an emblem of authority.

A third recent memory is at the inn embedded in the ruins at Llanthony Abbey, where, idly watching a snail trailing across a low stone-tiled roof, amid moss, stonecrop, and cranesbill, with his horns advanced, it came as a flash that he was called the dodman because he carried the two sighting staves on his head (Fig. 73), and that the Long Man was the dod-man, the prehistoric surveyor.

Glance at the use and necessity of two such staves to the primitive surveyor on the ley, and note that Codrington and Belloc have explained it much as is here given. Picture then, as an illustration of this use, two distant sighting points A and B in the diagram Fig. 94. A mountain ridge comes between, so high that the two points cannot be seen one from the other; but it is necessary to plotting out a ley that a spot be found in the ridge which aligns with the two points. Here comes the use of the staves. An experimental trial is first made at a guess-work spot, and staff C is stuck in the ground. A dozen or so yards away staff D is planted so that it aligns with C to the distant point A, this being shown on the line marked 1st trial. On glancing

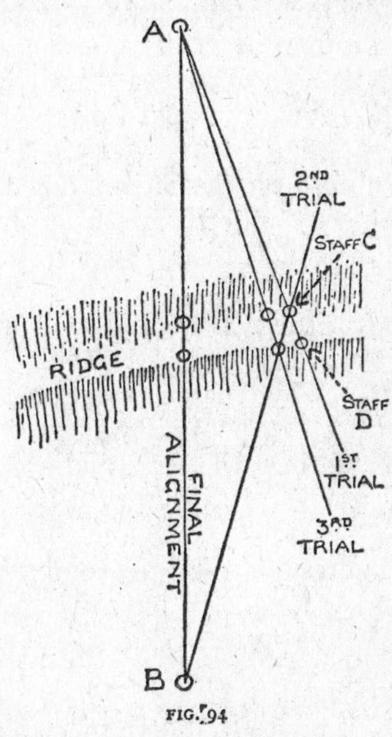

FIG. 94

backward from C to D it is seen that the alignment is not right for the other distant point B. So leaving C in its place, staff D is moved until both staves align to distant point B, this in the diagram being the 2nd trial. This again will not align backwards to distant point A, and a 3rd trial is made by moving C for that purpose, although to no avail as regards alignment to both points. In short, a final position for both staves is found (as marked final trial) in which they align both ways to both distant points; and it is on this ley that a mound, cairn, or cutting, as the case may require, is formed. This frequent dodging or doddering was not so troublesome in practice as might appear, for with two ley-men (whether called dod-men or not) each carried a staff, and they walked with frequent side-glances until very near a final position.

Every mark-point on a ley between two mountain peaks could be settled by this method, without climbing the peaks, provided that two known ley points (whether initial or not) can be seen for the trial. By marking the chief "high places" first, all the others could follow.

In primitive days men of the skill and knowledge to do this work would be men of position and power, and their staff would become a sign of such a position.

Thus it is that all down the ages we get fitful glimpses of the survival of the rods or staves which the Long Man to this day is seen to hold on the Sussex down. It is always men who in some way inherit or carry on a survival or development of the ancient ley-man's work, or of the authority he possessed.

The king in the statue which Layard found at Nimroud carries the long plain wand as his emblem of power. An illustration from the Babylonian account of the Flood ("The Dawn of Civilization," p. 569) shows two figures shutting up the Assyrian Noah into the Ark, and both these carry a long staff, clearly not a spear, but with a knob and a loop at the top.

The two black figures guarding the tomb of Tutankhamen (Fig. 90) each held a long staff having a ferrule—like the halo in a tilting lance—just below where the right hand grasps it.

Another glimpse of the rod as an emblem of authority is in the records of the election of early Irish and Scotch chiefs (Gomme, "Primitive Folk Moots," p. 172): "One of the conditions of Celtic inauguration was the laying aside by the chief of his weapons, and the placing of a straight white wand in his hand by the Brehon (lawyer) of his district."

"The staff of a priest" is specified in the Welsh Triads as one of the "three relics to swear by," the others being "the name of God, and hand-in-hand with the one sworn to."

There is internal evidence that the "priest" here mentioned was a Druid, and the triad goes on to say, "After that was introduced the blessed cross."

A bishop's pastoral staff is one of territorial authority, as he does not use it outside his own diocese. Its original form was without the present crook.

Early Christian saints carry a rod with a cross capping it; and Romily Allen ("Christian Symbolism"), speaking of ivory carvings of the sixth century, says, "The chief feature to be noted in the ivories is the substitution of the cross for the rod as the symbol of supernatural power."

The Chief Druid illustrated in Rowland's "Mona Antiqua" carries a long staff.

Strabo, writing in the first century, speaks of the inhabitants of the tin islands adjacent to Britain as "men in black cloaks, . . . walking with staves, thus resembling the Furies we see in tragic representations . . . leading for the most part a wandering life."

Roman centurions carried a short staff of authority; but the equipment of their assistant, called the "optio," is shown on a tombstone from Chester (Fig. 92), a tall staff, man-high, grasped in right hand, traveller's staff way; the left hand holding the strapped tablets for writing or notes. This would be right equipment for laying out the straight entrenchments when the legion halted for the night and "dug themselves in" according to rule.

Josephus ("Wars of the Jews") tells us the marching order of a Roman army under Vespasian: "Next followed that part of the Romans which were completely armed. Next to these followed ten out of every hundred, carrying along with them their arms and what was necessary to measure out a camp withal; and after them such as were to make the road even and straight." Now, the work of such men required a ganger, and thus it comes about that the working surveyor's staff of the Romans is depicted on the Chester tombstone.

An obsolete meaning of the word "rod" given in the "New English Dictionary" is "a path, a way, a road," once again a link with the old straight track, for an earlier form of our present word road was "rode," and we have in Herefordshire a Rodway place-name.

It was with a staff that Jack Cade assumed the mastership of the City by striking London Stone (surely a mark stone!) with it; and like evidence is to be seen in the fact that to this day the newly-elected mayor of Bovey Tracy claims his position by striking an ancient stone with a stick. Another survival of the association of the sighting staff with the ancient stone is that when "beating the bounds" of the City of Hereford in 1870 the party carried "about half-a-dozen rustic wands with many coloured ribbons at the top," and with these they tapped the stones.

The deacons and directors of ceremonies of Freemasons carry a wand of office, and in the annals of the old Scotch lodges are found details of the use of a sighting rod under the direction of the Master Mason when the alignment of a church was fixed by sunrise on a specified day.

In old prints of eighteenth-century funerals in England the man leading the procession (whether undertaker or beadle) carries a long wand decked with ribbons.

Churchwardens on occasions of ceremony, such as the induction of a vicar, still (in this ancient City of Hereford) carry a long wand. The wand of office, indeed, appears at many periods of English history, together with the fact that a sign of the voluntary relinquishment of the office was the breaking of the wand. In the Bible it was an emblem of power often harshly used (a "rod of iron") by kings.

Mythology gives a glimpse of the same symbol. Professor Steuding ("Greek and Roman Mythology") says of Hermes (the god of the trackways and their mark stones, and of market traffic): "He carries as herdman's god the hooked stick to catch the cattle, which was also used as a traveller's staff. . . . The herdman's stick passes over into the herald's staff (*caduceus*). After the transformation of Hermes into the god of luck this finally becomes the magical wishing-rod which raises treasure and bestows fortune." The wand continues as the badge of heralds. Black Rod, the messenger of the House of Lords, knocks at the door of the Commons for leave to enter.

The pilgrim's staff of the Middle Ages had the ferrule just below the hand-grasp and (usually) a knob on the top. Clark's "Heraldry" shows this form on a shield (Fig. 91), and side by side with it—also as a pilgrim's staff—a plain one with a cross strip on the top: a surveyor's staff pure and simple. Jusserand illustrates the first form (Fig. 93) and gives the inscription on a brass plate "with a cross" on the top of one: "May this direct thee in safety on the way."

To follow up the survival of the sighting staff: in the final chapter of "The Antiquary," the use of the cross-staff for beacon observation is vividly described.

Hermits carried a staff, as Piers Plowman notes when he writes, "Hermits a heap of them, with their hooked staves." This is verified by the picture in Jusserand of a hermit at his cell with a staff shaped like a crozier or a shepherd's hooked stick, not like a pilgrim's staff.

A curious legend connecting surveyors and sighting staves with tumuli is related by Nennius (a ninth-century historian) regarding Wormlow Tump, Herefordshire: "The man who is buried in the Tump was Amr. And men came to measure the Tump, it sometimes measures in length seven feet, sometimes fifteen feet, and sometimes nine feet. Whatever measure you may make it at one time you will not again find it the same measurement." Then in Gomme's account of the Free Court of Corbey, an out-of-door assembly held in Saxony three centuries ago, it is related how the accurate laying out and measurement of the court with the aid of "mete wands" is an essential part of the opening ceremony. It seems probable that the prehistoric surveyor, concealing the real use of his sighting staves, allowed the people to regard them as measuring rods.

The tutti-men of Hungerford are also a survival of to-day, linking up the Tut-hills or Toot-hills with the sighting staff, for when at "Hock-tide" (April 29th) they parade the town streets claiming the ancient privilege of kissing anyone they meet, they carry a six-foot staff decorated with flowers and ribbons.

A memory of the two sighting staves in use is mentioned by Mr. W. Simpson, R.I., in a paper on "Orientation" published in 1897: "Mr. Pettie painted a picture, which was in the Royal Academy a few years ago, of monks beginning to build a chapel, and they were in the act of fixing its orientation by means of a couple of rough poles, which they were placing in a line with the rising sun."

An alternate development in the history of the sighting staff is that it became the wizard's rod. This was quite an early phase, going back to the time of Moses, for did not

Aaron use a wizard's rod in his trial of skill against the Egyptian sorcerers? And in Ezekiel (xxi. 20) it is recorded that "the king of Babylon stood at the parting of the ways, at the head of the two ways, to use divination." This brings us very near to the sighting staff origin of magic, for the place selected was a sighting point, the purpose of the test to decide which way to go, and the method the shaking up (and drawing out one) of two short rods—arrows. The sighting method described in the beginning of this chapter was evidently always kept a mystery, and developed into magic. In Layamon's "Brut" the sorcerers go to the cross-roads (a sighting point) to practise divination.

The Irish Druids, who became mere magicians in their later days, used divining rods of yew.

All down the ages the magic rod has been the wizard's emblem of power; also of the witches, as we know from their possession of the broomstick. Mrs. Leather relates how in living memory children would go past a witch's door riding a broomstick, for they knew that this broke the spell of the evil eye, and the old hag could only shake her fist in impotent rage. And as regards the evil eye (did it not originate in sighting methods on leys?), the Italian peasants of to-day ward it off by holding up two vertical fingers in front of their own eyes—folk memory of the two sighting staves.

Old Burton in his "Anatomy of Melancholy" speaks of a witch "riding in the ayre upon a cowle-staff out of a chimney pot"; and this cowle (or cole) staff brings us back again to the cole-man and his methods.

The church—always antagonistic to Druids, wizards, and the like—classed heretics with them in the time of the Spanish Inquisition, and sent them to the stake dressed in a fantastic conjurer's robe and steeple hat, and carrying a long wand.

CHAPTER XIII

TRADERS' TRACKS

"Tafarn Goch, the Red Tavern?" said I. "How is it that so many of your places are called Goch?"
—George Borrow: "Wild Wales"

It may be that all the first straight ways were made for trading, for man must have very early had need for necessities, such as salt, flint, and (later) metals, not found in his own district.

One such type of roads—the salt way—has left place-names so loudly proclaiming the meaning that observers have long recognized it; and Alles in his "Folk Lore of Worcestershire" attempts to follow several leading from Droitwich. He mentions a number of field names, Sale (four of these), Salt Moor, Salt Way (piece, barn and coppice). Salt place-names abound: Satley, Salford, Sale (Cheshire), Saltash. Probably they originated in Romano-British times, for philologists trace our word "salary" to the *salarium* of the Roman soldier, being an allowance for the purchase of salt; and an inefficient salaried man is even now said to be "not worth his salt." It seems, therefore, plain that when the salary was exchanged with the trader for salt the transaction came to be called a sale, and, as will be seen when we come to the "chip" and "cheap" places, it was not the only instance of the evolution of trading terms from early products.

But there were at least two other types of names, probably of different periods, peculiar to the salt tracks.

The instance given in "Early British Trackways" of an alignment ending at Droitwich and passing through these two types of names illustrates this. The ley, starting from the Black Mountains, passes through Whitfield House, the mound at Hereford Castle called Hogg's Mount, White House (Tupsley), White Stone (Withington), Westhide Church, Whitwick Manor, and White House at Suckley.

Radiating from Impney Hill, Droitwich, were found leys (one sighted on the Worcestershire Beacon) passing through the many " wicks " in the district, as Kenswick, Knightwick, Duckwick, Henwick Church, Lower Wick, and Wick Episcopi; also through Whitton and Wittington Churches, the Lower Wych, and the Upper Wych—the last being the well-known pass or cutting through which a main road passes in the centre of the Malverns.

A short typical salt ley comes through Droitwich town, over Whitton Hill (in its suburbs), lies exactly on a long stretch of Rainbow Hill Road in Worcester City, crosses the Severn at the Cathedral Ferry, through Lower Wick, crosses the Teme at old Powick Bridge, and going through a moat (Moat Court) and Burston Cross (at Winds Point) terminates in the Herefordshire Beacon.

Two types of names now divulged, namely, the " whites " or " whits," and secondly the " wicks," " weeks," " wiches " or " wyches," have been found to align in other districts, to all appearance being on salt tracks.

To take the " white " group. There are White Houses by the score. White Wells, White Stones, White Rocks, and White Crosses (two each of the last three items in Herefordshire alone). Then White Ways are found in Gloucestershire, Ludlow district, Dorset and Lulworth, the first an important road called the White Way. Most of these places are quite plainly not so called because they have ever been white. Near Cradley is a Whitman's Hill, perhaps most significant of all, for it was the Whitman who carried the white load of salt and gave name to so many places he travelled through.

The Whiteacres (whence the familiar surname Whitaker) were not called from the whiteness of the ground. Whitehouse Hill, Essex (close by is Salcot and Abbott's Wick), Whiteway Hill, and Whitley Ridge bring us in touch with the high places of the sighted track and the leys passing over them. There is a Whiteley place as well as a Saltley.

The " wick " group of names have been stated (wrongly, it is here claimed) to be derived from the Latin word for village. There is overwhelming evidence of their connexion with salt production and transit. Alles (p. 310) gives Droitwich as being named Saltwic in A.D. 716 and 888.

"Domesday Book" repeatedly mentions Manors as being possessed of salt pans or pits at Droitwich—always called "Wich"—and among these is Topsslage (Tupsley), passed through in the first salt track here detailed, and Ullingwic (Ullingswick) which had "part saline in Wich."

Wick, Wich, and Wych, are forms of the same name. The salt producing towns of Cheshire are Nantwich, Middlewich, and Northwich. The other source of salt was from evaporation at the salt marshes, which are plentiful—under that name and as Salterns and "Wick Marsh"—on low coasts—as off Essex, and on great river estuaries. The several Wick Marshes have no houses on them, nor has Wick Down, inland on high ground. These places never have been villages. Round Worcester, on the way to Droitwich, the "wick" places (as Henwick, Rushwick, Northwick) are thick on the ground, and it is impossible to note how the "Wick Farms" cluster round the coast salt places and ignore the connexion. There is a Wick Lane and a Wick Moor in Somerset, a Lee Wick close to the salty Essex coast; and Wicksters Brook and Bridge, Frampton-on-Severn, might well name the salter or white man.

A well-confirmed salt ley near Weston-super-Mare is sighted toward the channel from Stride Shelve Hill (732 feet), near Axbridge; it touches the western entrenchment of Banwell Camp, lies on about a mile of straight road marked on the map as Wick Way, and goes down to the mouth of the River Banwell at the end of an embankment marked Wick Warth—the same word as Wharf. It is certainly not a "village way" leading to a "village wharf," but a wharf amid salt pools and pans.

In Devon a salt ley comes through three crosses near Sticklepath, West Week, East Week, Way, Great Week, Bishop's Cross, Whitestone, Bovey Tracey Church; to a spot on the shore of the Teign estuary which was surely salt producing, for to it also comes another ley from an 815 height near Whitestone Church, through Whiteway Wood, Whiteway House and (5 miles further), Whiteway Barton.

Wick Ball Camp (Salisbury), Wickbury Camp (Worcester), and Wick Barrow (Somerset) are names which indicate the sighting of the prehistoric salt track over tumuli on high places, for prehistoric man had organized his salt supply long before the Romans came, and Wyck Beacon, a round barrow in the Cotswolds, threw a light to lay out the white track.

There are two instances which appear to be folk memory of salt tracks over artificial mounds. The first is that in the Tower of London, not indeed on the White Mount (on which was built the White Tower), but in near proximity, is a tower called the Salt Tower.

The second is that of Eton Montem, fully detailed in "Hone's Year Book" of 1848. An artificial mound near Eton is called Salt Hill, and to this, until the nineteenth century, the Eton scholars made a triennial ceremonial excursion on Easter Tuesday, of which one feature was that a number of the lads, called "salt bearers," scoured the neighbourhood asking for contributions for the cost of the feast, which money being paid to the captain of the school was called "salt." It has been said that the custom was handed down from some adjacent dissolved priory, and that the monks, in a procession to the hill at the same season, "then and there sold consecrated salt."

Wick is probably the earliest of the salt names, for the combination in Whitwick (Herefordshire) and Whitewick (Somerset) suggest that its earlier meaning was lost sight of, and that by Saxon times really had come to mean in many cases a homestead, or, as Mr. Grundy thinks, a dairy farm. Salt roads continued to be made and used, and probably places named from them long after the old straight tracks had decayed. It is curious that there are few Wick names to be found round the Cheshire salt towns.

Another early necessity which (in the West of England) gave a colour name to the track was the pots or crocks—locally of red clay. The fortunate discovery of the scrap-heaps of an ancient pottery in the Kiln Ground Wood, Whitney-on-Wye, gave me a clue to the origin of a number of "red" place-names on leys—verified in several cases by fragments of present-day roads, which radiated from it. No further discoveries have been made of these since the earlier book. The principal ley ran from a hill beyond Newchurch, through Redborough, the pottery site, Red Lay Cottage, on two miles of the present high road (marked on map "Roman Road"), and ultimately through an old house at the Friars, Hereford, called the Red House. Other "red" place-names seemed to align to this pottery on other leys, as Redley, Maes Coch, and the Red Gates, Eardisley. And there is a Red Hill (referred to in the Place-Name chapter) and an ancient Red Lane amongst the hills behind.

Iron is not a plentiful place-name, but there is some slight indication that the iron-man might have given names to a track on a fairly well confirmed ley running along the cart track connecting Iron Cross with Ironhill Farm; it passes also through Berryhill Farm and a moat at Stoneton, all in Northamptonshire, on its Warwick border. There is another Iron Cross in Leominster town, an Iron Acton, Glos., and Kits Iron, Worcs.

Our native metal—tin—was of great importance in the Bronze Age, and the earliest records concerning Britain speak of its transport along roads. There are Tin and Tinker Hills and Tinker Crosses, but no real evidence as yet of tracks linking them up.

The twin facts that "knap" is a constantly recurring name for a sighting hill, and that a knapper is the name for the skilled worker who "knaps" off flakes from the crude lump of flint, caused a surmise that as flint implements were absolute necessities in early days, and in many districts had to be imported, the knaps were the places where the consumers met the knappers or flint pedlars. That, in fact, they were the earliest trading points. There are many places called Knap or Knapp, two Knap Barrows in the Isle of Wight, a Knapper's Barton in Somerset, a Knapper's Farm, Glos., a Flinty Knapp on Salisbury Plain, and a coast tumulus Belas Knap. Then the flint hawker seems to be indicated in Flintsham (Herefordshire), Flintsham (S. Notts.), Flinton (E. R. Yorks), and the town and county of Flint.

However, an effort to link up "knap" names towards the chalk and therefore flint-producing districts led to a failure. But something else resulted. The available map did not go as far as the chalk, but on the edge the words "6 miles to Chippenham" made a suggestion which at once led to results. If *knap* is an onomatopœtic word—created by the sound of the action it describes—so is *chip*. And both signify the same action. But there is a matter on which philologists have prepared the ground. Backwards from *chap-man* and *cheap* they come to the Anglo-Saxon *ceape* or *cepe*, a sale or bargain, and agree that the "Chipping" places are the market-places to which the chap-men came, and that although chap is "a word of difficult history," it is akin to chop and chip, and to the later word cheap.

Thus it is that there came a Cyp or Cype Street in old Winchester, Cheapsides in London, Manchester and Beaulieu (Hampshire), a Mealcheapen Street in Worcester, and Chipping Camden, Chipping Norton, and other "chips" from the same block of market towns round about the chalk country where the flints are found. To these the cheap-jacks still travel. Chepstow and Chipstead (Surrey) and Chepenhall Green in Suffolk are all from the trading name, and surely the first trade was in flints chipped or knapped from the lump.

Now to connect this with the old straight track and its sighting points. J. R. Mortimer particularly remarks upon the abundance of flint flakes as well as pottery shards to be found in barrows, not merely in the burial, he notes, but scattered through the whole of the earth of the mound. If flint flakes were traded here it helps to explain it.

Mr. O. G. S. Crawford in his "Andover District," referring to the "Ceapmanna del," or Chapman's Dell, and Chapman's Ford on the Harroway, says: "Place-names compounded with 'chapman' are almost invariably associated with prehistoric roads or earthworks." On the western edge of Exmoor Forest there are planted at 1,572 feet above the sea a group of five tumuli arranged like the pips of a playing card, and called Chapman Barrows. They act as pointers in their indications of several traders' tracks, one seemingly sighted on the cliff headland at Countesbury, and passing over a camp close there, in the other direction through Challacombe Church, and a barrow on the south of Bratton Down.

The names of several stones, such as the Pedlar's Stone, or Cross Llanigon, and the Huxter's Stone on the Shropshire Longmynds (there is a Hucks Barn near Ludlow), indicate the trader's track. High Hucklow in Northumberland was certainly a sighting mound on a trader's track.

In the chapter on Mark Stones it is shown how the mark, merch, or march stone in time settled the place of the market (often "merchet" in old documents) and created the term of merchant, or marchant, as it often remains in surnames. There is a Marchant's Cross on Dartmoor.

Half a century ago, pulling up my horse to pay the toll-gate at Birtley (Berkley) cross-roads, against Deerfold Forest in the north of Herefordshire, I found a group of country-women, and was told that it was "Nut Fair" that day, the one day in the year when the dealers came to the spot to buy their harvest of hedge nuts. It may be that the mark stone of this cross-road is still there buried in the bank, for, like Mr. Dutt's friend, I have so found at least one half-buried example—near Credenhill.

The delightful old timber market-house at Pembridge (Fig. 95) still has its original mark stone (of the same squarish shape as others proved to be on a ley in the district) close to the oak pillars.

The tradition of trading at a stone, revived in the time of the Black Death, and commemorated by the erection of a cross, is recorded in the White Cross, close to Hereford.

Outside Winchester, on rising ground near the Westgate, in like manner, an obelisk is raised to commemorate the spot where during the Great Plague of 1666 the country-folk brought provisions, and the identical flat stone is built into it on which the exchange—with due precautions—was made.

Such "plague stones," where the exchange of goods for cash was made, are recorded in many parts of England. Those at East Retford (Broad Stone), near Manchester (Giant's Stone), and Stuston (White Stone) indicate by their names that it was an ancient mark stone, not a more recent boundary stone, which was thus made a market point for the time being.

At Grosmont, Mon., is a small town hall built in 1832 by the Duke of Beaufort as Lord of the Manor and owner of the chief market tolls. It replaced an older wooden building. In it is the large table-like fourteenth-century stone shown in Fig. 97, perhaps an adaptation from some previous use. On it some of the women stood their baskets, and the first comer who did so escaped toll. My friend, Mr. Whitney, who lives in this quaint townlet, thinks that this stone is part of the old parish cross. Opposite the market hall is the unworked stone shown in Fig. 96, which to me is a most convincing mark stone settling the site of the market; and on writing Mr. Whitney he says: "The upright stone is a landmark; there was formerly another of these stones further up the street which was destroyed many years ago. At all fairs held here formerly the occupiers of the houses were entitled to charge toll upon all articles deposited upon the land between these marks, whilst all other tolls were invested in the Lord of the Manor." Another inhabitant tells me it is called the toll stone.

Here is record of the actual gathering of a market round mark stones, of a later market house, and of a market stone in that house.

Markets and crosses had close connexion; most of those outside churchyards were used for trade, and those inside did not always escape. Practically all the ancient crosses align on leys. One of the many books on crosses deals with Scottish market crosses, and the "Butter Cross" is a familiar spot in many an English town.

At Pembridge a socket stone of a cross (of the usual fourteenth-century type, with a bit of its stone shaft still leaded in) is used as a support (Fig. 98) for one of the wooden pillars of the little market house, which is of sixteenth-century date. Here apparently are the three stages —the prehistoric mark stone deciding the site of the market, the market cross, and the later market shed. The place was granted a charter for a market by Henry I.

There are many records and legends of money payments being made on an open-air stone, as at Knightlow and Colwall.

At the ancient corn market of Bristol (Fig. 100) there stand on the pavement outside (the market was an open-air one until the last century) four handsome brass standards—3 feet 3 inches high, with circular table tops 2 feet in diameter, rimmed to keep coins from slipping over. These were called "nails," and used for counting cash when corn in sacks, "pitched" for sale on the stone pitching near by, was sold for "cash on the nail." They vary slightly in pattern, and are not in their original position. One—the most northern (Fig. 99), with no inscription—seems to be recorded as at the old Tolzey (adjacent) in 1550. The others, dated 1594, 1625, and 1631, have inscriptions and seem to have been gifts from merchants when business had outgrown one "counter." I think that the earliest one, akin in shape and purpose to the Grosmont market stone, was a successor to an earlier mark stone.

At Bodenham, Herefordshire, is a fourteenth-century socket stone on a makeshift base. It stands at a cross-roads close to the Cross Well, and is fitted with a shaft known to be brought from Dewsall Hope quarry last century. The vicar has discovered that it stands on the site of a timber market house as at Pembridge, the tradition of women bringing goods for sale here being told me by the old lady of ninety-three who lives at the Cross Cottage.

The largest mark stone in the district—the Whetstone on Hergest Ridge (see Fig. 16), Kington—has also a tradition of trading. It stands about 3 feet 6 inches in height, and its flat top (irregular) is about 6 feet 6 inches by 3 feet. The "History of Kington" (1845) says that "tradition handed down from our ancestors, informs us that a market was held weekly on this ground during the time of the pestilence in the reign of Edward III in the year 1366, and that it was the custom to place wheat and other kinds of grain for sale around this stone." But there is a doubt how much of this is really tradition and how much the surmise of an early antiquarian. The stone is on a non-populated mountain ridge 1,300 feet above sea level, and wheat (a bulky product) is only sparingly grown in this district at a far lower level. The stone shows as a pimple on the sky-line from certain approaches to the Radnor Forest, in which district natural slips of stones which to this day are used as whetstones are to be picked up. A few years ago an old man used to come to Radnor from a distance to collect them.

Whetstones of the same size and shape are frequently found in ancient barrows (see Pitt-Rivers' "Cranbourne Chase"), and it seems more probable that the Whetstone was on an old sighted track of the ancient whetstone pedlar, just as the knaps were probably on the track of the knappers or flint pedlars. There is a circle of stones called the Whetstones on Shropshire hills near Clun, Whetstone villages in Middlesex and Leicestershire, and an ancient occupation street or terrace on the northern side of Lincoln's Inn Fields in the heart of London is called Whetstone Park.

CHAPTER XIV

SUN ALIGNMENT

> There stood I on the cairn of the Grey Giant looking around me. I thought on the old times when Mona was the grand seat of Druidical superstition, when adoration was made . . . to Wyn ab Nudd, Lord of the Unknown, and to Beli, Emperor of the Sun. I thought on the times when the Beal fire blazed on this height, on the neighbouring promontory, on the copestone of Eryri, and on every high hill throughout Britain, on the eve of the first of May.
>
> —George Borrow: "Wild Wales"

A STUDENT following up the actual topographical evidence regarding the ley, inevitably finds himself getting into touch with other important factors in the early history of mankind, however ill equipped he may be to treat of these branches, such as Anthropology, Astronomy, Magic, and Religion.

In Britain of to-day, where we still devote a weekly Sun-day for the discharge of our religious duties, there is scarcely need to labour the assumption that some at least of our ancestors must have brought sun alignment into their religion. I had not gone much beyond this point when I wrote "Early British Trackways," which does not allude to sun worship or to beacons, and I had not then read Lockyer's "Stonehenge." But now it has become plain that the topographical sites used for sun alignment and those for the ley are in some cases identical, and that the alignment is often the same for both uses.

I do not attempt much beyond this, and refer the reader to Lockyer's books (including the "Dawn of Astronomy"). The important link which I have found between this and the ley is best told by a statement of the sequence of evidence which in my own case led up to it. It starts with the Giant's Cave on the Malvern Hills.

I first visited this cave (Fig. 102) about forty-five years ago, and was puzzled at the shallow-cut panel at its back, but had no suspicion as to its prehistoric origin. It lies at the top of the Herefordshire side of the ridge, near the Herefordshire Beacon on its Eastnor side. Below it is a large rough igneous stone (Fig. 101), which appears to be a natural outcrop, but might be detached. This is referred to as the Sacrificial Stone in the Woolhope "Transactions" of 1889, and is supposed to be the same as the Shew Stone named as a boundary in old documents. A local tale is that it is "the door of the Giant's Cave thrown down." The cave itself is always called as above locally, but marked on the map as Clutter's Cave.

Mr. P. H. L'Estrange's researches and paper on "Sun Worship on the Malvern Hills" brought up the subject anew, he having made many solar observations regarding this cave, stone, and other points. The one now to be followed up is that at six o'clock on Midsummer Day morning the sun, rising over the ridge at the cave, falls on the stone, at which instant "the sacrifice" was assumed to have been made.

Visiting the stone in November, 1922, I discovered that although it was generally rough and "knobbly," one face sloping southward was smoothed, although not flat; and that it so exactly fitted a human back that almost every inch from neck to heel touched the stone when limply reclining at an angle of 45 degrees. The position shown by the figure—the neck bent back and the chest expanded—is right for the purpose.

On a surmise that the sighting line from cave to stone might have been also used as a ley, the photograph was taken on that line, the angle taken by compass, and plotted out on the six-inch map. But no confirming points were then seen on the limited area of this large-scale map, and the investigation dropped.

But in January, 1924, paying a visit to the Ridgeway in order to exactly locate the Gospel Oak (which stands close to this old track at the end of a quarter mile straight piece from Park Lodge, but is not marked on the map), the oak was found to be exactly on the spot where the above trial ley crossed the ridge more than a mile from the stone.

Both the stone and the oak are marked on the one-inch map, and on plotting out the ley it was found to go to Woolhope Church, lying on several bits of present roads. After thus marked, the line was found to pass exactly through Holme Lacy Church (Fig. 103). Taking another map with the two churches as fixing the ley, and again plotting it out, it passes through Aconbury Church, and on to Aconbury Camp (Figs. 13 and 85), striking the highest point of the camp at its western end.

Aconbury was a beacon station, for in the Scudamore MSS. is a document endorsed "Things belonging to Aconbury Beacon in Kydley's hands 1625," namely, an "iron potte, piche, and Rosen, and tallowe and towe."

Since writing this I find by the 6-inch Ordnance map that both Woolhope and Holme Lacy Churches are oriented to the angle (14° N. of E.) of this ley. This fact is more fully discussed in the Orientation chapter, for here is a ley passing through a traditional sacrificial stone with its angle decided by sunrise at the stone, and the same angle repeated in the orientation of both churches, although it is an abnormal angle due to the position of the stone under a mountain ridge. In addition to the churches there is a gospel oak and a beacon point on the line. It cannot be regarded as a mere series of coincidences.

Finding myself sighting upon Midsummer Hill, in the Malverns, and May Hill (there are three in my district) I have felt that these names denoted a sunrise line for Midsummer Day and for May Day, and I found by spade excavation that Midsummer Hill, although not reputed to be a beacon hill, had been used as such. Other place-names indicate the same idea: Sunset (close to Kington, Herefordshire), Dawns Men (a stone circle in Cornwall), and Cronk yn Tree Laa, Isle of Man, or Hill of the Rise of Day. Mr. Johnson, who gives this last in his "Byways" (p. 71) explains that cronks in the Isle of Man are "equivalents of our toot-hills," which means that they are artificial sighting mounds.

In plotting out a ley (Radway to Chipping Norton) given elsewhere, I found it pass over the highest point of Sun Rising Hill, (704 feet) on the Edgehill ridge. This ley was not at any sunrise angle, but putting a pin through the 704 point and experimentally trying the Stonehenge Midsummer Day angle, I found within a degree of it a line passing through the point, the two nearest churches (about 1½ miles), namely, Middle Tysoe and Ratley, and on through the Three Shire Stones to a 728 hill point near Charwelton, about 4 miles beyond the spot where three counties still meet. At daybreak on May Day the choristers assemble on the top of the tower of Magdalen College, Oxford, to sing a hymn. A ley through this tower, Bury Knowle (Headington), and Oxford Cathedral is worth investigating. It is at the May Day angle.

Stonehenge is a very striking and convincing example of the connexion between sun alignment, long-distance tracks, and the use of the beacons.

Stone circles are only touched upon in this book in the same way that churches are—in as far as a ley system has settled their sites. I claim no expert knowledge of their purpose, a subject well treated by Sir Norman Lockyer in his book on " Stonehenge," which seems to show very convincingly that certain alignments through its centre—or perhaps the slightly different centres of successive structures on its site—are sunrise (or sunset) alignments for different seasons. Indeed, if this skilled astronomer had never written, the fact that for centuries, and up to now, the people of Wiltshire have come at daybreak on Midsummer Day to see the sun rise over the " Friar's Heel " and along " The Avenue " would be evidence in the same direction.

That Stonehenge is at the crossing point of long-distance alignments was really indicated by Lockyer, but he did not follow up the clue. He points out that Stonehenge, Old Sarum Mound, Salisbury Cathedral, and Clearbury Ring (the edge of this) precisely align. I found this (which I will call alignment *D*) before seeing his book; and also noted that two miles of it lies approximately on the modern road from Salisbury to Oldstock. I found the alignment to run on northward to St. Anne's Hill, a point the old name of which is Tan Hill (denoting a fire or beacon point); on it is still held a fair on August 6th. I have seen no sunrise significance in this alignment. Lockyer also indicates that the main axis of the circle is a long-distance alignment by his note that if extended it strikes three of the long-distance points I am about to detail.

The sketch outline of Stonehenge (Fig. 105) indicates two alignments, *A* and *B*, and the map diagram (Fig. 104) three alignments, *A*, *B*, and *C*, with those barrows within 2 miles which come on them. Lockyer specifies *A* and *B*, but not the barrows in alignment, although in another place

(p. 110) he remarks that barrows sometimes take the place of stones in marking the direction of alignments from the centre of circles.

It should be noted that the mark-points I am about to give are exactly of the type which would be evidence of leys (or tracks) through them, even if no Stonehenge existed.

Alignments through Stonehenge, starting from northern ends:

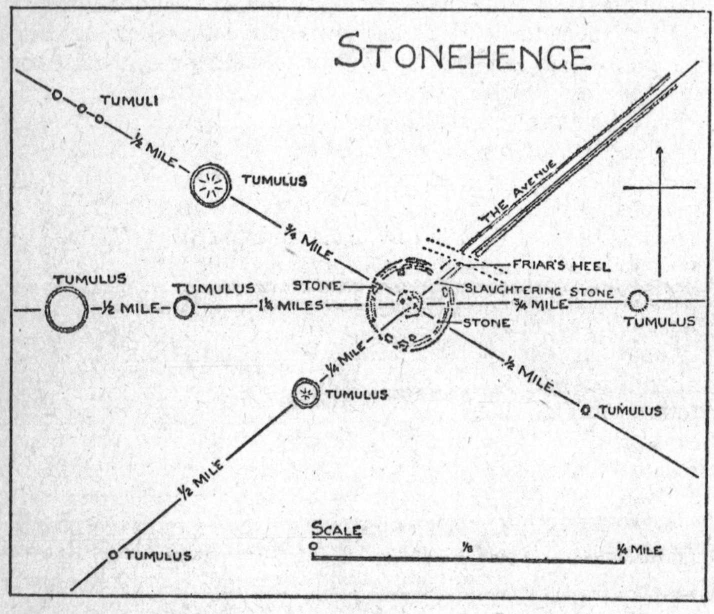

FIG. 104

A. Winterbourne Camp, Tumuli on Inkpen Beacon, Bacon (formerly beacon) Farm, Shear's Inn (cross-roads), Sidbury Camp (S. E. edge), The Avenue, Friar's Heel Stone and Slaughter Stone at Stonehenge, large barrow at a quarter of a mile, and small barrow at three-quarters of a mile from Stonehenge centre, Stapleford Churchyard, south-east edge of Grovelly Castle, south-east edge of Castle Ditches, and across Dorsetshire through Cerne Abbas to Puncknowle

Beacon, a 434 feet hill on the coast. This is the Midsummer Day sunrise alignment.

B. Tinhead Hill (over 700 feet), Tilshead Lodge, three small barrows (in alignment) one and a quarter miles from centre, a large barrow three-quarters of a mile from centre, the centre of Stonehenge, also exactly through the "two smaller untrimmed sarsen stones lying near the vallum" (Lockyer's "Stonehenge," p. 88), a tumulus half a mile from centre, and earthworks near Stockport and on Idmiston Down. This is a May sunset or November sunrise alignment.

C. Not indicated by Lockyer, and not based on sighting stones within Stonehenge, but the result of a trial for

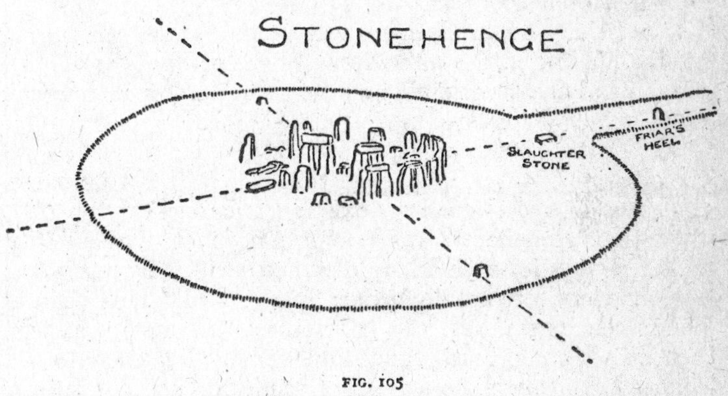

FIG. 105

the equinoxial sunrise alignment. It is about 1° N. of true E. Its main points are (from west) Shear Cross, Cross-road at Sutton Veny (then, near Stonehenge) barrow or circle one and three-quarter miles from centre, barrow one and a quarter miles from centre, Stonehenge, barrow (centre of the "Seven Barrows") three quarters of a mile from centre, Ann's Farm, a mile of present road near Cholderton, and south edge of Quarley Camp.

D. This alignment has been given.

Lockyer ("Stonehenge," p. 40) mentions that in Brittany fires are still lighted on Midsummer Day (or Eve) on the tumulus at Carnac and at other spots, and are called Tan Heol. This is Celtic, and in modern Welsh means "road-fire." Now the "Friar's Heel" stone, over which Midsummer sunrise is sighted, is on a beacon (or fire) track, and I have little doubt that *heel* was originally *heol*.

I must disclaim any local or expert knowledge of Stonehenge, but the points named are to be verified from an Ordnance map, and the sketch map is accurate except that the barrows are drawn in towards the centre to combine compactness with large scale of detail.

It is unnecessary to give details of the widespread practice —even up to recent times—of lighting hill-top fires at the quarters and half-quarters of the year, chiefly on the eves of Midsummer Day and May Day, the latter being called "Beltane," which means "Baal Fire." Sir James Frazer's "Golden Bough" details this.

I must leave Stonehenge (and stone circles generally), having illustrated the three desired points:

1. That the sunrise alignments of Lockyer are identical with long-distance leys.

2. That Stonehenge (and probably other circles) is at the crossing of several leys, and that it is far more probable that two of these were pre-existing and decided the site, than that Stonehenge was the primary fact, with all the radiating leys for such a long distance decided by its site.

3. Several of the alignments (perhaps all) have beacon points on them. In *A* (Midsummer sunrise), Inkpen Beacon, Beacon Farm, and Puncknowle Beacon. In *B*, Tinhead Hill might be a form of Tanhead. *D*, not on the sketch map, terminates in the highest hill on the Wiltshire Downs, Tan Hill, and tan in modern Welsh means "fire," although corrupted to St. Anne's Hill. Probably the Ann's Farm in *C* has the same meaning. The suggested derivation of "Friar's Heel" assumes *A* to be a "fire heol" or track.

It seems very evident that the direction of sunrise on one day in the year, not being a convenient standard for other times, there were established as sun substitutes beacon lights on the ley. This is why, digging a pit hollow on Midsummer Hill, I found it to be a beacon site. This sequence seems to suggest that the utilitarian trackways might have been the primary ones, that sun alignment followed, and then beacons evolved. Lockyer thinks that the utilitarian need of seasonal information for agricultural operations was the origin of priest-astronomers and sun alignments.

A bit of folk-memory connecting up the sun with artificial mounds is to be found under the word "caer" (a camp, a mound) in Pugh's Welsh Dictionary. There is quoted the vernacular phrase, "mae yr haul dan ei gaerau," as meaning "the sun is set or gone down." The word for word translation of this is, "Exit the Sun below his camps." This clearly describes the observer standing in alignment with the setting sun and a hill-top camp (caer or gaer), and infers that other camps have also a personal relation to the sun.

Since writing the above there has appeared in the paper by Admiral Boyle Somerville on "Orientation in Prehistoric Monuments" ("Archæologia," 1923, Vol. LXXIII) strong and convincing evidence that a number of stone rows, circles, and dolmens in Ireland and the Hebrides have orientation over certain stones to sunrise and sunset on the quarter days and half-quarter days. This is as found (on other monuments) by Lockyer. But the interesting link with my subject is that in five cases Admiral Somerville notes that such alignments continue to hill summits several miles distant, marked by cairn or earthwork, and in one case to an "abrupt" hill gap. Two cases are also given in which a barrow has a sunrise orientation to a hill summit with cairn, and one to a large spherical boulder on a hill crest. All these appear to be from eye observation, taking the monument in question as a starting point. It is confirmation of my conclusion (1) above, although the Admiral does not appear to have made further extension of these alignments on the map.

One of these alignments from the stone circle on Beltany Hill (Donegal) to a hill summit "is precisely that of sunrise on Bealltaine (May 6th)."

We have only one known stone group in Herefordshire capable of internal sighting; a dolmen, Arthur's Stone, already illustrated (Fig. 15) and partly described, with the leys through it, in Chapter II. I now note its possible connexion with this chapter.

The main axis of Arthur's Stone—the line along its central chamber—is approximately magnetic N. and S., and there are no indications of its stone structure having been made for sighting to sunrise or sunset at any time of year. But there does seem a possibility of some of the upright stones being adjusted for a midday sun (maximum elevation) observation in connexion with the large " blocking " stone shown in the foreground of Fig. 15. This flat stone—approximately at right angles to the axis, and planted in front of the opening to the dolmen, 3 or 4 yards away—has two notches on its western edge, and at least one of the upright stones at the rear of the dolmen could be aligned with this edge. There is also a stone which when upright would be central with the axis; it stands between the " blocking " stone and the mouth, and might have acted as a pointer stone in connexion with a notch on the top edge of the blocking stone. But as I could not get within the enclosure no exact observations were possible.

Most certainly the round mound in which this dolmen was once enclosed was on a Midsummer Day sunrise ley. I gave this line, which is 50° E. from true N. (practically identical with the axis of Stonehenge), in my first book, as through the Golden Well and the Gold Post; I have recently again traced it on the map and find that it is sighted on the Cefn Hill (1,593 feet), not Pen-y-Beacon. The two " gold " place-names on a sunrise ley demands further investigation.

It was Mr. Walter Pritchard who called my attention to this being a sunrise line. He worked out " on his own " (theoretically) the angle of sunrise on Midsummer Day, marked it on his map through Arthur's Stone without considering any other mark-point, and showed it to me. It passed through identically the same distant points (Devereux Wootton, for example) as the " golden " line I had marked on my map from purely topographical data. It was a strange bit of confirmation, as the " golden " points are not marked on the map on which he worked.

I commenced this chapter with preconceptions towards sun worship in Britain. I finish by striking out the word " worship." It might have been there, but I find no evidence for it in material things, with the slight exception of the prevalence of the name " Bel," detailed in the Place-Name chapter.

The material facts indicate gigantic sundials in ceremonial use, but most certainly for utilitarian—that is, season fixing—purpose.

It is much like the facts concerning " stocks and stones,"

(detailed in other chapters) with their orderly and perhaps reverential placing, but purely for utility ; their " worship " exists in assumptions. We dig up scores of idols in Egypt ; none in Britain.

Although I have treated sun alignment, orientation, and beacons in separate chapters, they are practically one subject.

CHAPTER XV

BEACONS

> Many roads thou hast fashioned:
> All of them lead to the Light.
> —KIPLING: "Song to Mithras the Sun God"

THE prehistoric purpose of a beacon fire was to guide and direct. Not until sun alignment and the sighted track had decayed came the entirely different use in mediaeval days as a warning signal.

It probably had its first use to fix the point of seasonal sunrise, for when a place had been found from which the sun could be seen to rise over some Beltany Hill or May Hill on May Day, the fire on their summit took position as a symbol—for the sun itself rose somewhere else a week later—and as a means of laying out the alignment and the track which was made.

A large number of beacon hills and points are found in any part of the Kingdom, most of them lofty hills with unmistakable names, as Pen-y-Beacon, the Breconshire, Worcestershire (Fig. 78), and Herefordshire (Fig. 79) Beacons, Treleck Beacon. Other hill-top names (elsewhere explained) seem also to indicate use as fire beacon points. Such are Firle Beacon, Tan Hill, Solsbury Hill, Black Hill, Cole's Hill (Fig. 80), Midsummer Hill, May Hill, The Beck, Bexhill.

Evidence is clear as to the early use of these fires. The words "beacon" and "beckon" (both Anglo-Saxon) are from identical roots, and both mean "come to me." Macaulay has hammered into our minds forcibly the mediaeval use of beacons as danger and warning signals. "Till twelve fair counties saw the blaze on Malvern's lonely height," is good, sonorous declamation, although it raises a smile to those who know that the writer could never have really noticed the serrated ridge of the Malverns, with the Worcestershire

Beacon saved from loneliness by its near neighbour, the North Hill.

But other British poets (and all the seers of the Bible) see the true origin.

John Henry Newman, and not Macaulay, is the true modern poet of the beacon light, as a guide:

> O'er moor and fen, o'er crag and torrent till
> The night is gone.

Sir Walter Scott—an instinctive student of early facts—in his tribute to Pitt in the introduction to "Marmion," very carefully limits the beacon light to being a guide, as his hero is made to use "the trumpet's silver sound" as the warning signal:

> Hadst thou but lived, though stripped of power,
> A watchman on a lonely tower,
> Thy thrilling trump had roused the land,
> When fraud or danger were at hand;
> By thee, as by the beacon light,
> Our pilots had kept course aright.

It was not until a year after the publication of "Early British Trackways" that constant repetition of beacon spots aligning on leys, frequently as initial points, began to suggest to me the conclusions with which this chapter commences. I soon realized that in planning the track the beacon fire must have played an important part as an optical weapon, and that there exists a whole string of evidence to prove it.

To begin with, there is the remarkable evidence found on the Chute Causeway in Hampshire, noted in 1760 by R. Willis and in 1898 by G. Knowles, and given in Codrington's "Roman Roads in Britain" (p. 323), in which burnt ash or powder was found in quantities on the original road, under such local conditions as to give rise to the following conclusion: "They must date from the making of the road, as they were covered by the upper layers, and the supposition may be hazarded that we have here traces of fire lighted on the flint foundation of the road, to make a smoke as a beacon for the laying out of the 16 miles of straight road from the south." Here it may be noted that in the Somersetshire Quantock Hills is a Smokeham Farm, and that there are six or eight hill points in this charming district with names indicating fire beacons.

I give other evidence indicating that beacons were on ley sighting points, and therefore must have thrown a line of light by night, or a signal of smoke by day, straight down the track.

Mr. Hippisley Cox records in Dorsetshire, " From a tumulus on Shapwick Hill a road known as Fire Barrow Lane branches off to Musbury Camp." There is a tumulus called by Ormerod a " Fire Beacon " in Sedbury Park, Chepstow, and another labelled with the same name on the map in the Quantocks. The cases in which I found leys (mapped out by other evidence) terminating in hill points with beacon names are innumerable. I give one because the ley is given in Lockyer's " Stonehenge " (p. 412), and because I had found it quite independently.

An alignment runs through Clearbury Ring, Salisbury Cathedral, Old Sarum Mound, and Stonehenge. On plotting this to the north-west I found its termination to be at St. Anne's Hill, 958 feet, the highest point on the Wiltshire Downs, and later I found this to be Tan Hill, where is held a traditional fair on August 6th; also that Tan is modern Welsh for fire, and that its Celtic use for beacon fires is proved by the fires lit in Brittany " at the time of the summer solstice " on the top of Mount St. Michael in the Carnac alignments, being called " Tan Heol " (" Stonehenge," p. 40). This name also connects the beacon fire with the track, for " heol " is modern Welsh for " street," " road," " lane."

Fire Stone Cross, Dartmoor, Flamborough Head, Flamstead (West Herts.), Flamstead End, and Flamstone (South Wilts.) are all significant of places on the beacon track, and as regards the first named, a ley runs through Brandis Cross (another fire name), Fire Stone Cross, the northern tumulus on Causand Beacon, to Willhays, the highest peak of Dartmoor.

Brent is an old English form of " burnt," and the following four " Brent " place-names have situations which suggest a beacon fire: Brentor, an isolated hill rock on the north edge of Dartmoor with an ancient church (St. Michael's, as is usual in such situations) on its point. This Brent Tor of 1,100 feet elevation is used as a mark for vessels entering Plymouth Harbour. There is a similar point—Brent Hill—crowned by a chapel, on the other side of Dartmoor, and a Brent Knoll (Somerset) overlooks the mouth of the Bristol Channel. Brent Point is a coast promontory near Flamborough Head, and perhaps served the same purpose. There are others, high up in Dartmoor, as Brent Fore Hill and Brent Moor, and quite a number of such towns or villages as Brentford (Middlesex), Brentwood, South Brent, East Brent, etc. A mile or two away from Brentford is the ancient hamlet name of Brent Street.

Good proof that the beacon light was part of the mechanism of the old straight track lies in the number of proved instances of church towers being used as beacons, and, as already shown, churches were built on ley sites.

Old Radnor Church, already described and illustrated, is locally reputed to have been a beacon.

It was the retired Radnor schoolmaster who told me that at Barnet, many years ago, he had seen the iron beacon cresset in a church tower. This I found by a guide-book to be at Hadley Church, and it was stated to be used to direct wanderers across the adjacent Enfield Chase. Other beacon churches are recorded at Alnwick, St. Catherine's (Milford Haven), and Bedwelty (Mon.).

About a dozen examples of churches known to be provided with beacon lights is given by Mr. Walter Johnson in his "Byways in British Archæology" (p. 127). Of these, two (St. Aldhelm's chapel on St. Alban's Head, Dorset; and St. Catherine's on Abbotsbury Hill, Dorset) are built expressly as beacon chapels or chantrys, as is the chapel on Lantern Rock, which even now has on its roof the lantern for Ilfracombe Harbour, in the midst of which it stands. I find a proved ley using this Lantern Rock as its terminal.

Royston (Barnsley) and St. Nicholas (Newcastle) both have beacon lanterns fitted to their towers. The stone cresset still left among the ruins of Llanthony Abbey, Mon. (Fig. 46), with its three hollows to hold melted fat or oil, might perhaps have been for use within the church; for just as the early church took over in many cases the much earlier beacon lights, so also they took under their patronage the semi-sacred need fires, one of which in each district must never go out, that the household hearth might be renewed. Our present bonfire (boon-fire), with its hill-top traditions of feasting and dancing and jumping over, is a survival. But this is an aspect which many pages of Frazer's "Golden Bough" are written to expound.

Now to come to the severely practical question why the hill-top beacon should in so many cases align with the old straight track. The answer is found in the perplexing fact of the old roads going through ponds and moats. A beacon fire on a lofty hill can be seen from anywhere. But to be seen *reflected* in *water* (which is a level plane surface) can only happen if the observer stands in alignment with the beacon and the piece of water (and also at the right angle of altitude). If, therefore, a small pond—or a moat—is placed at a low point on the ley, an observer on higher ground beyond can mark the next sighting point accurately by this night signal. It was the early use of a beautifully accurate plane mirror for surveying. The beacon fire would not be for nightly use, but for laying out and checking the sighting points, and for special occasions afterwards, such as (in many cases) the day (or night before) when the sun rose on the alignment.

"What imaginative stuff!" I can hear some reader exclaim. But pause to consider the very remarkable string of evidence. In many parts of England small ponds (of just the type through which leys are found to run) are called "flashes." There is a Flash Dam on Matlock Moor, and I have often noted a stream dammed up to form a pond without apparent reason; Flashbrook Wood (Salop) and Flash, a village in Staffordshire, record this. The "New English Dictionary" states that "low watery marshy places are frequently called 'flams' by persons in or about Oxford"; and it also gives us an obsolete meaning of "leye" to be "flame or fire." The root element in "lake" also means reflection, as in lacquer, and in a poetic name for the ruby, "a lake of wine." In Herefordshire, Letton Lakes, Sutton Lakes, and Withington Lakes are not large sheets of water, but sluggish streams with ponds on them; and adjoining the first is a similar low place called Tumpy Ley, while adjoining Letton Lakes is Tumpy Lakes. An obsolete meaning of "lay" (lei, ley) in the "New English Dictionary" is "a lake, pool."

Rudyard Kipling, writing from local knowledge, makes

Puck say, " It was Weland's Ford then ; a road led down to it from the Beacon on the top of the hill," thus connecting a prehistoric ford with a beacon light by a track.

Bunyan, in describing Christian's start on the straight track, makes it clear that the way is not only straight towards a beacon light, but also straight through a pond.

Then while " beorh " is the Anglo-Saxon for a moated mound, " beorht " is an adjective meaning " bright, gleaming, shining, radiant, shimmering," and " mote " is not only a water-ringed mound, but a speck of light or something in the eye.

Other place-names supporting the connexion between the beacon and the ley and its sighting points are: Beacon Stone (Northumb.), Becontree (Essex), Bicknoller Hill, Bicknoller Post (a mile distant), and Fire Signal Pitts in the Quantock Hills. Also Beckbury, a Gloucestershire Hill Camp, " from which can be seen twelve counties."

Cole names come into touch with beacons in the surnames (originating from places): Colbeck and Colebeck. More direct and nearer the Celtic origin is the fact that *coel certh* in modern Welsh means " omen of danger, beacon, bonfire."

Bringing the word cole nearer still to beacon facts, it is recorded that when in 1898 the Woolhope Club visited Cole's Hill, a 1,000 feet point in north Herefordshire, the only find recorded is that on the summit are hollows supposed to be beacon pits. I have only had one opportunity to put spade to lofty hill-top since there dawned the connexion between beacon and ley, and there, on Midsummer Hill, a hollow on the top I proved to be a beacon pit. It would take but little delving to test all the Black Hills and the Cole Hills.

Although so many Beacon Hills are lofty terminals on the ley, there is nothing in the mechanism of their use which involves the assumption that all must be at the end of a sighted line, and as a matter of expediency it is quite probable that a series of beacon fires were used on one ley when it was planned. The proved example at the Chute Causeway indicates this. There is a " Beaconshill " near Dymock on a bank, scarcely a hill, and this applies to many of the " Beacon " or " Bacon " farm place-names.

The question whether rock basins were not made and used for beacon purposes, utilizing perhaps " the fat of rams," is discussed in the Initial Points chapter. Mr. H. R. Watkin of Torquay is emphatically of opinion that the granite rock basins about Dartmoor are excavated by the disintegration of the stone by fire action, not by tools.

That hollow basins in stone were used for illuminating purposes, is shown by the early mediaeval stone cressets (see Fig. 122), which may have been a survival.

A most fascinating account connecting the beacon light with orderly sighting methods, is that in the last chapter of Sir Walter Scott's "The Antiquary": "Old Caxon, perched in his hut, with an occasional peep towards the signal post with which his own corresponded, was not a little surprised by observing a light in that direction. He rubbed his eyes, looked again, adjusting his observation by a cross-staff which had been so placed as to bear upon the point. And behold the light increased. . . . And he lighted the beacon accordingly."

CHAPTER XVI

CHURCHES ON MARK-POINTS

On the Sussex Stane Street . . . you can walk for some three miles on the actual embankment of the Roman Way, with the solitude of the Downland around you and the tapering spire of Chichester Cathedral, marking the heart of the old Roman city, always in the centre of your vision as you look along the dead-true line of the ancient road.

—REGINALD WELLBYE: "The Motor," June 3, 1924

THE evidence that ancient churches in Britain were in most cases built upon those points of antiquity which I have shown to be mark-points on alignments amounts to overwhelming proof, and only part of that available can here be found room for.

Church building commenced in historic times, and there are at least two documents clearly indicating this site origin. The first is the letter (A.D. 601) from Pope Gregory to Abbot Mellitus (given in Bede's "Ecclesiastical History") sending a message to Augustine that pagan "temples" ought not to be destroyed, but purified and converted to churches. The second is referred to on page 35 in Johnson's "Byways in British Archæology": "It is on record that Patrick, Bishop of the Hebrides, desired Orlygus to build a church wherever he found the upright stones or menhirs."

To follow up at once the evidence of actual instances (excluding for the moment evidence of alignment) in which ancient stones decided church sites, Mr. O. G. Crawford says: "Under the western end of Constantine's Church (Harlyn Bay, Cornwall) are two partially buried boulders of Catacleus stone. They are doubtless the sacred nucleus round which the chapel was built." Mr. Johnson discusses similar examples in "Byways."

An ancient church near Halifax is named Cross Stone.

It is natural that actual instances of ancient stone originating the site are rare, as such stone would be embedded in the foundation of the church and never seen until demolition. The writer has seen none in his district, which contains few derelict church sites. But the custom of "laying the foundation stone" of a church is probably a bit of folk-memory recording the fact, for it is usually overlooked that from the builder's point of view there is no such thing as "a" foundation stone, every stone laid below ground being of equal importance as a foundation. The "foundation stone" is a symbol of the ancient mark stone which "founded" the site, and the coins or valuables deposited under the stone are another survival in folk-lore.

A Roman altar which was apparently a link between the prehistoric mark stone and the Christian Church was found about 1837 "inside the west end" of Michaelchurch (Ross) Church by Rev. John Webb. It is the only known inscribed altar found in Herefordshire. The inscription reads DEO TRIVII BELLICVS DONAVIT ARAM—"To the god of the three ways Bellicus gave this altar." It is still to be seen in the church. Roman altars have also been found in churches at Daglingworth (altered to a Norman window head), and at St. Swithin's, Lincoln, found beneath the tower when rebuilding (Johnson's "Byways," p. 6). These three instances point to a Roman (pagan) altar taking the place of a mark stone, and this in its turn deciding the site of the church; the inscription on the one at Michaelchurch clearly indicates the first stage in this evolution, one translator rendering "trivii" as "crossways."

Mounds were the other type of mark-points which sometimes decided the site of churches. Cascob Church, Radnorshire, has its square stone and wood framed tower (Fig. 106) built on (or in) a mound to which a ley was found to be sighted. Another church (Bleddfa) a few miles away has also its tower in a similar mound. Mr. J. R. Mortimer records the finding of a barrow with its burial contents beneath Fimber Church, Yorkshire, and Mr. Allcroft says that within the south-west angle of the stone footings of the wattled church of Arlington, Sussex, was found a sepulchral urn of coarse fabric.

In Shore's "History of Hampshire" it is stated that "a number of ancient churches in Hampshire are built upon artificial mounds," and examples are cited at Corhampton, Burton, Sopley, and Cheriton.

Mr. Hadrian Allcroft's delightful "Downland Pathways"

describes similar instances in Sussex. Alfriston Church " is a mound of earth—so small that the great cruciform church almost fills it up . . . and finally one surmises that the original garth had been quite circular." Berwick Church " crosses a little knap, and within it is a perplexing mound of great size, which impinges on the south-west corner of the tower. . . . Field paths converge on it from the most unexpected directions." Wilmington Church is " perched as usual on a mound." At Rottingdean, " the sanctuary is built upon a knoll." At Falmer " the churchyard is mounded up, for all the world like a barrow—the popular notion that churchyards rise by reason of continuous burials will not explain these bigger examples."

In all parts of England are found churches built on a bank or hill point, often apart from the village. " The decent church that topped the neighbouring hill " is not confined to the " Deserted Village." It is needless to labour examples of this: Harrow, Churchdown (Glos.), Lincoln. Wigmore (Herefordshire, Fig. 107) is a typical example on a bank. All these are explained by the fact that a ley sighted across country would have its mark-points—whether stone, tree group, or mound—on the highest points touched. It is a curious fact that in so many cases the churches or chapels on a lofty peak are dedicated to St. Michael.

All the St. Michael's Mounts, Brent Tor, Dartmoor, Brent Hill, a former chapel on the Skirrid (Fig. 51), and Glastonbury Tor are examples of this.

Chapels are often built on isolated rocks or small islands a little away from the coast. These are in most (or all) cases terminal points of leys: the two St. Michael's Mounts, St. Tecla's Chapel in Severn mouth, The " Lantern Rock," Ilfracombe, Caldy Island.

Mr. Walter Johnson in his " Byways in British Archæology " devotes a hundred pages to various evidence that churches were frequently " on pagan sites," that is—in the light of the present investigations—on ley marking points, and indeed the word " pagan " signifies " country."

Forty Herefordshire churches have mounds or moats adjoining, or almost adjoining, the churchyard. My surmise as to the cause is that a mark stone near the mound indicating the direction of a track passed through both, and that the church (or its cross) is on the site of the stone.

At Cirencester the ascertained course of Ermine Street, as traced by Mr. Collingwood in his "Roman Britain" (p. 49), through the town goes through the west end of St. John's Church.

The evidence of the alignment of churches, not only with each other but with all types of original mark-points and with ancient roads, occurs all over the Kingdom. It is too abundant to give more than a selection. Strangely enough it is most abundant (as regards churches aligning with roads) in old towns, perhaps because here tenements lining the road keep its site fixed (often widened on one side) all down the ages. In every such old town a church tower can be seen closing the vista down a straight bit of road, and often there are several examples.

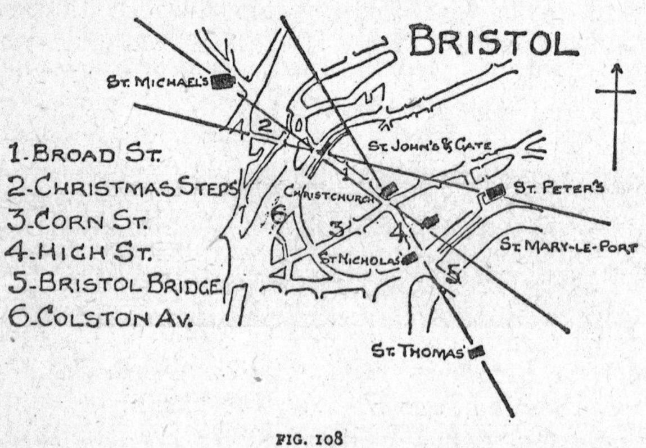

FIG. 108

At Shrewsbury, St. Julian's and St. Alkmund's precisely close up the end of Fish Street and Grope Lane.

Bristol has many vistas of a tower or steeple closing the end of an ancient street or lane. All Saints' Passage (off Corn Street) with St. Nicholas spire; Small Street also with St. Nicholas; Lodge Street (from Park Row) with St. Mary, Redcliffe; High Street with Christchurch spire. This last alignment runs to the south-east through the site of St. Nicholas Gate, over which stood the chancel of old St. Nicholas Church, and on over Bristol Bridge to St. Thomas Church; to the north-west through the Grey Friars, Redland Green, where a guide-book reports "a large prehistoric stone, supposed to stand on the site of an old Roman or British road," and, some three miles away, to the Roman Camp (with site of St. Blaze Chapel) near Henbury.

The most striking set of examples of church alignment in Bristol (shown in the diagram Fig. 108) is that where a four church ley—St. Michael's, St. John's, Christchurch, and St. Mary le Port (lying on Broad Street which, however, swerves a little)—crosses with another church ley passing through Christmas Steps, the site of a monastery at the top of this, St. John's Church and gate, and St. Peter's. The photograph (Fig. 109) shows how Broad Street actually passes under the spire of St. John's Church, which is built on the city wall, and has no east or west windows; it was photographed a bit on one side of the ley to show St. Michael's (on a hill, as usual) aligning; and Fig. 110 shows the view in the contrary direction through the archway (city gate) under St. John's, with Christchurch aligning.

The fact of these two leys passing through the tower site indicates that before being that of a city gate it was a prehistoric mark-point. Bristol, with many prehistoric sites aligning, is rich ground for ley hunting.

At Oxford, the churches of St. Giles, St. Mary Magdalen, St. Martin's Carfax (partly demolished), and St. Aldate, align through the Northgate in the city walls, and over the Thames "Oksna Forda" (thus on a coin of Alfred), alongside the present Folly Bridge. Crossing this ley is another through St. Peter's in the Castle (demolished), St. Martin's Carfax, All Saints, and St. Mary the Virgin.

These leys cross in St. Martin's Carfax (on the highest part of the gravel bank), which was the traditional assembly point for common council, justice, and market; they are the basis of the present main streets, which are altered so as not to go through the church sites, as the sighted leys do.

In Hereford City, Offa Street, which is obviously ancient, because two vehicles cannot pass each other, has the tower of the cathedral precisely blocking one end of the street looking south (Fig. 111). Looking north, from the other end of the street, the tower of St. Peter's Church precisely aligns in the same way (Fig. 112). On high ground overlooking the city the two towers can be brought into alignment, and when this is done from the right spot in a meadow, four sighting points align, namely, a small pond, the two churches, and, beyond, a circular wooded knowl called Beechwood, situated in the King's Forest of Haywood, outside the city. This last aligns on other leys and (containing perhaps 10 acres) is a perfect circle in plan. These three sighting points are shown (not quite in alignment, to indicate their separate form) in Fig. 113 and aligning with the pond in Fig. 114. The trees of the wood will be seen on each side of the cathedral tower, and it will be kept in mind that a street (naturally hidden in the photograph) has its whole length precisely on the ley.

Another Hereford ley through churches is to be seen down Portland Street, which aligns on All Saints' Church tower (Fig. 6). The alignment, continuing, passes, without surviving mark-points, over the city; but in the opposite suburb, lies in succession on the site of old St. Owen's Church (demolished in the Civil Wars, but its site shown in an old map), St. Giles' Chapel, and an old house site on a mound called The Crozen, which tradition states to be "on a Saxon burying ground." Three churches and a reputed mound are thus on a ley along which a length of a main road lies, with slight deviation to avoid two of the sighting points. St. Giles' Chapel is so awkwardly placed at a cross track (motors head straight for it from three directions) that public opinion is demanding its demolition, and it is interesting to reflect that the trouble originated in our ancestors planting a mark stone in the centre of a cross track four thousand years—or more—ago.

Looking up Broad Street—still in Hereford—from its southern end near the cathedral, All Saints' spire is at the northern end. In this line of sight four churches precisely align within five miles, namely, All Saints', Holmer, Pipe and Lyde, and Wellington; the ley continuing through spots called Kipper Knoll and Cold Oak. Southward the ley crosses the Wye at or near the Palace Ford, and through Aconbury Church. It lies within the whole length of Broad Street, but at the northern end close on one side of it, exactly where was situated up to 1787 the Northgate, a narrow passage entering the pre-Conquest city over the King's Ditch.

Another Hereford instance to be verified by eye is to stand on the knuckle earthwork of Dinedor Camp (Figs. 47 and 84), and note how the tall spire of All Saints' Church appears to spring up between the pinnacles of the cathedral tower, so exactly do the two churches align with the ancient mound underfoot.

To take East Anglian examples. A correspondent gives this information: "The Rector of Kirby le Soken took me to the tower and showed me the remaining three towers (left out of five) once dead in a line from Walton-on-the-Naze." In Norfolk are many examples: the four churches at Swardeston, Yelverton, Ashby, and Carleton St. Peter align; and so do Colney, Norwich Cathedral, Great Plumstead, and Fishley Churches. Fig. 13 shows a ley passing through Woolhope, Fownhope, Little Dewchurch, and Much Birch Churches, marked on the Ordnance map itself to show its exactness. All these are within eight miles. This map also contains that part of the Giant's Cave to Aconbury ley (see Chapter XIV) which passes through Woolhope, Holme Lacy, and Aconbury Churches. A study of this map disproves the "accidental coincidence" argument. For Bucks church leys, see the Appendix.

A church ley convenient to verify is to be found in the map which is part of Mr. O. G. S. Crawford's "Andover District, an Account of Sheet 283 of the one-inch Ordnance Map," a monograph which contains special information invaluable to ley hunters. Here five churches—Tidcombe, Linkenholt, Faccombe, Burghclere, and Sydmonton—align precisely, and on the ley are homesteads with the ancient names of Folly Barn, Bacon's (formerly Beacon's) Farm, and Curzon Street Farm, with fragments of present-day road in approximate alignment. There are also on this map eight alignments, each with four churches.

Within a mile north of this ley lies Highclere Castle, from which in April, 1923, there was carried the body of the Earl of Carnarvon to his final resting-place within the British Camp on the summit of the Beacon Hill, only half a mile south of our ley. It is a strange thought regarding this great and persistent explorer, dying almost in the height of his triumph amidst the tombs of the ancient Egyptian kings, with the most brilliant of all Eastern discoveries to his credit, that his thoughts went back to the quiet hills of his native soil, that to him the beacon beckoned, and that he, like the chieftains of his prehistoric ancestors, craved for the wind-swept grave on the mountain-top.

There are some differences in mapping out leys through churches from what occurs with earlier and more definite sighting points. Present churches are not always on the ground plan of their predecessors. Three instances of this can be specified. A ley precisely down Lower and Upper Church Street goes through Hereford Cathedral, not through any special part of the present building, but through the site of the Chapel of St. Catherine, reputed to be the earliest site of all. A north and south ley through Leominster was found, which, passing through the churchyard, just escaped the present building. But it passed through the foundations of a Saxon apse which has been excavated.

Staying at Paignton I found on the map indications of a ley which passed through a corner of the churchyard, but not through the church. On visiting the spot there was seen in a churchyard corner, quite away from the present church, the uncovered undercroft of the earliest church. This corner was the exact spot through which the ley was already marked on my map.

London church alignments are many, but should not be accepted as final until the structural history of each church is verified as being on an ancient site.

(*a*) St. Martins-in-the-Fields, St. Mary-le-Strand, St. Clement Dane, and St. Dunstan's, Fleet Street, align to the site of an ancient mound (approximately at Arnold's Circus, Shoreditch), described by Borrow in a chapter called " The Mount " in " Romano Lavo-Lil," and this is verified as a track by lying approximately on part of the Strand and Pall Mall.

(*b*) St. Paul's, Covent Garden, The Temple, St. Bride's, Fleet Street, church on Ludgate Hill, one near the Guildhall, St. Stephen's, Coleman Street, all align to St. Botolph's, Bishopsgate.

(*c*) The Temple, St. Paul's Cathedral, and St. Helen's, Bishopsgate, align to St. Dunstan's, Stepney, which has pre-Conquest remains, while two other churches and the bank site (where was a church), are on the ley. There are further features of these London alignments dealt with in the Orientation chapter.

There are some strange instances of churches being built on a track, which instead of curving round to avoid the church actually continues under it. The chapel over St.

John's Gate, Warwick, is one instance, and a narrow lane leading out of the main street at Exeter actually passes under the altar of St. Stephen's Bow, which is very much higher than the nave to make the accommodation possible. In a portfolio of the Architectural Detail Postal Club, a fellow member—Mr. F. E. Howard—makes some notes about public footpaths under or through church towers, and mentions instances at St. Mary's (Warwick) and St. Michael (Coventry), also mentioning that several Saxon towers show doorways or arches through both north and south walls.

Working on a street map of Warwick before reading Mr. Howard's note, I had marked a ley passing through the great mound of Warwick Castle and the tower of St. Mary's, the track appearing to lie on the footpath in the line of the present road, which path is the one passing through the tower.

In Bristol, Broad Street goes under the tower of St. John the Baptist, which forms a gateway (see Figs. 109 and 110) in the city wall, the church being on the wall. Three other Bristol gateways, now demolished—St. Giles, St. Nicholas, and St. Leonards—had churches over them. There is the Hanging Chapel over a gate at Landport, Somerset.

The tower of St. Magnus, London Bridge, is hollow at the lowest storey, and formerly a footway through it led on to old London Bridge.

Although this chapter refers to Christian churches, it is very evident that the practice of building them on the sighting points of tracks is one of continuity handed on from a similar practice with earlier places of worship. Pope Gregory's letter to Augustine refers to "temples of the idols" as something more than a few grouped stones, and they were probably roofed. Stonehenge I have shown to be on the crossing of tracks.

Three Roman pagan temples in England, one of those at Silchester, one at Weycock, and another at West Mersey, have indications of evolution from the stone circle, being polygonal or circular in plan.

We should expect, therefore, that as pagan temples are in the same line of descent from ley mark-points as churches have been proved to be, that, like churches, they would align with each other and with ley mark-points. Their sites, or remains, are so infrequent that actual evidence of this was not expected, and the striking proof now to be given of their alignment is all the more gratifying.

Silchester, in Hampshire, on the Berkshire border not far from Reading, is the site of a town built by the Romans on a previous town of a British tribe. There being now no buildings on it except a farm and a parish church, it was possible to excavate it, which has been done thoroughly by the Society of Antiquaries and others. The Roman walls with six gates still remain.

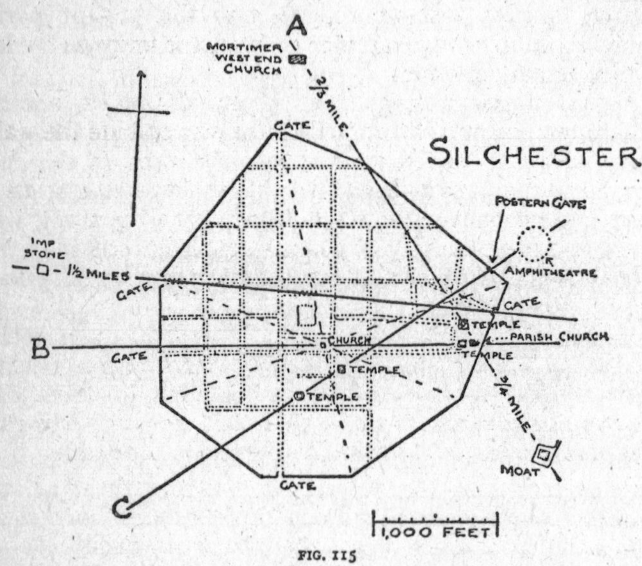

FIG. 115

The sites and foundations of four pagan temples, and of one presumed early Christian church were found, and, as is shown on the plan, Fig. 115, these align with each other, with the two parish churches near, and two other ley mark-points.

It happens that on the six-inch map, which includes the town, there are so few ley mark-points besides the excavated temples and church, that all of them (namely, two parish churches, one moat, one mark stone, and an amphitheatre) are given on the plan—three of them drawn nearer to the town than their proper distance, to save space.

It will be seen that all of these (except the stone) come into alignment on three leys, that there is no surplus, and that the argument of "accidental coincidence" is almost, if not quite, outside possibility.

Ley A on this plan is a four-point proof, unusual in the short limit of a six-inch map. In this a line intersecting the only two parish churches (Mortimer West End and Silchester) on the map, also goes through one of the pagan temples in the Roman town, and on to the only moat in the map.

Ley B, only 2½° N. of E., goes through the small early church, a square pagan temple, and the present parish church. All three are oriented to the same angle as the ley, a very remarkable fact.

Ley C passes through the polygonal temple, another square temple, and the amphitheatre just outside the walls. Thus, all seven of the ancient religious sites on this map fall upon the above three leys. The above leys seem to have little connexion with the planning of the town, with the one exception that ley C intersects no less than five street corners, and mark stones on it might possibly have decided their lay-out.

But there is one strange fact which appears to show that the exact site of the early Christian church was decided mathematically. It is at the intersection of three lines (shown dotted) from angle to angle and from angle to gate. The intersection is through the presumed altar site.

CHAPTER XVII

ORIENTATION

> We must lay his head to the east;
> My father hath a reason for 't.
> —"Cymbeline"

TO orient a temple, a church, or a trackway must be done in its first construction, and it is to decide the axis of the structure by taking a sighting line from the spot where the observer stands, to the spot where the sun (or a star) is seen to rise on a chosen day. It is obvious that this varies enormously according to different times of the year, but the sunrise direction on a level plain when day and night are equal is true east. It is also obvious that an observation taken in a valley with the sun rising over a hill ridge also makes a great difference in the angle, and that this is not theoretical only is shown by the fact that there is a difference of 26½° between the orientation of Stonehenge and that of the sunrise line I have described over the Giant's Cave on the Malverns, which settled the orientation of two churches, although both angles were settled by sunrise on Midsummer Day.

The vague idea that ancient churches were built east and west is quite wrong as regards this district, where they are to be found at every angle between 50° N. of E. (Llancillo) and 38° S. of E. (Dore). Two out of three are N. of E.; and true east, or within a few degrees of it, is not so common an orientation as 10° or 20° north of it. From 30° to 40° N. of E. is frequent, especially on the Welsh border, where for example, Llanigon (41° N. of E.), Clyro (32° N. of E.), and Llowes (28° N. of E.) adjoin.

The subject is so complicated and there is so little proof of uniformity of procedure that Mr. W. Johnson, who devotes thirty-eight pages to the subject in his "Byways of British Archæology," comes to no definite conclusion in summing up the evidence. In particular the supposed practice of taking the birthday of the patron saint to decide the orientation is neither general, nor proved for early times. Mr. Johnson does not find it mentioned before the middle of the seventeenth century.

The subject is introduced here because there is clear indication that in some cases trackways were oriented, and that the angle was the same as certain sun temples or churches on the track.

This is indeed indicated by St. Paulinus of Nola writing in the fifth century—again quoting Mr. Johnson—who states that the outlook of a particular church was not directed towards the east, following the more common practice, but towards a certain basilica, containing a tomb—that of the martyred presbyter, St. Felix.

All sun temples were oriented, and Sir Norman Lockyer has probed deeply into those of Egypt and Britain.

Stonehenge is an example of the connexion with the old straight track. Its avenue (Fig. 104), even as marked on present-day maps, extends far beyond the temple itself, and is on its axis, that is, the orientation to Midsummer Day sunrise. The point I wish to make is that it is a trackway, even if also a processional road. Let us suppose that (as probably was the fact) it were necessary to get a fixed beacon point at convenient distance to stabilize the sunrise line; a more distant point than Sidbury Hill (7½ miles) would be unnecessary, and the beacon alignment which I have shown to continue for very many miles both ways is for some other purpose than for this temple, an actual track being the only explanation. I know of no evidence which decides whether the orientation of this track (and of Stonehenge) was first laid down at Stonehenge itself or at some other point on the alignment.

The Malvern Hill alignment (Giant's Cave to Aconbury), which I have detailed in the Sun Alignment chapter, does afford very clear and very important evidence as to the place where the orientation of this ley was decided from Midsummer Day sunrise. The angle of this orientation, although fixed also by Midsummer Day sunrise, is about 14° N. of E. instead of the 40½° N. of E. given by Lockyer for Stonehenge; this is because it was observed at a steep upward angle over a high mountain ridge from the Sacrificial Stone, which lies in a hollow. None of the other sighting points on this alignment would give the same, and the two churches which the six-inch map shows to have this orientation could not possibly have had it fixed by a sunrise observation at their own sites. It follows that if the observation was made at the Sacrificial Stone it must have been in some way communicated to the church sites. There is no evidence of use of angle instruments, here or elsewhere, but there is here full evidence of a sighted line having been laid down across country through the church sites to Aconbury beacon. There are six other churches in the same map, and, as will be seen by the statement below of their orientation, the facts that out of the eight churches Woolhope and Holme Lacy are the only ones which align on the sun worship line named, and are also oriented to its exact angle (14° N. of E.), cannot possibly be a mere coincidence.

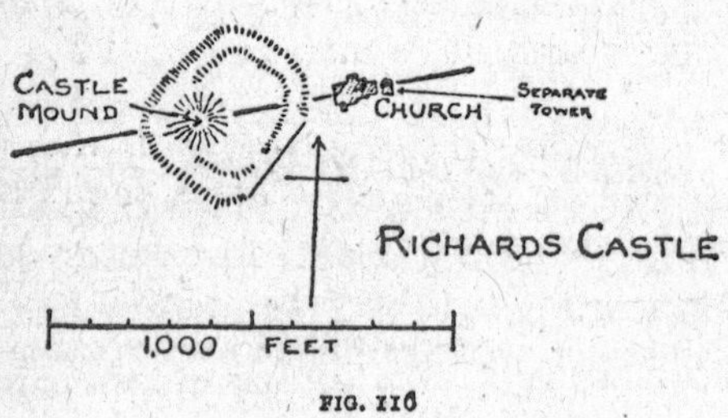

FIG. 116

Soller's Hope	6° N. of E.	Fownhope	2° S. of E.
Bolstone	30° N. of E.	Dinedor	3° N. of E.
Hampton Bishop	9° N. of E.	Mordiford	11° S. of E.

Here then are two churches which are oriented (see Figs. 13 and 103) by the ley on which they are built, and not by solar observation on the spot; nor are they dedicated to the same saint. It is a new aspect of orientation and might prove to be a most important one, although it is unlikely to be universal.

Forty churches in Herefordshire have mounds or moats practically adjoining the churchyard, or with a field between. In ten cases the churches orient through these, in two cases (Richard's Castle and Eardisley) through the centre, in the others not central but within the moat or the trench of the mound. With these moats and mounds in all positions round the church there must be accidental coincidences. But these, I estimate, could not be more than one in fifteen cases, and actually one in four have the orientation through them. Six out of these ten cases are recorded castles, including the two earliest Norman castles (Richard's Castle and Ewias Harold) built in England, and of the six all but

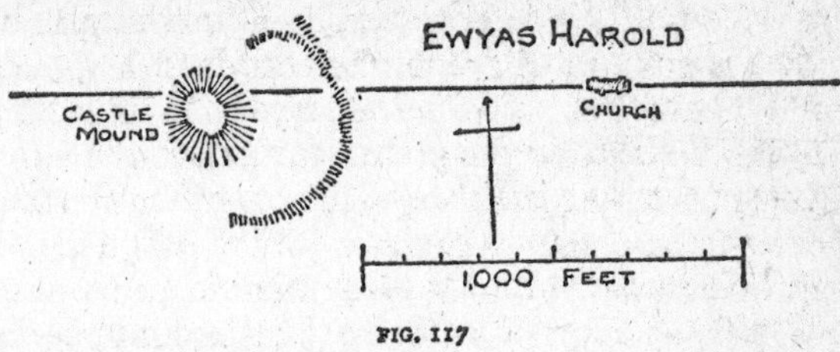

FIG. 117

one (Lyonshall) have the orientation to a mound. The list of churches orienting to moat or mound is:

Richard's Castle Church	oriented	8°	N. of E.	See Fig. 116.
Ewias Harold	,,	2°	S. of E.	See Fig. 117.
Ashperton	,,	5°	N. of E.	
Eardisley	,,	5°	N. of E.	
Lyonshall	,,	28°	N. of E.	
Kilpeck	,,	30°	N. of E.	See Fig. 118.
Shobdon	,,	2°	S. of E.	
Burghill	,,	24°	S. of E.	
Walterstone	,,	$1\frac{1}{2}$°	S. of E	See Fig. 81.
Whitbourne	,,	13°	S. of E.	

FIG. 118

There are thirty identified castle sites in Herefordshire, and the above list shows that one-fifth of them have an adjacent church orienting to them. This cannot be all accidental.

The following churches in Herefordshire orient to an adjoining church: Hereford Cathedral to old St. Nicholas, Richard's Castle to Wigmore, Whitbourne to Doddenham (site of), Grendon Bishop to Wackton, Mansel Lacy to Old Yazor, Kingstone to Vowchurch, Longtown to Llanthony.

Other churches, such as Brinsop, Callow, Dewsall, Aconbury, Soller's Hope, Longtown, Yatton, Marden, Madley, Mathon, apparently orient on leys. This information is all taken from the six-inch Ordnance maps, which show a small plan of all churches, and has therefore no high degree of accuracy. Nor has a complete search been made of the county, and the suggested leys have not been completely traced.

It is well to mention that the number of churches observed not to orient on a ley far outnumber those which do; also that I see no evidence that leys were usually aligned by sun; there are too many in a northerly direction. Probably the great majority of leys were initiated for utilitarian purposes, a few only by sun, and the utility tracks were the first ones.

Freemasonry affords a most striking link between ley sighting methods and orientation of buildings; for their lodges were formerly oriented, and annals of some of the Scotch lodges (says Mr. W. Johnson in "Byways") describe the exact procedure followed for the alignment of churches. "The site of the altar having been decided upon, a pole was thrust into the ground, and a day appointed for the building to be commenced. On the evening previous, the Patrons, Ecclesiastics, and Masons assembled, and spent the night in devotional exercises; one being placed to watch the rising of the sun, gave notice when his rays appeared above the horizon. When fully in view, the Master Mason sent out a man with a rod, which he ranged in line between the altar and the sun, and thus fixed the line of orientation."

The exceptional orientation of Llanigon Church (Brecon) to the midsummer sunrise angle caused me to try a map ley through the church at that angle. Within a few miles it passes through the conical mound of Brontllys Castle, the hill-top earthwork of Castleton, and Winforton Church.

There are curious facts linking up orientation with the ley system illustrated by some London churches. In the seven-church alignment (*c*) given in the Church Alignment chapter, St. Paul's, St. Helen's, Bishopsgate, and Stepney Church orient on the same angle (4° N. of E.) as the ley, the last two as exactly as can be judged on the six-inch Ordnance map, but St. Paul's with a slight difference of about one degree. In ley (*b*) two churches—the Temple, and St. Bride's—orient on the ley. Another orientation fact was revealed in plotting out a line from the white mount (Tower) to Southwark Cathedral, which also goes through St. George's in the East. This alignment goes to Westminster, and converges with a line down the middle of Tothill Street, to a point in Wellington Barracks. Lines on the exact orientation of Westminster Abbey and the adjacent St. Margaret's Church were then laid down, and they too converge to the above point. Here, then, are four indications (one of them Tothill Street) of convergence or orientation to one point, and it leaves a strong presumption that this was the point at which was situated the tot, toot, or mound, which gave its name to Tothill Fields and Street.

CHAPTER XVIII

CASTLES ON MARK SITES

I will go to the mount of Reir, and rear there a castle.
—LAYAMON'S "Brut"

I SPEAK of castle sites—to begin with—in the present-day conventional sense. It will be seen later that the origin of the word was different from its present meaning.

The evidence now to be given indicates that ancient castle sites line up with mounds and moats, and therefore were decided in prehistoric times. There are far fewer castle sites than there are church sites, and it is therefore scarcely ever possible to find a ley proved by three or more castles aligning, the proof rather lying in their alignment with other undoubted sighting points.

Ewias Harold Castle and Longtown Castle align to Castell Dinas.

Monmouth Castle and White Castle align to the Skirrid Mountain.

Raglan Castle and Monmouth Castle align through Dingestow and Dixton Churches and Courtfield Mound or Hermitage.

New Radnor Castle, Kington Castle, and Weobley Castle align in a ley described in the Radnor Vale chapter.

Almost every castle in the above list appears from personal inspection to have an obviously artificial mound on its site, the castle keep being usually built upon it. In the thirty-six identified castles enumerated in Robinson's "Castles of Herefordshire" thirty appear to have such artificial mounds, and the exceptions might possibly have had such, now demolished.

In my experience of local ley tracking, a castle site (its mound or keep) aligns almost as surely as does a prehistoric mound, and these combined facts make out a prima facie case for almost (if not quite) all castles to have been built on the sites of such mounds.

The remainder of this chapter proves this to be so, even where historical evidence dates the castle to a Norman period.

There are many castles which have an earlier mound name than the castle name. Hereford has its Hogg's Mount at a corner of its embankments. Layamon's "Brut" (early thirteenth century) speaks of "A castle named Glenowre, upon a high mount; Cloard hight the mount, and Hergin hight the land, near the Wye, that is a fair water" (this description could only apply to Hereford, Wilton, Goodrich, or Penyard).

Exeter Castle is on the Red Mount, Normanized to Rougemont; and Grosmont Castle also indicates in its name the great mound previous to its building.

Raglan Castle site was called Twyn-y-Ceiros (Cherry Tree Tump) before the castle was built, and it is to-day a moated mound.

London Castle—The Tower—had its White name settled before William built it, and before the Roman settlement, as will be proved.

Richard's Castle (Fig. 116, its keep on a mound) was Aureton (a prehistoric name) in "Domesday Book." Other castles with names suggesting prehistoric mounds are Burglow (Sussex), Conisborough and Bolsover (Yorks.), Knockin and Wattlesborough (Salop), half a dozen Caer-Castles (as Carmarthen) and Carew, all meaning "camp" and all in Wales.

Totternhoe is classified by Mr. Allcroft as a Norman earthwork, but its tot-howe name—far earlier than Norman times—proves it to be a look out or sighting mound or barrow in its first existence.

The traditional account of the building of a castle on a previous mound given by Layamon in his "Brut" is most illuminating: "Then came a wise man, who well could counsel—Listen to me lord king—upon the mount of Reir I will advise that thou work a castle with strong stone wall, for there thou mightest dwell and live with joy. Then answered the King I will go to the mount of Reir and rear there a castle. . . . When the dyke was dug and thoroughly deepened, then began they a wall on the dyke over all, and they laid together lime and stone. . . . In the day they laid the wall, in the night it fell over all; in the morrow they reared it, in the night it began to tumble." Merlin the sorcerer is brought. "The dyke was dug seven feet deeper; then they found there right the stone fair and broad." Under the stone was a pit of water and when the water was drained and the pit was empty, then came out two dragons and made great din and fought fiercely.

In this account a previous mound, which ultimately proves to be a barrow—for it has its stone chamber and its dragons—is selected for the castle site. The spade is freely used to deepen the trench and perhaps enlarge the mound; the tumbling of the walls is probably folk-memory of the result of building on the newly enlarged mound.

In Caerleon (Mon.) is a mound with Norman castle remains on it. But Roman articles were found at its foot and all about it. The mound was there before the Normans came.

So at Worcester, when the great mound of the Norman castle was demolished (see Alles, "Folk Lore," p. 15) it was Roman relics which were found buried in its substance, and in the black earth at ground level a prehistoric bronze celt. The Normans as usual had built upon an older mound.

The mound of the great Norman castle of Duffield—a castle long destroyed—has been found to contain Anglo-Saxon remains.

Mrs. Leather in her "Folk Lore of Herefordshire" gives five instances of legends that the mounds of local castles contain hidden treasure, and such legends have an earlier origin than Norman times. Longtown is one of these, and the schoolmaster there, whose house within the bailey is nearest to the mound, also tells me of a vivid dream he had recently that he and a scholar were shovelling gold from within the castle mound. He has not been there long and vows that he never heard of the legend; but that is as it may be.

Although a mound—which I have shown to be prehistoric—was almost always the nucleus of a castle, an enclosure (either earthen bank or stone walls, or both) had to be added to secure enough accommodation. This is now known as the bailey, and began to be added in Anglo-Saxon times, probably most of them being Norman. Usually the walling of the enclosure came into the flank of the mound, which was often in one corner, as in Longtown Castle (Figs. 63 and 88); but sometimes in later Edwardian castles, as at Skenfrith (Fig. 120), the mound (and keep) is in the centre and the walling encircles it.

In most castle sites it is very clear on close inspection that the bailey vallum (wall) was a later addition to the original mound, which often still stands as a distinct structure. This is very striking at Longtown, where the bailey vallum also aligns to the mound, but stops short of it.

In several cases, as at Hereford, Lewes, Lincoln, and Ripon, there are two original mounds. The development of a castle enclosure from a prehistoric mound nucleus follows exactly the same lines as the development of a camp and of a walled city, also from mounds.

Mr. A. Hadrian Allcroft in "Downland Pathways," referring to the town name Lewes being derived from the Saxon for grave-hill, says, "There is one at least beneath what is now the Brack Mount." He describes later how William de Warenne about 1087 built his second castle of Lewes on the same Brack Mount.

Mr. W. Johnson in "Byways in British Archæology" calls attention to "castle-mounds" at Penwortham, Arkholme, and Warrington which all have been raised or enlarged at different periods, and in two of them pre-Norman objects have been found. He also remarks that although a mound at Pirton (Herts.) has been classified as a "Norman motte," its common name is Toot Hill, and this brings out his comment, "There must always remain the doubt whether an earlier mound was not enlarged and entrenched by the builders of the castle-hill," for "toot" or look-out hill is an Anglo-Saxon word. In the same way the moated mound adjoining Almeley Church, which I have described in the Alignment of Mounds chapter, is Almeley Castle on the map, but Ameley Twt (toot) to the villagers. Mr. Johnson also mentions "the Castle Hill, at Hallaton in Leicestershire, an earthwork of the mound- and court-type, yielded traces of British, Roman, and Saxon settlements."

There can be no doubt that, in the words of Professor Freeman, "The Red Mount of Exeter had been the stronghold of Briton, Roman, and Englishman" before William the Norman built or rebuilt its castle henceforth known as Rougemont Castle.

It was the late Francis Bond who, in his architectural lectures, called attention to the Saxon windows which are still to be seen high up in the walling of the castle close to the gateway from the town. It is idle to urge that these (which I illustrate in Fig. 119 from my own tele-photo) are part of the original Saxon walls of the city, for they are not on the line of the city walls, but are part of the Saxon period castle defences, probably of the Athelstan period, when a "wall of square stones, further strengthened by towers," was made to encircle the city. To bring Rougemont under the official classification of "Norman motte and bailey" is wrong.

A puzzling fact is the frequency of places with no sign of ever having had defensive buildings, still bearing a "castle" name, such as The Castle, Red Castle, Ragged Castle, and Castle Farm. A mound or ring earthwork far earlier than the Norman period often bears the name.

It seems certain that the word "castle" originally indicated some kind of earthwork, and that the defensive building placed on such was a secondary use.

I think that in most towns possessing a castle its keep and mound will be found to align with one of the streets, which was on the old track. A small street at Dudley illustrates this; the mound of Totnes Castle aligns down Fore Street, the White Tower of London's fortress down Great Tower Street, and Shrewsbury Castle mound down Castle Street and through The Cross.

No more important castle was built in England by William the Norman than the White Tower of London, and there is clear evidence, both in legend and in topographical fact, that it was built on the site of a prehistoric mound.

The traditional Welsh poems produced about the tenth century, but attributed to the sixth-century bard Taliesin, refer to the White Mount as a Gorsedd or seat of justice. Rowland's "Mona" (second ed., p. 90) devotes two pages to this White Mount or *Bryn Gwyn*.

Then in the later traditional tales of the Mabinogion, that of "Branwen the Daughter of Llyr" (the second of the "Four Branches") relates how "Bendigeid Vran the son

HOLLOW ROADS

FIG. 56. DOWN TO A WYE FORD AT MUCH FAWLEY

FIG. 57. UP TO A SKY NOTCH, WORMSLEY

WATER SIGHT POINTS

FIG. 58. MOATED MOUND, EARDISLAND

FIG. 59. CAUSEWAY THROUGH POND, TEN HOUSES, HOLMER

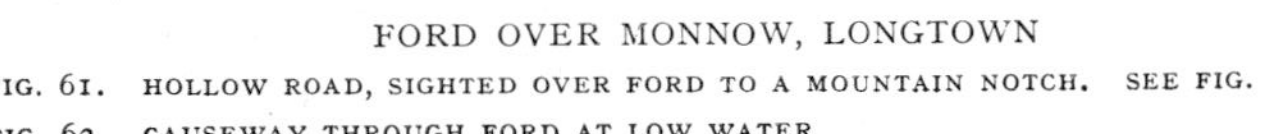

FORD OVER MONNOW, LONGTOWN

FIG. 61. HOLLOW ROAD, SIGHTED OVER FORD TO A MOUNTAIN NOTCH. SEE FIG. 70

FIG. 62. CAUSEWAY THROUGH FORD AT LOW WATER

FIG. 63. LONGTOWN CASTLE KEEP ON EARLY MOUND

FIG. 64. LONGTOWN CHURCH AND CASTLE ALIGNED TO BLACK HILL

FIG. 65. LONGTOWN CASTLE MOUND ALIGNING WITH EARTHWORK OF CAMP

SIGHT NOTCHES

FIG. 66. IN DESERT, GHAZA   FIG. 67. PANDY   FIG. 68. CWM-Y-YOY   FIG. 69. LLANTHONY

FIG. 70. BLACK DARREN, LONGTOWN   FIG. 71. COLDMAN'S HILL   FIG. 72. RHIW-CWRW, LONGTOWN

FIG. 73. THE DODMAN

FIG. 74. BWLCH-Y-EFFENGYL FROM SIX MILES DISTANT

FIG. 75. LLANTHONY-LEY SIGHTED THROUGH THE ABBEY TO A STEEP TRACK

FIG. 76. LLANTHONY. THE SAME LEY AND STAVES SIGHTED BACK TO NOTCH ON RIDGE

FIG. 77. LLANTHONY ABBEY. WITH MOUNTAIN TRACKS BEHIND

INITIAL POINTS

of Llyr was the crowned King of this island, and he was exalted from the crown of London." And how, after disastrous fighting in Wales, being "wounded in the foot with a poisoned dart," he addressed the seven companions (including Taliesin) who escaped with him and commanded them that they should cut off his head. "And take you my head," said he, "and bear it even unto the White Mount in London and bury it there, with the face towards France. And a long time will you be upon the road. In Harlech you will be feasting seven years, the birds of Rhiannon singing unto you the while." All things came to pass as he commanded and predicted, and in the fullness of time, "because of their perturbation they could not rest, but journeyed forth with the head towards London. And they buried the head in the White Mount, and when it was buried, this was the third goodly concealment; and it was the third ill-fated disclosure when it was disinterred, inasmuch as no invasion from across the sea came to this island while the head was in that concealment."

Imaginary as the events in such romances may be, the places named are real places, and there can be little doubt that an early "White Mount" in London was a reality, and the story indicates a burial mound.

The second piece of evidence is of a ley sighted from the knowl of Primrose Hill to the White Tower of the Tower of London. It lies precisely along Great Tower Street, passing through a spot within the precincts of the Tower called Cole Harbour in a map (1597) reproduced in Green's "Short History." It also passes through the ancient site of "The Stocks Market" on which The Mansion House now stands. Beyond the Tower it goes to the Thames at a spot—now much altered by dock construction—called Hermitage.

The fact of the eastern and southern sections of the Roman walls of the city aligning to the White Tower (Fig. 123) is also evidence that the mount was there long before Norman times.

It will be seen that the facts detailed in this chapter are in contradiction to the archæological view adopted about 1902, which may be summed up in the words of Mr. Gilbert Stone ("Wales," p. 227): "We may perhaps assume that the motte, equally with the castle, was of Norman or

Continental origin, and that before the Norman had introduced moated mounds and castles proper, England knew but the ancient earthern ramparts." From the first acceptance of the fact that Norman castle sites align with other mounds, moats, and mark-points in a ley, a revision of the present classification of a certain type of mound and earthwork as "Norman motte and bailey" becomes inevitable.

At the same time it is plain that what is called the bailey is a post-Roman addition to the prehistoric mound, and this is clearly shown in the photograph of the "Castle Cruger" of Giraldus's "Itinerary" (Fig. 124). But although G. T. Clark was correct in tracing the site origin of Norman castles to an earlier period, I am in no way endorsing his opinion that such first origin was a Saxon "burgh." It is also possible that some of the later castles were built on entirely new sites, although in the case of Raglan Castle, built long after Norman times, there is the clearest possible evidence that its site was settled by a prehistoric mound by the fact that I found its citadel (which is outside, and separate from the main castle buildings) aligning with other sighting points before I knew (from visiting it) that this citadel was a moated mound, and (from a paper by Sir Joseph Bradney, C.B.) that it bore the name of Cherry Tree Tump before the castle was built.

The evidence that Normans actually "heap up a mound as high as they are able, and dig round it as broad a ditch as they can excavate" ("Acta Sanctorum," quoted p. 227, Gilbert Stone's "Wales"), and the similar evidence in the Bayneux Tapestry, is no doubt quite correct. It confirms, but does not go as far as the description which I have quoted of castle building in Layamon's "Brut," which, however, makes it absolutely clear that this throwing up of earth was the improvement of an earlier mount, which settled the site.

Spade excavation is required to investigate this. At Lingen Castle mound, which has a Scotch fir on it, there is the appearance of an addition of newer earth on one side of the first mound. At Kilpeck, standing on the castle keep mound, and getting the axis of the adjacent church in alignment (see Fig. 118), it came to the mound, but on one side, not the centre. The same is the case with the orientation of Ewias Harold Church (see Fig. 117) to the mound of the early Norman castle. In each case the early mound seems to have been enlarged, but to one side.

It seems often to be assumed that the word "castle" is of Norman origin. The "New English Dictionary" states that it came into the language at two different periods, the first well before A.D. 1000.

Most of the local "Castle Farms" in my district (and there are many) await investigation. I began with the Castle Farm at Madley, which no one had noted as an ancient site, and found the farm-house built on an obvious mound with unmistakable signs of a moat round it, especially at the back. From the mound centre a narrow, straight, cobbled causeway crosses the moat site (where the farmer reports black mud deep down), and this is sighted on Aconbury Camp 7 miles distant. Both on the map and by sight the ley lies on the northern entrenchment of this camp, and defines part of its course. Eastward the ley goes through Tyberton Church, 2 miles away, and westward, beyond Aconbury, through Little Dewchurch and Aston Ingham Churches. Figs. 125 and 126 illustrate the farm, causeway, and its sighting.

The Castle Farm here (probably the Cublington Castle of Robinson's "Castles of Herefordshire," no site being there indicated) has all legends appropriate to an ancient site. The inevitable "underground passage" leads to Madley Church, a mile distant; a skeleton is said to have been dug up in the mound; a ghost haunts the house and disappears at a certain spot in the floor. Above all, only eighty or ninety years ago a somewhat poverty stricken tenant was suddenly enriched to a substantial extent (enabling him to stock his farm) by a workman finding in a hole in the cellar what is locally said to be a "pipkin of gold" or a "crock of French gold." It was kept secret, but the man was off to London—or some say Paris—a day or two later, and prosperity commenced on his return. It is a fairly well known tale, verified by my informant's grandmother, relating what she knew in after years, she being a servant maid in the farm kitchen at the time of finding.

The map, Fig. 15, shows that part of the above ley passing through Aconbury Camp and Little Dewchurch Church, while beyond, the ley passes through the house now called

Hill of Eaton, which I have identified as the Eaton Tregoz Castle of Robinson's "Castles of Herefordshire."

The evening light photograph (Fig. 124) of the mound and bailey on a magnificent vantage point high up (1,250 feet) on the Radnor Forest, close to the main road, indicates plainly the transition of a cast-up mound (a "beorh") with the after-addition of a bailey to form either a camp, a "burgh," or a castle. It is not easy to say which of the three this one was. It is marked Tomen on the map, is known locally as Tomen Castle, and has been identified as the Cruger Castle of Giraldus's "Itinerary," which Baldwin made a halting point in his recruiting crusade in 1188. Its pure conical outline shows plainly that no building—not even a stockade—was ever perched on the mound itself, whatever buildings might have been within the bailey. The two distinct curves of the ditch round the mound, and that round the vallum, indicate that the two were dug at different periods. Then whenever spade excavation has been applied to such a case, the mound has usually proved to be the earliest.

Examination and comparison of the plans and photographs of the camps as at Capler, Hundred House, and Dinedor, with those of castles, will show that both camps and castles had in most cases a common origin—a mound—and that there is little essential difference between the early stages of their development by adding an earthwork enclosure.

CHAPTER XIX

ASSEMBLIES AT MARK-POINTS

Then sent the King, by Ælvere, abbot, his writ to the Gemote at Cwicelmes-hlaew, and there greeted all the Witan that were there assembled.

—Saxon Charter quoted in GOMME'S " Folk Moots "

A HEALTHY primitive people do not advance far towards civilization before they develop communal gatherings for special purposes. These may be divided into five classes—Religion, Legislation, Administration, Commerce, Recreation.

A separate volume would be required—and has been written in several cases—to enter fully into each of these classes of assemblies, and the object of this chapter is merely to indicate that they were all, with very few exceptions in early days, located in Britain at those ley sighting points (mound, stone, hill-top, tree, moat, and ford) which have been described, and all in the open air.

It is obvious that only very faint evidence of assemblies having been held can be found in the purely topographical inquiry which is the main theme of this book ; and that such evidence as is not found in early records (which do not touch prehistoric times) must be sought in place-names and legend, in later revivals of such meetings, and in their survival in a few cases to the present day.

Religion, including pre-Christian forms, has been touched upon in the chapter on Churches, the assemblies being all at mounds, mark stones, or hill-top. Biblical references make the " high places " (with clear indication that the height was topographical, not spiritual), the meeting places for worship, and the stone for sacrifice.

Legislation and administration were combined in one meeting in early days, but separated later, and this branch has the advantage of very complete and concise treatment in Gomme's " Primitive Folk Moots."

In that book practically all the assemblies recorded are on such spots as are now known to be ley sighting points. Whether called Birlaw Court, Folk-moot, Gemot, Hundred-moot, Hustings Court, Shire-moot, Thing, or Witenagemot, they were held in the open air, which fact carried with it, as Sir Lawrence Gomme points out, the condition that anyone could attend. Mounds or barrows were perhaps the most usual points selected, fifty-three of the Hundreds in " Domesday Book " bearing names which show that they were so held.

The Court-Hills and Law-day Hills in Scotland were numerous. " A hill called Law at Lawton is said to have been the place where Macbeth dispensed laws." Here it may be noted that Gomme found that, in Scotland, " lady " in place-names was a corruption of " law-day," and also in Hampshire, where the court leet for the Manor of Pamber is held in " Lady Mead," at Chester, where there is a Lady Barrow, and on the road from Shrewsbury to Wenlock, where there is a Lady Oak. If this is thought to be fanciful, take note of the " Laugh Lady Oak " and spring in Brampton Bryan Park, Herefordshire, and then turn to the account (pp. 160–170) of the Law-tings of Shetland, presided over usually by the lawman or laughman. We have several " Lady " place-names in Herefordshire—Lady Lift (see Fig. 40), Lady Harbour, etc.—and law days are mentioned in Leominster town records. A natural conical hill near Hereford is called Thing-hill. There are survivals of out-door courts on mounds to this day. At Knightlow (Warwickshire) the Hundred Court is held at a cross on an artificial hillock at sunrising on November 11th, dues collected from the parishes and deposited in a hollow in the stone. The most famous survival is that in the Isle of Man, where every year all the laws passed by the House of Keys are proclaimed in solemn court from the summit of the Tynwald Hill, an artificial mound.

To turn to Saxon charters: there is given the record of the gemote held in the reign of Æthelred at the hlaew or " law " of Cwichelm (a West Saxon King), now called Cuckamsley in Berkshire.

The moot-hills or mote-hills often had " a trench or watercourse " round them, and the gallows hill not far away. As elsewhere noted, there is a close link between the barrow (hlaew) and its ring trench (halo), between the moot-hill and the moat. Gomme's book abounds in moot hills for legal assemblies, and describes one (p. 170) of the Law-ting (the althing or great law-gathering of the Shetlands), held in " an island in the middle of a fresh-water lake . . . the entrance by some stones laid in the water, and in the holm there are four great stones upon which sat the judge, clerk, and other officers. The inhabitants that had law suits attended at some distance, and when one was called, he entered by the stepping-stones, and being dismissed, he returned the same way." Here, then, the moot was held at a moat, as it also was in the Hundred of Avelands, Lincolnshire, where the sessions were held under a tree in a moat. In "The Times" of November, 14, 1923, it is recorded that " a moot was held at Gray's Inn on Monday before the Lord Chief Justice of England," and that an academic debate took place upon an imaginary case, involving a doubtful point—a moot question.

Examples of law assemblies at stones abound in the book just quoted.

Many Domesday Hundreds, such as Golderonestone, Stane, Kinwardstone, Dudstone, Tibaldstone, Whitstone, clearly indicate that courts were held at mark stones. The instance of the Grand Court of Shepway, held out of doors at a stone or a reputed cross site, all down the ages, and held again in 1923, is given in the Mark Stone chapter, as is that of a shire-mote held at a stone in Cnut's reign.

Similar strong evidence occurs as to courts and legal assemblies being held at trees which were ley mark-points. The Herefordshire Domesday Hundred Courts at Webtree and Bromesese, a cross-road spot now Broom's Ash.

In other counties, at such significantly named points as Doddintree (Worcs.), Becontree (Essex), and Horethorne (Somerset). Canon Bannister mentions that in Herefordshire " Cutethorne is a very perplexing Hundred, which seems to have run through the whole county from north to south."

There was also a court at Cutthorn, near Southampton. Courts at Shire and other oaks, at elm, ash, beech, and every kind of tree are abundantly recorded.

The gemot of Ecgfrid of Northumberland was summoned at Twyford, and the charter plainly states that it is at the ford on the river. Other courts at fords are mentioned by Gomme: at Brothercross, at Eynford, and at Depwade, or Deep-ford.

To turn now to assemblies for commerce. Mere trading along the tracks by chap-man and merchant, and also the transition of the mark stone to being a market, have been dealt with elsewhere. The larger assemblies for trade—and often for pleasure at the same time—were called fairs, partly products of the Middle Ages, and are only introduced here to show how they tended to be created at mark-points, chiefly barrows and hill sighting points. Even as late as the time of Henry VII the Abbess of Amesbury obtained the king's patent to establish a fair on Danebury Hill, as Shore relates in his "History of Hampshire," and the great fair at Winchester was held on St. Giles' Hill. One of the most celebrated fairs in the Kingdom—Weyhill—almost explains in its name that it clustered round a "hill" on the track or way. Another fair is held on Stone Green Hill, in Lincolnshire. and Miles in 1827 speaks of the fair on St. Anne's Day, celebrated at Tan Hill, Wiltshire, as being of the most early period. This is, of course, a "fire" or beacon hill.

Assemblies for recreation probably commenced quite early in prehistoric times, and the persistence of folk-memory as regards the type of spot at which they were held is illustrated by the fact that two or three years ago Caple Feast was revived to take place as of yore on the Wednesday in Whit week round Caple Tump (Fig. 1), which is a large medium height tumulus (described in another chapter) in an open space adjoining the churchyard—with the road between—of King's Caple. I went to see and record it this year (1924), but was a day too late, as the date had been altered to Tuesday. Round the mound, the grass all nicely cut, were signs of where the stalls had been, and the shy village child playing on the horse block at the churchyard entrance told me how they had been dancing on the top of the mound the night before. Indeed, there were the modern signs of such outdoor recreation—confetti—to prove it, some of it to be seen on the elm tree bole in my photograph (Fig. 2). And what a pretty circus-like ring it was, with its low parapet of earthen banking for sitting out, fine elms all round the rim, but none within!

Here, then, is a true survival of a folk-meeting at the mound for amusement.

Another Herefordshire instance, but of the past, is St. Weonard's, where the large flat-top tumulus was stated by Wright ("Arch. Camb.," 1855) as "until recently the scene of village fêtes, especially chosen for Morris dancing."

Mr. Allcroft tells how at a now demolished barrow at Hove, Brighton, on Good Friday, was held—on into the nineteenth century—a local fête, with games and dancing.

Mrs. Leather ("Folk Lore of Herefordshire") cites a "Nonagenarian" writing in 1879 whose memory went back eighty-seven years: "We used to go every May-day to Broomy Hill, and dance round the May-pole, and play at stool-ball and have cake and cider, and the milk-women used to dance with pails on their heads." There are other instances of a May-pole on high points, although in late years it was put up anywhere. At May Hill, a well-known landmark on the Hereford-Gloucester border, there was, according to Rudder, "on the first of May, a custom of assembling in bodies on the top of that hill from the several parishes, to fight for the possession of it." Such a procedure, in the view of young manhood, would probably come under the head of recreation.

At the Dane Hills on Easter Monday, and at Burrow Hill (both in Leicestershire) on Whit Monday, there were assemblies for sports and merrymaking, the latter "within the earthworks at the top," and a wake now kept at Nanpanton was "formerly kept at Beacon," obviously an ancient high point. At Messingham, Lincolnshire, the young people assembled on May-day even at Perestow Hills for all kinds of games, and on Good Friday they ascend St. Martha's Hill, Guildford, for similar amusements.

There are Dancing Hills in Middlesex and near Bridgewater; all over England there abound places, as Merrystone, Merryhill, Merrivale (or Merryvale), Merrylands, Merripit, and Merrymeet; and there is at Worcester a Merryman's Hill! There are also two stone circles called The Merry Maidens. Stone circles are rather kept outside the sphere of this book, except as being points on a ley—which they are. Their construction makes it obvious that they were built for assemblies; whether legal, administrative, religious, trade or amusement will not here be discussed, but the ancient Gorseddau was one type, revived in the modern Welsh Eisteddfod.

CHAPTER XX

ROMAN ERA

> The Roman has passed from Britain as though he had never been. He has left no name on hill or river; he has not even bequeathed a few drops of Roman blood. Racially, topographically, culturally, ancient Rome has nothing to do with modern Britain.
>
> —PROF. F. HAVERFIELD: "The Roman Occupation of Britain"

> The foundation of England is a Roman foundation, . . . the civilization . . . of Britain . . . is a Roman thing; nor is it possible to prove one institution or one inherited handling of material things to have descended to us from the outer barbarism.
>
> —HILAIRE BELLOC: "Stane Street"

IT is a sore temptation to leave this chapter (and, indeed, the next) unwritten. It will contain far more destructive than constructive matter, and will afford openings for much criticism. I feel much in the position of a man inheriting an ancient but ill-built mansion, falling to pieces by constructional weakness, of which he has to pull down the greater part and can only re-roof or fit up a few rooms for altered conditions.

If the main theme of this book is a truth and not a myth, then the fundamental idea with which many writers (as the second one whom I quoted at the head of this chapter) approach the subject is destroyed. They seem to assume, if not state, that the Romans landing in Britain found British road communication so feeble and incoherent that they made a new beginning in the matter, and planned on their own routes roads from station to station, with a characteristic which differentiated them from native tracks, in that they were for the most part straight in sections.

The new fact which upsets this is that they found Britain a network of cleverly planned straight tracks, although perhaps in a state of partial decay, and that the improvement which they could introduce was widening, perhaps diverting, in places, and laying down their own splendid surface engineering.

For years, in my own county, which possesses four or five small Romano-British towns or settlements, I have, when making efforts on the spot and by actual survey to link up gaps in the supposed " Roman roads," been much struck by their apparent unsuitability for direct communication between the known stations.

Take, for example, the supposed Watling Street between Church Stretton and Magna, passing through the Roman station (Bravonium) at Leintwardine. What a hodge-podge and muddle it is! How could competent engineers like the Roman road-makers have possibly designed it afresh as a communication between these places? In the last stretch at Credenhill it is a straight piece of road, and here at least, will be said, is a Roman road; yet it does not aim at Magna, the chief town of the district at all, but goes past it with the width of a field between it and the town gate. The name Watling Street is not only traditional in the district, but is found in old documents. But does not this piece look as if they had chiefly taken previously existing roads and tracks?

The assumption usually made that because a number of bits of road which can be linked up together are known by one ancient name, there is one definite main highway along that route is really very weak.

Look, for example, at the course of " Watling Street " in any map of the Roman roads of Britain. It is roughly east and west in part of its course in Kent, leaves London for St. Albans a little to the north of north-west, veers round, until approaching Uriconium in Shropshire, it is again circling east and west, bends towards the south for Bravonium, and then it has doubled back on its supposed track near St. Albans, and is going towards Magna a little to the east of south. The fact is that " Watling Street " is a generic name; whether it is taken with its guesswork meaning lined with wattled fencing, or Mr. J. G. Wood's interpretation of Gwaith-y-lleng, i.e. the work of the legion (we have a " Legion Cross " at a cross-road near Eardisland, Herefordshire); and because bits of road quite genuinely bear that name, it does not follow that they are part of a single organized route. In the same way Stane Street is a generic name; we have three or four of them in our county, as Stone or Stony Street, and the Stanways and Stone Ways in other counties are not part of Mr. Belloc's Stane Street. Ermine Street, running north out of London, bears the same generic name, but has no other connexion with the Ermine Street which runs through Gloucester (Glevum).

Imagine investigators a thousand years hence saying, "We find that in the nineteenth century there was a road called the King's Highway; we will trace out the course of this particular road." To be quite frank, a lot of recent investigation has started from just as weak a basis.

There is in late years a tendency of other observers to doubt the supposed poverty of communication in pre-Roman Britain. Dr. Williams-Freeman ("Field Archæology of Hampshire," p. 220), speaking of the Lepe Road (which, by the way, I make to be sighted over the Solent, through Gurnard and Northwood Churches in the I. of W.), says: "The pre-existence of a British track along the direction of a Roman road seems to be the rule rather than the exception." He is speaking of the pre-Roman tin traffic in Britain, concerning which there is every reason to assume one or more well-organized roads for a heavy traffic over a long distance.

In a letter to the "Weekly Westminster Gazette" (April 28, 1923) Mr. Denis Pater says: "If the roads in pre-Roman Britain are negligible, of what use were the horses and chariots which bulk so largely in 'Celtic' poetry and in Roman and other descriptions? The Briton had neither the steppes of the Cossacks nor the deserts of the Arabs over which he could gallop at large. . . . It is manifestly absurd to deny the capacity of making roads, to the people who carted enormous masses of stones to erect at Stonehenge and elsewhere from far-away sources, carried their tin from Cornwall to the Isle of Wight, prepared those dewponds which still serve upon a thousand hills, and raised up earthworks which must have required labourers by the thousand and garrisons as great."

Dom. Ethelbert Horne, of Downside Abbey, Bath, wrote me: "In opening up the Roman road on the Fosseway here, I found beneath it signs of other paving that may easily have been pre-Roman."

Writers on Roman roads in Britain have largely based

their assumptions on the "Itinerary of Antoninus." Valuable as this might be as long as it is assumed that all the roads available were those made by the conquerors, does it not lose that value if it is found that there was a choice of routes between Roman stations, and it is more the record of the way one traveller went than of all that existed?

There is one exceedingly valuable source of evidence not yet explored as to whether the Romans introduced straight sighted roads into Britain. The Romans never landed in Ireland at all, and if the ley system is found there, it was not introduced by them. As a commencement for such an inquiry let me quote Wakeman's "Handbook of Irish Antiquities": "Alignments of forts are an important feature in Ireland, and will be found especially on the sea-coast from Waterford westward, and round to the north of Mayo, and also in many inland districts."

Major Thomas Coulson, M.C., told me that when at Belfast he had noticed a curious fact concerning the Giant's Ring, which is a hill-top near the city capped by a circular earth walling, in which are gaps. Through these gaps, when standing on a stone heap within the circle, the tops of certain hills were exactly sighted. A Belfast correspondent afterwards confirmed this: "When I was up there in July, 1922, I noted that by sighting through the dips in the earthwork ring from the dolmen in the middle of the ring one could get, through one, the Priest's Hill, through another the Standing Stones Hill, and so on."

Now to the very limited constructional information I possess, for I have paid no special attention (in this alignment investigation) to "Roman" roads more than other tracks, and, as said before, have done no excavation. Spadework to ascertain the surface details is, I think, the main, almost the only, reliable source of real evidence concerning Roman roads, and recent work in this direction by Mr. G. H. Jack is not yet available.

In the Herefordshire Roman settlements only two—Bravonium (Leintwardine) and Magna (Kenchester)—have any indication of the outline of their boundaries. As regards the first, it is a rectilinear camp, and the chief sighted tracks appear to pass through its centre. But as regards Magna the case is different. The map (Fig. 83) and the details given in the Camps chapter show that its six sides (four of them straight lines) are dictated by sighted leys the evidence for which is to be found miles away. One of these leys (the one on the south side, pointing north-west) was found by me in Radnorshire by sighting over the tops of a pair of the "Four Stones" in the Radnor Vale, and is verified at Magna by lying on bits of the modern road leading to the camp from the New Weir. The "Four Stones" mark-point on this ley proves it to be pre-Roman. The other leys bordering the camp must also be pre-Roman, if the general basis of this book is sound. Here then is a Roman settlement of polygonal outline, which outline has been decided by straight tracks which were there before the Romans came and which, enclosing a space on elevated ground, provided an eligible site. It settles the question whether the Romans did or did not find organized roads when they came to Britain. Incidentally it explains the reason why so many Roman settlements have a polygonal outline, the subject of two long papers with many diagrams in recent volumes of the "Archæological Journal." This conclusion also agrees with the experience of the contact of leys with British camps of earlier date. It is also confirmed by the approaches to Magna being curiously inconsequent if it is assumed that the town was built on a freely selected site and newly planned roads made to it.

The planning of the Roman walls of the city of London was in straight lines, their outline, as decided by the late Professor Haverfield, being shown in Fig. 123. In Chapter XVIII I give the evidence (including the ley marked B, which runs from Primrose Hill, aligns on Great Tower Street, and through the White Tower), which indicates that William the Norman built his castle (the White Tower) on the site of a prehistoric mound, the White Mount. The plan of the Roman walls shows that two of their straight outlines (A on the south, and C on the east) align precisely to the south-east corner of the White Tower, where the White Mount, smaller than the subsequent building, is shown by the converging of the three alignments (A, B, and C) to have been.

These two sections of the wall (A and C) evidently had their positions decided by pre-Roman trackways sighted on the White Mount, and, judging by the evidence at Magna, the other straight pieces of the Roman wall were also decided by pre-Roman trackways, of which the present streets London Wall and Bevis Marks are fragments, and the church All Hallows-on-the-Wall a confirmation.

Another apparent example of a mound in the corner of a Roman town, having the walls aligned to it, will be found in the map of Caerwent, Mon. (Venta Silurum), in "Archæologia," Vol. LVII, where a mound is marked in the south-east corner of the walls.

The walls of the Breconshire Gaer—illustrated in the Appendix—are also decided by earlier alignments.

To return to Magna: it may be useful to speak of the road which has been found by excavation to run through its centre—a few degrees to the south of east. The ley comes from a hill point behind Clyro, through Bredwardine Castle and Brobury Church, lies on a mile and a half of the present Bishopstone-Kenchester road, through the centre of the Roman town, lies approximately on half a mile of the well-known "east and west Roman road," and then through a sighting mound in Holmer Lane.

Only a little over two miles of this alignment is reputed to be "Roman road," and yet it has most convincing sighting points extending far beyond that two miles.

The reputed Roman road which appears to "come straight" for Kenchester from the east of the county (joining on to the last-mentioned ley half a mile to the east of Magna) is, like almost all such roads, only straight in sections of a couple of miles or less. Such are exceedingly difficult to investigate, and I cannot say decisively whether the Roman surveyors sighted them in short sections by local mark-points, or whether they laid down their superior paving or surface on the top of pre-existing tracks. I have found evidence tending to both conclusions.

Another piece of supposed Watling Street—that between Aymestree and Mortimer's Cross—has an alignment which to the south comes through the great moated mound at Eardisland (Fig. 58) and down to the Wye at Bridge Sollars in a deep, straight cutting which has to be bridged by the main road and is often wrongly thought to be Offa's Dyke, that being a few hundred yards to the west.

Another example of a proved Roman road continuing for miles through pre-Roman mark-points is the Colva Hill to Birdlip Hill ley given in "Early British Trackways."

It lies on five miles of that well-known stretch of Ermine Street which runs alongside Gloucester city.

The inconsequent planning of Roman roads in Herefordshire leaves me in perplexity each time I investigate any bit of it. It is all "in penny numbers," and yet most stretches of it obviously aligned by sighting. Take the 2¼ mile stretch of the almost straight highway (part of Watling Street) between Stretford and Bush Bank. It is quite obviously aligned with the isolated peak of Pyon Hill (the Canon Pyon "Butt") to its south, that initial point being seen fixed in front when motoring down the road. Northward it can be traced in the fields in the same alignment, but not quite as marked on the Ordnance map. Crossing the road between Golden Cross and Bainstree Cross, it is as marked on the map and still aligns, along the edge of a wood, through Moss Hill Farm, over the Arrow by a ford, and along a short lane to the Crown Farm on the Eardisland to Kingston road.

This last part has been traced and verified as an actual Roman causeway by Alderman H. Gosling, who has opened up parts and walked through the ford. What I want to point out is that from the Crown Farm the actual Roman track starts off on a slightly different new alignment for three miles, the last part on Hereford Lane to Mortimer's Cross, while the previous alignment is a ley to the left passing through Wigmore Castle and sighted on the highest point of Brandon Camp. The road as used by the Romans is five miles on one alignment, three miles on the next, then on to a new straight bit at a new angle only two miles this time, and this is the Mortimer's Cross to Aymestree road whose alignment as a ley southward I have already given.

The Roman frontier walls in North Britain show signs (like most of the Roman roads) of being founded on a number of intersecting straight tracks of earlier date. It is not that the wall itself is in straight sections, but that certain lengths of the forts seem to align.

There are traces of this in Hadrian's wall, but it is more plainly indicated in the sketch map of the Antonine wall (north of Glasgow) given on a small scale in Sir Bertram Windle's "The Romans in Britain." The subject requires investigation with larger scale maps, but the following are apparent indications of fort alignment, and of forts with churches:

1. Barhill, Westerwood, Castlecary, and Roughcastle Forts.
2. Renfrew Church, Kirkintilloch, Auchinolavy, and Barhill Forts.
3. Balmuildy, Cadder, Kirkintilloch, and Mumrills Forts, with Clyde Bank and Cumbernauld Churches.

I only go on very incomplete investigation as to Roman roads, but it looks very much as if the Roman surveyors still used sighting methods, but methods based on local expediency, without the magnificent long-range vision of the Neolithic or Bronze Age people; that finding a network of sighted tracks and having to traverse them between their own stations (sites being settled by these old tracks), they laid down their new paved or gravelled surface on such old stretches as suited them, but in a difficult county like Herefordshire, desiring easier valley routes, they linked up such old stretches with new bits of their own sighting.

I must leave it at that.

CHAPTER XXI

PLACE-NAMES

Past Tott Hill Down all snaked with meuses,
Past Clench St. Michael and Naunton Crucis,
Over short sweet grass and worn flint arrows
And the three dumb hows of Tencombe Barrows.
By Tencombe Regis and Slaughter's Court
Through the great grass square of Roman Fort;
By Nun's Wood Yews, and the Hungary Hill,
And the Corpse Way Stones all standing still?
—JOHN MASEFIELD: "Reynard the Fox"

IN noting place-names on the straight track it gradually becomes evident that the local characteristics of the spot are often a minor influence; the track itself, its character, the men who made it, who came along it, or the goods they carried giving names to places all along the line.

It is amazing how this fact has been neglected so much by philologists, for it was well known, for example, that the ancient salt roads gave names to a great variety of spots past which the salt was carried.

There is another fundamental difference in the approach method of the ley-hunter to place-names, compared with that of the philologist. The first deals with evidence created at a period when words were spoken in Britain but not inscribed, and therefore works forwards towards written records. The second commences with the earliest written record centuries later, and his investigation is a deplorably incomplete one. Both types of students make blunders; they are on different types of inquiry, and an expert knowledge of both is rarely combined in one person, certainly not in me. The topographical student and the language student are both necessary to get at a prehistoric word meaning.

To give an example: In the early epic "Beowulf" occur the two similar words "beorh" and "burh," the first used only for a tumulus or barrow, which was a burying place;

the second for a fortified or protected dwelling or enclosure; and the two meanings are not confused. Philologists adopt these meanings, and extend "burh" to include the hill-top camps, and also later to enclosed settlements or towns which now are called -bury. And on this evidence they decide that -bury in a place-name is derived from "burh" and not from "beorh."

But as a ley student I find that the earthwork enclosures called "burh" (camps or castles) in most cases originated from the nucleus of an older tumulus or "beorh" to which they are akin in fact as well as name. Moreover, I find that farmers wishing to protect their roots call the earth-mound which they use for the purpose a "bury," but that the same heap of roots protected in a barn is not a "bury," the earth covering being the essential point in the word. Moreover, our modern verb "to bury" has the earth covering (and the mound still persists) as an essential, for cremated remains are not buried if enclosed and protected in an urn, and placed on a shelf in a chapel. Can there be a doubt that this instinctive use of "bury" shows that the word originated in the tumulus or barrow, and that the philologist has not gone far enough back in its history, but commences where it had already split up into two branches?

I avoid interpretation of place-names as much as possible in this book, and only do so where it aids in the explanation of the sighted track, but then give the evidence with some fullness.

The word ley, which (rightly or wrongly) I have adopted for the sighted track, must be so dealt with.

The name, whether spelt ley, lay, lee, lea, or leigh, is stated by philologists (and correctly, if investigation is confined to historic times) to mean pasture or enclosed field of some kind. But if the word existed in prehistoric times, it could not then have had such a meaning, because no enclosed fields or pastures then existed.

The prehistoric meaning is well suggested (if unintentionally) in the following extract from Dr. Williams-Freeman's "Field Archæology," describing the ancient track the Harroway: "We cross the Bourne or western Test at Chapman's Ford . . . and on getting to the top of the rise see Quarley Hill away in the distance. This was evidently the landmark on which the earliest travellers set their course. I know of no road which gives one a clearer idea of walking on a mark. At the top of each fold in the down the track heads straight for the hill, then as the traveller descends into the valley the road wanders a little to the right or to the left. . . . No map and ruler laid out the line for the Bronze man. . . . We can see the edge of the forest called Harewood Peak to the left . . . on the right . . . the outlying copses of Doles Wood. Between . . . the only gap in the forest for ten or fifteen miles. Through this gap—in Saxon times, the 'ley' or clearing of Finkley —passed the ancient road."

Mr. Hubert Reade, in a paper read before mine, refers ("Woolhope Club Transactions," 1921, p. 20) to the Herefordshire woods of oak, "with their thick undergrowth of thorn and briar, rarely broken by those open glades, those 'leys' or 'lawns,' which in the New Forest are so gay with gorse and heather."

The sequence seems clear—first, the straight sighted track, then a clearing of the woodland, through which it passed, then the fields which evolved in the clearing, the same name ley, lay, lee applying to each stage, a logical sequence.

Now to evidence indicating that "ley" did not always mean pasture or field. Ley Hills and Leys Hills are frequent, and hills are not likely to be named from pastures.

There is a Ley Rock in the sea off Tintagel, which can scarcely be so called from a pasture on its surface.

In the "Chesterfield" sheet of the one-inch Ordnance map is a Ley Fen on the top of the moors, well over 900 feet level, and another open moor near Bonsall called "Leys" at a 1,060 feet level. On the south Devon coast is a pool or mere close against the sea. A stream empties into it, and it is called Slapton Ley. It can scarcely be so called from a piece of cultivated land.

In "Scottish Lake Dwellings" by R. Munro, two lakes are mentioned having artificial islands in them, their present names being Loch of Leys and Loch Lee. They could not be so called from cultivated land. Mr. Munro gives many instances of causeways (chiefly under water) to such island dwellings, and in the chapter on Water Sighting Points in the present volume it is shown that islands in lakes and ponds are constantly found on the straight sighted track.

Leye is given in the "New English Dictionary" as an obsolete word meaning island.

In Marden parish, Herefordshire, is a Laystone Bridge, and north of it, about a mile away, a Layfield Green with a straight and direct footpath connecting them.

The Red Lay Cottage (mentioned in the chapter on Trade Routes) is on a well-proved track. It is also called Red Ley, and a few miles away is a Redley cottage farm, which is always pronounced as two words exactly as is the previous example. This brings us to the fact (amply proved in old documents) that the termination -ley and the separate word ley are identical in meaning. Each of the last-named places is on a track (or ley) to the ancient (red) pottery in the wood at Whitney.

An open-air man in a new district will take the first chance to get on high ground to "see" or "spy" "the lay of the land." It was particularly noted on the last occasion of hearing a farmer spontaneously use this phrase that it was "lay" and not "lie, as recent writers have tended to give it. Even to-day "the lay of the land" is not used to mean the "pasture of the land," but something akin to a survey, or the result of one.

In the "New English Dictionary" the present words lea, lee, lay, and ley (practically identical) have the same spellings in early records with many other forms as leah, leaz, lez, legh, leye, lai, etc., and is defined as "a tract of cultivated or uncultivated land." The present investigation probes earlier than this meaning, and is helped by the "New English Dictionary" notes that the word is etymologically connected with O. H. G. "lôh," and Latin "lucus," grove; also "leug," to shine, "in spite of the difference of sense." The scholastic Latin tag "Lucus a non lucendo" attempts to explain that a "grove" of trees is "light" because it has no light. Students of the sighted track will see that a grove is so called because it is on the light track, and that there is a constantly recurring connexion (as there is in the Old Testament) between track and light. For example, the "New English Dictionary" gives an obsolete word "leye" as meaning flame, blaze, fire.

The "straight" meaning of ley is indicated by the fact that to "lay" a gun in artillery is to aim it. Also that the batten of a loom is called a "lay," and the crossing of the threads is called the "lease"; it should be noted that warp threads stretched for weaving are straight as a sighted track, and that the weft thread is made straight (in one plane) by the beat of the batten or "lay."

Such names as Fishley, Saltley, and Whitley do not fit the orthodox -ley interpretation, for pastures are not likely to be named from such commodities, or because they are white. But both fish and salt (white) had to come along tracks, and Fishley Church aligns with three other churches and a castle in a direct route from Norwich to its near fish-port—Caister, next Yarmouth.

The fact that word elements in a large number of place-names are derived, not from characteristics of the place, but of the track on which it is situated, is illustrated in the chapter on the Ley Man, where the names (as cole, black, etc.) are generic, and therefore liable to occur on any track, and also in the chapter on Trade Roads, where the names are special, and indicate one particular type of track.

It is very evident that the "Red," "White," and "Black" places are not (in the majority of cases) so called from local colouring. The miller at Rhos Goch (Red Marsh), when asked the name of a hill point to be seen up a valley, replied, "They call it the Red Hill, and it often puzzles me why, for there's nothing red about it at any time." In the same way there are Whitewells and Whiteways and White Stones away from limestone or chalk districts, which have nothing white about them. But they are on a track with other places also called "white" from the salt carried past them.

Fig. 64 is a photograph of the mound of Longtown Castle aligning with the beautiful Black Hill (or Cat's Back) ridge which juts out from the Black Mountains, enclosing in its angle the Olchon valley. The tall, sharp point is the Black Hill (sometimes called "Great"), and low down where the ridge dies away is the Little Black Hill. Grouped round there are no less than seven Black Hill Farms. These are all on various sighted tracks, terminating in one or other of the above hills, and get their name for that reason, and because the "black" or "blake" man planned the track.

There is no difference in colour in the district, all being "Old Red" sandstone.

The " black " is a characteristic of the track—or rather of the man who planned it—not of the place.

The Great Black Hill farm is nearer to the " Little " hill than it is to its namesake, but it is on the track from the Great Black Hill to a well-known mountain point, Garway Hill.

Incidentally, a good ley runs from the Black Hill and lies on a present-day road for a bit, and passes through both Llanveyno and Longtown Churches ; also the very striking mound (Figs. 63 and 64) of Longtown Castle.

" Early British Trackways " detailed how four " broad " names aligned, the ley lying on stretches of present roads, and how this gives many place-names, as Broadmoor, Broad Oak, Bradley, Bradlow, Bradbury, Broadway, Broadstone, Bredwardine, Bredenbury, etc., all originally on a broad track wide enough for wheels, the oldest tracks being for " pad " and " pack " use only. It is often forgotten that chariots were in use in prehistoric Britain. But the narrow tracks still kept in use. " Little " or " luttel " in a place-name indicated that it was on the small (probably short) track as in Litley and Lutley, Luton, and Littlebury.

An interesting group of place-names is that which combines a name for an artificial mound with the name of the receptacle in which the earth and stones were carried to build it. In Herefordshire are Kivernoll, Kipperknoll, and Mount Skippitt, embodying three early names for baskets, and there are at least two other instances of the last name in the Home Counties ; it is also surviving in the term " skep " for a bee-hive. Hod Hill probably recalls that box carried on the shoulder with the aid of a rod which is still used by bricklayers' hodmen, and its connexion with the skilled mound builder has strange verification in the old nickname for a snail—*hoddy-man dodd*, or *hoddy doddy*, explained in another chapter.

We still use the same name for our earth-carrying implement—barrow—as we do for the ancient mound, and we call it a wheelbarrow because the earlier ones were carried by two men, sedan-chair fashion.

Again, the Sussex-made basket—the trug—is akin to crug, the Welsh or Celtic for mound.

Apparent proof that in at least one case King place-names indicate a road over which a king has travelled is shown in the New Forest map, which contains seven only such names. But five of them (King's Garn Gutter, King's Garden, North Kingston, Kingston, Kingston Lower Common) are on one diagonal straight line. When, many years ago, I photographed Mrs. Gamp's lodgings in Kingsgate Street, Holborn, then, as in Dickens's time, a barber's shop, I did not know that "gate" was "road." But by good chance Sir Lawrence Gomme did know, and the new great thoroughfare which obliterated this and other mean streets received the happy (and accurate) name of Kingsway.

This reminds us that in very old names "gate" was not a barrier on a road, but the road itself, and that there is an older form still—"yat"—which survives in the dialect word "glat" for a gap in the hedge.

Black Yat is among the Radnorshire hills, and Symond's Yat a well-known beauty spot on the lower Wye. Why Symonds should give his name to several places was a puzzle until a very evident ley passing over Symond's Yat (a high mark-point) and lying on the very direct road past Berry Hill and through Coleford, was traced down to the ancient seaman's port of Bristol. A Seaman's Corner place-name was noted in the New Forest, and Symond's Yat stood revealed as the seaman's road.

The general meaning of the termination -ton must remain uncertain and unproved in this present record. There is no sufficient coincidence of evidence. Yet a few indications exist to show that some at least of the -ton endings originated with a stone. Near Hereford such a meaning is now evolving. A boundary stone (on the highway) of the "Liberties of the City of Hereford" is known and marked on the map as the Franchise Stone. But the group of cottages near form a hamlet which is always called Franchiston, however it may be written. Places in Heugh, Northumberland, called in 1479 Bakstanes and Ravenstan-more, have become by 1622 Blaxtons and Ravenston Moore; this from "Notes and Queries," July 26, 1924.

A clue to the meaning of the termination -thorpe (found in so many places of Danish word influence) is in the "New English Dictionary" connecting it with the modern Friesian "terp," which is defined as "An artificial mound or hillock, the site of a prehistoric village, and still in many cases occupied by a village or church in parts of Friesland. Belongs to the Iron Age."

Hole is another ley place-name. There is a Black Hole Lane, Withington, Hereford, with no hole in its present sense, nor even a hollow road, and another Black Hole in Devon. In old Norwich City were four lanes—Blakestere's Hole, La Fulleres Hole, Craketayles Hole, and Smalberges Hole, which were also sometimes written as Lane instead of Hole. Hell Hole occurs in Herefordshire, Worcestershire, and Shropshire. A street in the border town of Hay, along which a leat runs from the Dulas Brook to drive Hay Mill, now called Brook Street, is still known to the older people as Heol Dwr (water lane). Heol is Celtic for road and hole no doubt a corruption of it.

Turning Way is a place-name in Titley, Herefordshire, and Turner sometimes forms part of a place-name (Turner's Boat, Turner's Tump, etc.). It is probably the point at which a transfer was made from one ley to another.

End is frequent as a place-name element. Coalway Lane End in Dean Forest, and Five Lanes End (at a cross-road) near Matlock probably give a clue to its meaning, not always perhaps the end of a road, but the end of some particular use. Thus Bacon's End near Birmingham was Beacon's End—as far as the use of the beacon applied. Writers on dewponds mention that up to this century there have been travelling gangs of expert pond makers. It looks as if Ponder's End, Middlesex, recorded the limit of the travel of such a gang. But its use in this way might be quite recent, for there is a Railway End place near Matlock.

Six or eight farms and places called "Hillend" grouped about the Malverns afford interesting evidence that they are at the useful end of a track sighted on a hill point. Few of these can be said to be on the end of a hill, or on relatively high ground.

In six cases I found leys passing through a Hillend, another hill place-name, and on to a peak.

In one instance I discovered the ley when motoring from Tewkesbury, the car heading exactly for the peak of Chase End Hill along a straight bit of the high-road, and the alignment (on the map) passing through Hill Court (which, like another Hill Court near Ross, is low down on a plain),

Pendock Moat and Hill End (Birtsmorton). Another instance is, edge of Towbury Camp, Hill End Court (Castle Morton), Hillworth House to Midsummer Hill. In a third case, Hillend Farm (Cowarne) aligns through a Hill Farm to the North Hill on Malvern Range. Then Hillend (Eastnor) ends a ley through Eastnor Church, Eastnor Hill (a point), and Hill Farm just beyond.

In all the above cases the "hill" element in the place-name refers to the distant hill on which the track is sighted.

Bel or bell is a frequent word element. There are Bell Hills in Dorset and Norfolk, the latter with a tumulus, and near it is Belton village. In Bellstone Lane, Shrewsbury, is the ancient Bellstone preserved in a bank, another Bell Stone near Powerscourt, Dublin, and a Belstone place in Dartmoor, which has also several Bell Tors. Blue Bell is a cross-road in Salop, and a place with an inn in Kent. Belfit Hill (Matlock) and Belfa Farm (Herefordshire) seem akin; there is a camp on Belsar's Hill (Camb.), a Belford in Northumberland, Bellimoor (Herefordshire), Belmore Farm (Salop), Belinstock a camp at Caerleon, and a Bella Port in Cheshire. The name attaches itself to barrows in Belas Knap in the Cotswolds, Beltout or toot or mound in a camp on a sea cliff in Sussex, and Belle Vue Barrow near Wimborne. But this is pure Norman! will be said at once. Rather, I think, an old British name Normanized, and I am not sure that this does not apply to the many Belmonts where they are not recent creations, for we have in Herefordshire at Preston Wynne a cottage farm and a coppice near it both called Belmount. There is a Bellman's Oak in Dean Forest and near it Oldstone Well, both, I think, sighting points on leys.

The Babylonian god Bel or Baal was undoubtedly introduced as a sun god in Britain, and the Beltan, Beltain, or Beltane Fires (or Fires of Bel, "tan" being Celtic for fire) which were lit all over Britain until the last century early in May, are fully detailed in Frazer's "Golden Bough." In the Sun Alignment and Beacon chapters I have shown the connexion of such fires on hill-tops with sighted tracks, and I feel certain that most of the "bel" place-names originate thus, not from our present bells, which are comparatively modern things.

The bael fires of Anglo-Saxon records at barrow sites are

phases of the same word and the same thing. It is interesting to note, on Frazer's authority, that "baal or ball is the only word in Gaelic for a globe," which thus connects it with these festivals of the sun. Before seeing this I had a strong impression from local place-names that "bel" and "ball" were connected. There is a Belgate (Shobdon) and a Ballsgate (Aymestrey) in adjacent parishes, "gate" meaning track. Ball's Cross, and an important hill in the Black Mountains to which many leys are sighted, is called Bal-mawr, or the "great ball," which it looks like from one end.

As regards these last two places, on the surmise that they were both on a sun ley, I tried one through them, and it was confirmed by passing exactly through the mound of Ewias Harold Castle, Wormlow Tump, and Much Birch Church.

Should it be thought unlikely that the name of a god of Babylon should find its way to Britain, let me mention that I have found one other of the Babylonian triad, namely, Ea, the goddess of water, recorded in the little brook Ea, which is close to Eau Withington (Hereford), commonly called Watery Withington, and pronounced Ee Withington.

One of the books of the Apocrypha called Bel and the Dragon refers to the god Baal.

Gold place-names are frequent. A well-proved ley sighted on the Cefn Hill passes through the Red Lay, Bredwardine Castle, Arthur's Stone, the Golden Well, Dorston (at the head of the Golden Valley to which it seems to give the name), and a mountain cot called the Gold Post.

There is another Golden Valley in the county near Bishop's Frome, one in Worcestershire just over the Holly Bush Pass, and one at Stroud. Goldhill farms occur in the county at Eastnor and Ashperton, a Golden Grove near Ewias Harold, a cottage on the highway near Clehonger called the Golden Post, and Golden Bank near Kington. Gold Cliff (Chepstow) and Gold Point (Dorset) are coast terminations; there is Golden Hill (Isle of Wight), Golden Farm (Bridgwater), a Goldstone (an ancient stone) in Hove Park, Brighton, and Goldstone Farm (Dorking). Golder's Green, Middlesex, seems to hint at a man's occupation, and is not the only such name, for in "Domesday" Golderonestona is given as the ancient name of a Dorset Hundred.

Goldsmith's Wood, Dixton, Monmouth, sounds modern, but might also denote the golder's track. There are four cross-roads in the county with the name Golden Cross attached to them.

I had surmised that these names marked the gold traders' track, for gold ornaments were prehistoric luxuries, and gold was found in England and Wales. But the fact that two "gold" names are found on a ley through Arthur's Stone, which is at the exact angle of sunrise on Midsummer Day, makes an alternate suggestion—that of the track line of the golden sun. But both surmises are pure guesses as yet.

CHAPTER XXII

FOLK-LORE

> Mr. Shillingford was soon discoursing—I shall interest you very much about the life of Neolithic man and woman—He continued steadily—and many slept; one even snored. . . . I hoped that he was going to be amusing, declared Miss Tapper, and tell us some funny stories, and make us all laugh, for of course many funny things must have happened in those days.
>
> —EDEN PHILPOTTS: "Widecombe Fair"

FOLK-LORE tales almost always contain some germ of prehistoric fact, mixed with much accumulated imaginings. What the germ of truth is, can best be found by comparing a number of similar tales from different districts, and the feature common to all is founded on historical fact.

Take, for example, that tale to be found in all counties, of an attempt to build a church on a selected site being frustrated every night by the stones being carried back by supernatural agency to another site, frequently on the top of a hill. The point which is common to all versions is that there is a dispute concerning two alternative sites, and both usually seem to be sites of previous antiquity, that is, mark-points on tracks. It is probably the struggle between early Christian leaders, who objected to "pagan" sites or stones, and the people who clung to them, and the defeated and winning sides would see the agency of the devil or fairies in the matter.

To give Herefordshire examples collected by Mrs. Leather. At Much Cowarne "the church was intended to be built on a hill north-east of its present position, but the materials which were collected there for that purpose were regularly conveyed by some invisible agent to the spot it now occupies." "Kingsland Church was first begun near Lawton, but the devil pulled down the work each night, and the site had to be abandoned." At Pencombe it was

" the spirits of those buried in the churchyard " who interfered to compel the use of the old site for a new church. At Garnstone the old mansion (not a church this time) was about to be built at the foot of the hill, but the fairies pulled down the work every night and carried the stones up the hill where it finally was built.

We have here only to do with such legends as bear upon ley matters. Such is the yarn about " old Taylor's ghost that used to walk about at the White Cross. He couldn't get rest, because he had moved a landmark " ; it brings in " two immense stones," and Mrs. Leather, who quotes it, says : " I have heard several similar stories, including one of a man who ' wasted away like,' until he died through remorse, and afterwards could not rest until the landmark was replaced in its original position."

The old tale of Wergin's Stone (Herefordshire) is that the devil moved it to a new place one night, and the Swedish legend of Jack-o'-Lantern is that he was " a mover of landmarks " and therefore doomed to be out at nights for ever and ever.

These last refer to disturbance of mark stones after they were in position. But there is a group of legends in all parts which explain how and why they were first placed, and all have these features in common, that the stones were carried by a giant or a wizard or the devil from a hill-top, or were thrown from the hill, thus getting fairly near to the fact of a ley-man fixing their position by sighting from the hill-top.

Here is the best of them, told by Mrs. Leather of Jack o' Kent, " a wizard in league with the devil " : " Why, one day he jumped off the Sugar Loaf mountain right on to the Skirrid " (see Fig. 51), " and there's his heel-mark to this day, an' when he got there he began playing quoits, he pecked (threw) three stones as far as Trelleck, great big ones as tall as three men, and there they still stand in a field " (see Fig. 38), " and he threw another, but that did not go quite far enough, and it lay on the Trelleck road just behind the five trees, till a little while ago, when it was moved so that the field might be ploughed, and it was always called the Pecked Stone."

Like unto this is the name of the stone called the Giant's Throw, and those various ones in different parts named

Hurlers. A Yorkshire friend, too, has just told me how Robin Hood once stood at Standing Stone near Sowerby, and across the valley of the Calder threw a great stone which fell at Wainstalls, four miles away, and this was known as Robin Hood's Pennystone, until they broke it up, time back, to make roads with. And as to this same Standing Stone, Watson, an eighteenth-century writer, relates how Robin Hood "is said to have used it to pitch with at a mark for amusement, and to have thrown it off an adjoining hill with a spade as he was digging."

Then there was the giant who lived in a cave near Adam's Rocks (up on Backbury Camp) who wanted to destroy the spire of Hereford Cathedral, so threw a big stone from the hill (it is five miles away), but it fell short and dropped in a field at Longworth. Likewise the other giant who also had his cave on the Malverns above Colwall, and his trouble was that he saw his wife with another fellow down at Colwall, and chucked a great big stone at her, which killed her. And the stone (or its successor), called Colwall Stone, is there now with heaps of other legends about it, going back centuries before the time of Francis Shuter, who late in the eighteenth century brought the present large stone down from a quarry.

The jumping from hill to hill and dropping a huge mark stone is told by Wood-Martin in his "Pagan Ireland"—of a witch this time—in respect of the Hag Stone; and another lady traditionally known as Moll Walabee, who is supposed to have rebuilt Hay Castle in one night, carrying the stones in her apron, and a big one (now a cross in Llowes churchyard) having got into her shoe, she threw it across the river in a temper. This early menhir-shaped cross is worked all over, but a local man told me of a tradition that it was brought from Bryn Rhydd Hill, where are hut-circles, and so it might have been an upright mark stone reworked in early Christian times. Such legends do not gather round objects without some shred of foundation.

The "Devil's Apronful" occurs in many parts of the Kingdom (and indeed of Europe) to explain artificial mounds of earth or cairns of stone (we now know them to be placed there as sighting mounds), and all the tales explaining "how it was done" are much on the plan of this one given by Mrs. Leather regarding the White Rocks

FIG. 79. HEREFORDSHIRE BEACON OR BRITISH CAMP. MIDSUMMER HILL IN LEFT DISTANCE

FIG. 80. COLES TUMP. WITH SKIRRID, SUGAR LOAF AND BLACK MOUNTAINS

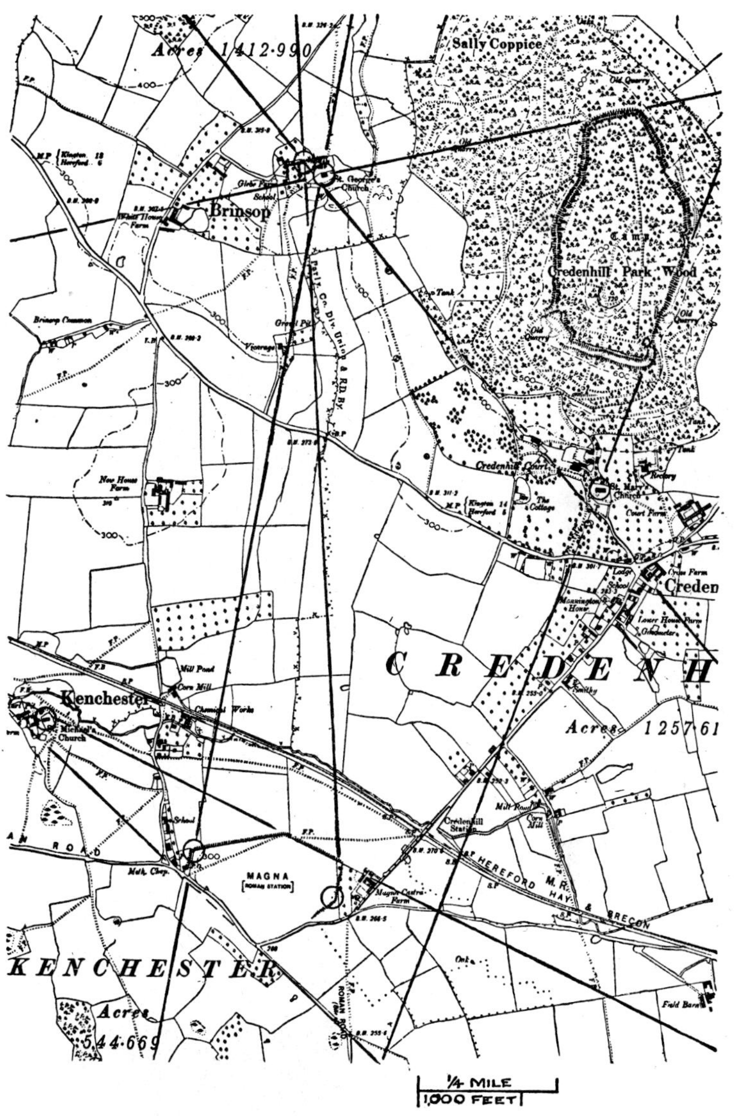

FIG. 83. CREDENHILL, MAGNA, AND BRINSOP CAMPS

FIG. 87. CAPLER CAMP. WITHIN THE VALLUM, EASTERN END

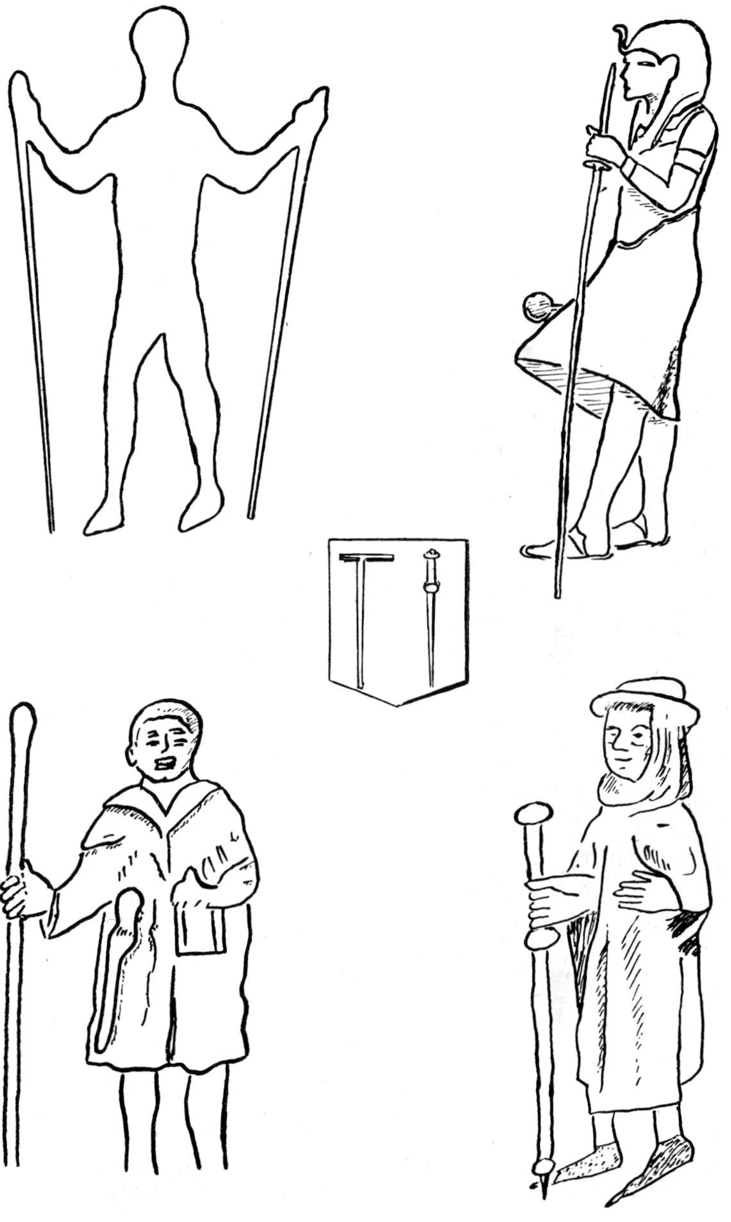

SIGHTING STAVES

FIG. 89. LONG MAN, WILMINGTON FIG. 90. STATUE, TUT-ANK-HAMEN'S TOMB

FIG. 91. PILGRIM'S STAVES

FIG. 92. A ROMAN OPTIO FIG. 93. A PILGRIM

FIG. 95. PEMBRIDGE. MARKET HOUSE AND MARK STONE

at Garway (there is another White Rocks spot on Vowchurch Common): "The devil was helping Jack to stop up the weir, at Orcop Hill, in order to flood the valley and make a fishpool. But as the devil was coming over Garway Hill his apron strings broke; and down fell all the stones he was carrying. Then the cock crew and he had to go home, so there are the stones to this day." In this case is a strange reference to the formation—by damming up a stream—of what are called "flashes" in some districts, which I feel sure were made as ley sighting pools. I have noted several not otherwise explainable.

And how Colwall Stone stands where it does is because—so a roadman told me in the kitchen of the "Yew Tree" at Colwall Green—the devil was carrying it in his apron, the string broke, and there it fell.

The "Devil's Jumps" are three conical hills near Hindhead, commanding (as do all high sighting points) "delightful views." There is "a row of Celtic mounds" of the same name near Privet, Hants. The legends attached to all such place-names are similar to this one, again from Mrs. Leather's "Folk Lore of Herefordshire": "Robin Hood bet Little John he could jump right over Wormesley Hill and clear the Raven's Causeway, monastery and all. Robin jumped and kicked a piece out of the hill with his heel: that's Butthouse Knapp. Then Little John tried. He took a longer run, and jumped better, but his foot caught the hill too, and kicked a piece out that is now Canon Pyon Butt. You can see the hole on the hill-side made by their heels now."

The number of "Robin Hood's" Butts (these are two of them) and hills and earthworks, including a pair of barrows on the Longmynds, absolutely disprove the idea that the original of this name was an outlaw of the Middle Ages. The name is assuredly far earlier.

The legend of the stone circle at Rollright centres round the couplet:

> **If Long Compton thou can'st see**
> **King of England thou shalt be.**

From the position of the King Stone (the upright pointer stone of the circle), Long Compton is just hidden by a long mound. A would-be claimant had just triumphantly declared

Stick, stock, stone
As King of England I shall be known.

But he had been brought by the witch within the seven prescribed strides of the stone site, and she declared, when he had taken these strides:

As Long Compton thou can'st not see
King of England thou shalt not be.
Rise up, stick, and stand still, stone,
For King of England thou shalt be none.
Thou and thy men hoar stones shall be,
And I myself an eldern-tree.

This is condensed from Dr. Evans's account to bring out the points that, firstly, the whole tale is about sighting; secondly, that three points—the King Stone, the mound, and Long Compton—align; and, thirdly, that the stick is not an essential part of the tale, but that the "rise up, stick, and stand still, stone," might be surmised to be folk-memory of sighting with an upright staff.

There is a strange map corroboration of this, for a ley through Long Compton Church and Rollright Circle goes on through the castle and church of Chipping Norton, a tumulus, and another church.

Legends of underground passages between ancient sites such as churches, castles, abbeys, and camps are amongst the curiosities of archæology. They are so frequent and persistent that it is unnecessary to give examples. It has never been my fortune to verify one, and other archæologists have had the same experience. But it is scarcely safe to say they do not exist. The distances which those tunnels are supposed to negotiate are often several miles, sometimes down steep hills with a stream below to dive under. A straight line between the points connected is usually assumed, as it was in one marked on a 1865 map of Hereford of a traditional passage which was supposed to connect the Priory of St. Guthlac with their vineyard on the steep bank of the Wye. Strangely enough, this "passage" had fallen in or been dug into on several occasions. I lived at the spot, and saw what appeared to be a small, unlined tunnel crossing the high road at the reputed place—a sewer being put in at the time.

Years later " it " fell in again on the reputed course, and a fellow-club member and I dug in to investigate. We found that it was some kind of natural " fault " or long crevice, not man-made. At Llanthony Abbey again the reputed underground passage was simply the abbey sewer.

This subject would not be introduced here but that I really think that I have hit upon the source of this universal tradition and that it is connected with the ley.

I was using a sighting compass on a tripod one day at Longtown Church, sighting by map aid to Llanthony Abbey (to which there is a ley), but which could not be seen, as the 1,800 feet ridge of the Black Mountains, on which I was trying to locate a cairn or notch, intervened. A working man passed and halted. " They do say, sir, that there's an underground passage from here to Llanthony." The solution to the old puzzle came to me like a flash. There was an imaginary hole through the mountain, and I was trying to look straight through it. The onlooker could not understand my work, and if I had told him (as probably my predecessor surveyor of prehistoric times, when he was mapping out the ley over the ridge by sighting rods, did to the ignorant inquirer of his day) that I was going to make a secret passage from the one place to the other, it would be a feasible explanation. No doubt the methods of the ley-men, like those of their successors the Druids, were kept secret. Hence the passage legend.

A queer bit helping to this view is on page 166 of Shore's " Hampshire ": " In the folk-lore of the district Cnut's barrow, lying about midway between the great camps of Danebury and Quarley, four miles distant from each other, marks the line of a subterranean way between these great fortresses." Here, then, is probably the sighted ley from one camp to the other over the barrow as a sighting point, on the top of the ground, while below is the legendary communication underground.

Two traditions link together the staff and mark tree of the old track. At Stow in Lincolnshire, St. Etheldreda, wearied with travel, struck her ashen staff into the ground, and with her maidens fell asleep in the noonday heat. When they awoke they found that the staff had taken life, and shot forth branches and leafy shade to protect the saintly queen. And on the spot was built a church.

Near Glastonbury a slight hill called Wirrall marks a spot where St. Joseph of Arimathea, sent with a band of missionaries to bring the gospel to Britain, tired with his voyage, sat down to rest, and planted his hawthorn staff into the ground. It struck root at once and became the sacred Glastonbury Thorn, which blossoms every Christmas Eve, the very cows in the pasture going down on their knees in adoration.

CHAPTER XXIII

HERMES AND HERMIT

There through the dews beside me
Behold a youth that trod,
With feathered cap on forehead
And poised a golden rod.

. . . .

Oh whence, I asked, and whither?
He smiled and would not say,
And looked at me and beckoned
And laughed and led the way.

. . . .

And 'midst the fluttering legion
Of all that ever died
I follow, and before us
Goes the delightful guide.

—A. E. HOUSEMAN : "The Merry Guide"

IT were unwise for one ill-equipped for the work to enter into surmises regarding the origin of Greek—or earlier—Mythology. But it is at least permissible to take the considered conclusions of experts regarding the attributes of these early gods and to compare them with the attributes of certain phases of human activity in Britain. The statements regarding Greek Mythology here condensed are from Professor H. Steuding's book on the subject in the "Temple Primers."

There are many links between these gods and the mark-points of early trackways. Of Eros it is stated that "his cult at Thespiai centered round a primitive symbol—an unhewn stone." M. Dulaire (quoted by Sir John Lubbock) considers "the origin of stone worship as arising from the respect paid to boundary stones." Steuding's description of the origin of the places of worship reads : "In the oldest times—so long as the gods themselves still dwelt in trees, springs, rude stones fallen (or reputed to have fallen) from heaven, and pointed columns . . . sacred groves furnished with a fence, served as the place of divine worship." The night haunt of Artemis, with her ghostly troup, was at the crossways.

The Greek god Hermes is my theme. Born in a cavern of Mount Kylene, on the summit of which he had from the oldest times a sanctuary, he became the patron of the skilled athlete. In the oldest places of worship, however, the good shepherd, bearing the hooked stick. He guides wayfarers on unknown paths. Stone-heaps with pillars in them, which serve as finger-posts, were hence sacred to him, so that the latter were often adorned with a head of Hermes; or on cross-roads even with three or four heads. As patron of market-traffic, he became the god of tradesfolk, and so brought his worship to Rome, where he was confused with the old Roman deity of Mercurius. Regarded thus he bears as the god of trade a purse as token. The herdman's stick passes over into the herald's staff (*caduceus*). After the transformation of Hermes into the god of luck this becomes the magical wishing-rod. As a wayfarer Hermes wears wings on his traveller's hat and his shoes to indicate swiftness. As an interlude he becomes the patron of thieves, and to him is ascribed the herdman's pipe, the lyre, and other inventions. He becomes the messenger of the gods, and the leader over unknown trackways of departed souls to the nether world.

It is a varied record of different activities for one personality, and Sir John Lubbock remarks that it is "difficult at first to see the connexion between these various offices; yet they all follow, I think, from the custom of marking boundaries by upright stones." Substitute the word "trackways" for "boundaries" and I think the true thread is disclosed which runs through the attributes of both Hermes and Mercury, and perhaps an earlier god, for Lockyer, speaking of "the Egyptian year-god Thoth," says, "In Greece he becomes Hermes, among the Romans Mercury."

Now to turn over centuries of record, and come to the Christian era and the Hermits in Britain. It is fortunate that Shore ("History of Hampshire") has gathered the records concerning hermits and hermitages for that county rather carefully, and summing it up he says: "The popular ideas concerning the hermits is very different from the true one. . . . In his cell the hermit lived his solitary life, but it was not a useless one, and he had some means of support." An example is given of William Gefferey, the hermit of the chapel of the Holy Trinity, opposite to the old ferry on the Itchen at Southampton, who was granted (with the mayor and burgesses) by Henry VII, part of the profits of an annual fair, probably as Mr. Shore remarks, as recompense for services—light or boat—rendered to travellers over the ferry. Mr. Shore enumerates eight hermitages in Hampshire, and in all eight cases the hermits were there at their stations to "help the traveller on his way." Two were lighthouse keepers. Three were stationed at fords or ferries, as at Havant, with "the duty of guiding travellers across the dangerous wadeway which led into Haybury Island." Three were in the ancient forests, that the hermit might, as at Stratfieldsaye, direct wayfarers through that part of the forest.

The early Cornish hermits, too—according to Rev. Thomas Taylor ("Celtic Christianity of Cornwall")—fulfilled similar duties. Richard, Hermit of Colemanshegg, is mentioned in a roll of 1258. Then in 1302 is a hermit at Chapel Carn Brea, a beacon-like site commanding views over channel and coast, with archæological evidence that the chapel stood over a "prehistoric chambered grave." The place-name in the first of these Cornish instances, and the tumulus in the second, give proof that both were on ley sighting points, laid out in the first instance by a cole-man ages before.

Piers Plowman, although down on the false hermits on pilgrimage:

"walking to Walsingham each had his wench with him,
Great long lubbers that were loth to work,
Clad in capes to be known for hermits,
To pass for hermits and have an easy life."

had still a better word for the true ones than he had for friars, pardoners, pilgrims, and palmers.

"Anchorites, hermits that held in their cells,
And coveted not to roam the countryside and beg,
Nor with dainty living their body to please."

In Worcestershire are names of three hermitages, and all are at "-stone" places on a trackway. Blackstone and

Redstone are at ferries over the Severn, and the hermit dwelt in a cave in the cliff; it was from the last place that Layamon came. The third Worcester hermitage was a cave in a curious isolated rock called Southstone near Stanford in the Teme valley.

Now there is every indication in all these facts that the hermits were not only stationed on trackways, but that they performed occasional duties to those who used the tracks.

In addition to the hermitage at Courtfield, unexpectedly discovered to be on a sighting mound, as mentioned in the Confirmation chapter, there is one other hermitage place in Herefordshire—Burghill—and on testing this I immediately found it to be on a ley which, sighted on Pyon Hill (one of the Robin Hood's Butts), comes down through Red Castle, the Hermitage, a piece of present road on the ley, and Burghill Church. A test of Southstone also indicated a ley to Woodbury Camp.

A slight bit of evidence connecting hermits with track guidance is that in the "New English Dictionary" is given Hermes, or St. Hermes, a name for the will-o'-the-wisp.

That hermits are successors to the work of the Greek god Hermes is not the claim, but that the attributes of both are folk-memory of earlier and prehistoric servants of wayfarers—those who made the tracks over stones and beacon points—I have no doubt.

Nearly a century ago a number of writers (of whom Bowles in "Hermes Britannicus," 1828, was the first, and Edwin Lees of Worcester, who contributed six pages to "Hone's Year Book" for 1848, perhaps the most accessible) rightly or wrongly connected the Egyptian god Thoth with the innumerable artificial Tot or Toot hills in Britain. The link seems to be that in the first place the gods Thoth, Hermes, and Mercury have a common attribute as being guides over pathways; that Cæsar, speaking of the gods under the Druids, says that Mercury, whom they regard as the guide of their journeys and marches and to have great influence over mercantile transactions, is their chief divinity. A Celtic god, Tout, or in its Romanized form Toutates, is supposed to be what Cæsar referred to, and this name has been found on a Romano-British altar. It is a fact that sighting mounds called Tot, Toot, Tout, Tute, and Twt abound all over the Kingdom, and the root is probably

Celtic, for on the Welsh borders natives call such a mound Twt and pronounce it toot. The fact that such mounds are mark-points on trackways strengthens the link, and I was interested to hear a competent lecturer on recent Egyptian discoveries pronounce the first element of the name Tut-ank-hamen as "Toot." The attendant figures at the tomb of this king carry a staff (Fig. 90), which I regard as evolved from the earlier sighting staff.

In the London districts are several places called from tot-hills, as Tottenham, Tooting, Tot-hill Fields (Westminster), and Totteridge.

CHAPTER XXIV

IN OTHER LANDS

> Both belong to that brotherhood of artificial mounds of unknown antiquity, found scattered, here and there, throughout Europe and the greater part of Asia, the most remarkable specimen of which is, perhaps, that which stands on the right side of the Way from Adrianople to Stamboul.
>
> —George Borrow: "Wild Wales"

THERE is evidence that the sighted straight track is in use in other parts of the world to-day.

In Sir Harry Johnston's "Uganda," he refers to "The broad native roads made as straight as possible, for their mark, like the roads of the Romans, seem to pick out preferentially the highest and steepest hills, which they ascend perpendicularly and without compromise."

In a travel article in "Blackwood's Magazine" (February, 1923) regarding a wild district in India, "Like all Chin tracks, regardless of gradients it followed the most direct line between villages. A Chin prefers a steep climb to a level road."

The "Toronto Star" of July 6, 1922, contains the following:

"In travelling over the plains of western Texas one now and then comes upon little isolated heaps of rock, in twos, that at first glance seem not at all remarkable.

"After a time, however, one notices that one heap is generally about three feet high and the other about a foot lower. The two are always within a few feet of each other, and usually on an elevation or a plateau commanding a view of the country for five miles or more. The rocks are roughly heaped together, as if left by children at play.

"You may see an Indian crouch down behind the taller heap, sight over the low one and mark the farthest object in a straight line, which is likely to be a clump of bushes on the horizon. Then he rides towards these bushes and finds

—not water, as he expected, but two other heaps of rocks.

" Sighting as before, and taking a rockfaced cliff, perhaps towards the south-west, as a goal, he rides a couple of miles farther, and there, trickling out from beneath the cliff's rocky brow, is a spring of fresh, clear water.

" It is said that whenever a band of Indians came upon a new spring they built the rock heaps along the trail. At any rate, it appears that these rude signposts lead either to water or places that show traces of a former watercourse."

The Rev. H. L. Somers-Cocks, who has worked among the North American Cree Indians, tells me that they often remarked, " We always know a white man's track because it's crooked, ours are always straight."

Mr. G. H. Harvey, of Leominster, who during the Great War served with the Herefords in Palestine, being in charge of a motor lorry, relates how—beyond Ghaza—he had to proceed to a spot forty miles away, and was given by his officer these instructions: " You see the clump of trees on that ridge (twenty miles distant), you will find a camel track goes straight for that, and when you get there you will see in front of you a similar clump another twenty miles, and that's the place you have to make for." And in his little collection of snapshots was the one in Fig. 66—native women bringing oranges to market. On attention being called to the notch that the road makes in the ridge he remarked: " We always made straight for that notch, and when we got there we made for a clump of trees on a hill about a dozen miles away." Mr. Harvey explained that it was only at the ridge (where a notch would be wanted) that the road was a sunken one, and that although the original track was straight, the motors often had to make a detour (as happens in this picture) to go round some obstacle or poor bit of road.

Major W. T. Blake, in a " Daily News " paragraph about a desert tour from Alexandria in a car, notes that he took as a guide " a shaggy Bedouin called Suleiman, who knew the way across the stony limitless waste by noting the little piles of rock set up along the caravan route," and also remarks on " here and there a cairn set up against the sky-line as a landmark for caravans."

There are many indications and references to what look

very much like evolutions from ley sighting points in other lands, the investigation of which seems worth while. It might or might not lead to results.

The stone cairns " exactly on the top of the ridge " which Mr. Alfred J. Swann in his " Fighting the Slave Hunter," mentions as " met with all over Africa," and to which his gun-bearer added a stone as a kind of tribute for a safe ascent.

The round towers of Ireland.

The pagodas of Burma and other lands, almost always on a ridge or peak, with a spiked head emphasizing them (as in the case of our English spires) as mark-points, and the curious fact that miniature ones are placed on the top of those logan stones, perched blocks, or rocking stones, which are points of superstition in most lands.

The pyramid temples of India.

The mounds which preceded pyramids in Egypt; those in other places in the East.

The mound of Cuicuilco in Mexico, described in the " National Geographical Magazine," August, 1923, as being proved (by a lava flow over it) to be 6000 B.C. in date, and evidently by its shape the forerunner of the later rounded stone pyramids of the sun and of the moon in the same land.

A text quoted by Messrs. Hubbard (" Neolithic Dew-ponds ") from the Pyramid of Pepi, B.C. 3223, seems clearly descriptive of an actual track based on a sunrise alignment: " Thy Mother Nut . . . giveth thee a path in the horizon to the place where Rā is." Competent students of the records of early Egypt might find further evidence in the same direction. Several forms of staves carried by ancient Egyptian figures seem to me to be evolutions from the sighting staff.

Major Conder in his " Syrian Stone Lore " (p. 126) refers to " the various local shrines connected with the worship of Jehovah, which originated apparently as tribal sanctuaries before the establishment of a sacred centre in Jerusalem—the *Bamoth* or ' high places ' where the kings of Israel and of Judah worshipped. These local centres exist throughout the length of Palestine, and are remarkable for one peculiarity, namely, the extensive view commanded from the sacred spot in almost every case." He details how this characteristic applies to such well-known Biblical spots as Dan, Carmel, Hermon, Bashan, Gerizim, Bethel, Nob, and Gibeon.

This slight chapter is one of mere suggestion.

CHAPTER XXV

BIBLE RECORD

. . . Confirmations, strong as proofs of Holy Writ.
—"Othello"

THE instances given in the last chapter of tracks sighted over mounds, tree clumps, and notches in use to-day in the East bring up what might be thought the most important evidence within the covers of this book.

The Old Testament contains, not in one but in dozens of places, not in one detail but in a number, references from which it is difficult to avoid assuming that the readers at the time it was written knew from then use, or from not long past use, all about the old straight track, linked up with high places, tree groves, and traditional stones.

A selection from these references (in the Authorized Version of the Bible, with two from the Apocrypha) is here given without further comment, except that where the reference is made by way of metaphor its pertinence to the present matter of historical fact is not weakened; for a metaphor is useless unless it refers to some fact or action familiar to the hearer. I see no alteration in accepted spiritual meanings.

BIBLE REFERENCES TO THE STRAIGHT TRACK

"I will go before thee, and make the crooked places straight."—Isaiah xlv, 2.

"Make straight paths for your feet."—Hebrews xii, 13.

"Let thine eyes look right on, and let thine eyelids look straight before thee. Ponder the path of thy feet, and let all thy ways be established, turn not to the right hand, nor to the left; remove thy feet from evil."—Proverbs iv, 25.

"Because the enemy hath said against you, Aha, even the ancient high places are ours in possession."—Ezekiel xxxvi, 2.

"Because my people hath forgotten me, they have burned incense to vanity, and they have caused them to stumble in their ways from the ancient paths, to walk in paths, in a way not cast up."—Jeremiah xviii, 15.

"Nevertheless the high places were not taken away; for the people offered and burnt incense yet in the high places." —1 Kings xxii, 43.

"Doth not wisdom cry? and understanding put forth her voice? She standeth in the top of high places, by the way in the places of the paths."—Proverbs viii, 1.

"For at the first she will walk with him by crooked ways, and bring fear and dread upon him, and torment him with her discipline until she may trust his soul, and try him by her laws. Then she will return the straight way unto him and comfort him, and shew him her secrets."—Ecclesiasticus iv, 17.

"Thus saith the Lord, Stand ye in the ways, and see, and ask for the old paths, where is the good way, and walk therein, and ye shall find rest for your souls."—Jeremiah vi, 16.

"Set thee up waymarks, make thee high heaps: set thine heart toward the highway, even the way which thou wentest."—Jeremiah xxxi, 21.

"Prepare ye the way of the people; cast up, cast up the highway; gather out the stones; lift up a standard for the people."—Isaiah lxii, 10.

"The Lord God is my strength, and he will make my feet like hinds' feet, and he will make me to walk upon mine high places."—Habakkuk iii, 19.

"And I will cause thee to ride upon the high places of the earth."—Isaiah lviii, 14.

"For he that hath mercy on them shall lead them, even by the springs of water shall he guide them. And I will make all my mountains a way, and my highways shall be exalted."—Isaiah xlix, 10.

"Prepare ye the way of the Lord, make his paths straight. Every valley shall be filled, and every mountain and hill shall be brought low; and the crooked shall be made straight, and the rough places shall be made smooth."—Luke iii, 4.

"Make thy way straight before my face."—Psalms v, 8.

"For the King of Babylon stood at the parting of the

ways, at the head of the two ways, to use divination."—Ezekiel xxi, 21.

" Their thoughts are thoughts of iniquity;
Wasting and destruction are in their paths,
The way of peace they know not;
And there is no judgement in their goings:
They have made them crooked paths."

. . . . .

" We wait for light, but behold obscurity;
For brightness, but we walk in darkness."—Isaiah lix, 7.

" And he maketh my way perfect,
He maketh my feet like hinds' feet
And setteth me upon my high places."—2 Samuel xxii, 33.

" The mountain of the Lord's house shall be established in the top of the mountains, and shall be exalted above the hills; and all nations shall flow unto it. And many people shall go and say, Come ye, and let us go up to the mountain of the Lord, to the house of the God of Jacob; And he will teach us of his ways and we will walk in his paths."—Isaiah ii, 2.

" And if thou wilt make me an altar of stone thou shalt not build it of hewn stone; for if thou lift up thy tool upon it, thou hast polluted it."—Exodus xx, 25.

" Lift up thine eyes unto the high places, and see where thou hast not been lien with."—Jeremiah iii, 2.

BIBLE REFERENCES TO THE GUIDING OR BEACON LIGHT

" Young men have seen light, and dwelt upon the earth, but the way of knowledge have they not known, nor understood the paths thereof, nor laid hold of it."—Baruch iii, 20.

" They are of those who rebel against the light, they know not the ways thereof, nor abide in the paths thereof."—Job xxiv, 13.

" And I will bring the blind by a way that they knew not; I will lead them in paths that they have not known; I will make darkness light before them, and crooked things straight."—Isaiah xlii, 16.

" Yet thou in thy manifold mercies forsook them not in the wilderness; the pillar of the cloud departed not from them by day, to lead them in the way; neither the pillar of fire by night to show them light, and the way wherein they should go."—Nehemiah ix, 19.

"Thy word is a lamp unto my feet, and a light unto my path."—Psalms cxix, 105.

"O send out thy light and thy truth: let them lead me; let them bring me to thy holy hill, and to thy tabernacles." —Psalms xliii, 3.

". . . till ye be left as a beacon upon the top of a mountain, and as an ensign on an hill."—Isaiah xxx, 17.

"The people that walked in darkness have seen a great light: they that dwell in the land of the shadow of death, upon them hath the light shined."—Isaiah ix, 2.

Bunyan's "Pilgrim's Progress" is based upon the Bible; its mechanical framework is a journey across country, and in referring to it I omit all moral or spiritual meanings, and only point out that Bunyan saw (as I do) in the Bible narrative a description of an actual straight track, the best for the special purpose for which it was designed, and that he took this as the path along which his pilgrims travelled in his allegory. I give merely the passages proving this.

At the start of the journey Evangelist sets Christian on his way. "Then, said Evangelist, pointing with his finger over a very wide field, Do you see yonder wicket-gate? The man said, No. Then said the other, Do you see yonder shining light? He said, I think I do. Then said Evangelist, Keep that light in your eye, and go up directly thereto; so shalt thou see the gate; at which when thou knockest it shall be told thee what thou shalt do." Before reaching the wicket-gate Christian meets distracting companions, and "being heedless" fell suddenly into a bog. He struggles to the other side and is assisted out by Help, who says "But why did you not look for the steps," and explains that in this Slough of Despond there are, "by the direction of the Lawgiver certain good and substantial steps, placed even through the very midst of the slough, but at such time as this . . . these steps are hardly seen; or if they be, men through the dizziness of their heads, step beside, and then they are bemired to purpose, notwithstanding the steps be there."

Before getting to the wicket-gate, Christian is again

beguiled by an evil counsellor who "said that he would show me a better way, and shorter, not so attended with difficulties," and turns out of the right way, to be brought back to it by Evangelist in order to gain the wicket-gate. He is there received by Good-Will who directs his further steps. "Look before thee; dost thou see this narrow way? That is the way thou must go; it was cast up by the patriarchs, the prophets, Christ, and his apostles; and it is as straight as a rule can make it." "But, said Christian, are there no turnings or windings, by which a stranger may lose his way? Yes, there are many ways butt down upon this, and they are crooked and wide. But thus thou may'st distinguish the right from the wrong, the right only being straight and narrow." He went on until he came to the foot of the Hill Difficulty, at the bottom of which was a spring. There were also in the same place two other ways besides that which came straight from the gate; one turned to the left hand, and the other to the right, but the narrow way lay right up the hill. This Christian, after refreshing himself at the spring, took. Many invitations and temptations to turn to either side are detailed, and a sighting mound is indicated when "he came to a little ascent, which was cast up on purpose that pilgrims might see before them"

Then the way led through a business and pleasure fair, "a thing of ancient standing," which pilgrims "must need go through," past temptations in by-paths, and to "a place where they saw a way which seemed to be as straight as the way which they should go; and here they knew not which of the two to take, for both seemed straight before them." Thus by the straight way to the Celestial City.

It is very plain that the "inspired tinker" got the "straight way" and the beacon light from the Bible direct. But the causeway through pond or slough, the steep track straight up the hill, the refreshing well on the path, the "ascent" or sighting mound artificially "cast up" and the pleasure fair, all spring from his own land, and are folk-memory of the old straight track in England. And a careful reading of the earliest part of the journey will show that from the start point, the pond, the causeway through it, the wicket-gate and the beacon light beyond, are all made by Bunyan to sight up in one straight line.

CHAPTER XXVI

CONFIRMATION

There is nothing in that which men say, to wit, that a thing happens by chance.
—KING ALFRED THE GREAT, quoted by BISHOP BROWNE

WORKING on the track and following up a ley often leads to disappointments, but vivid and strange bits of coincidence and verification are so frequent, and so convincing in their logical sequence, that it seems necessary to quote a few.

Visiting The Hermitage adjoining Courtfield, Herefordshire (the birth place of Cardinal Vaughan), in order to prepare for a visit by our local club, I not only found it to be on an unmistakable sighting mound, but precisely on a ley (detailed in my earlier book as through the Bewell Well), which, south of the Wye, runs as follows: Palace Ford, Dinedor Camp, Caradock Homestead, Pict's Cross, Hom Green Cross, Walford Church, Leys Hill, Hermitage at Courtfield, Speech House. It also (on another ley) aligned with Dixton Church, Monmouth Castle, Dingestow Church, and the early mound (the Citadel) of Raglan Castle. On this Woolhope Club outing, driving through the sighting cutting at Marstow (already shown in plate V of "E.B.T.") I asked members on coming back through the cutting to look out for a distant sighting point in alignment, as I had not worked out the matter. Simultaneously two members caught sight of a clump of trees on a hill point in alignment —Cole's Tump.

On the same day, passing Troy Station, Monmouth, I remarked that I remembered a map ley coming over the bank ridge, but had not visited the district to explore. Within half a minute after this, a tumulus was plainly in sight on the ridge pointed at—quite unknown to me until then, and not on the one-inch map.

A Hereford friend asked me if I had noticed a ley coming

down bordering Magna (Kenchester) and through Breinton Church; he only working on the local map. I found that this was the same ley which I had found by sighting over two of the Four Stones in Radnorshire, working on an adjoining map to my friend.

One of the most convincing experiences is to work out a ley on a map, but not extend it, then perhaps months later, having found a ley by evidence on an adjoining map and marking it out, to find on piecing them that the supposed two leys are one and the same. The following is an instance of this. The place-name "Lingen Bridge" applied to a Teme bridge between Bucknell and Brampton Bryan, with the village of Lingen four miles away beyond the last village, made me suspect a ley; especially as a straight bit of north and south road led to it. Sure enough there was one on the map, coming down from Hopton Titterhill and Castle Ditches Camp; then on through a tumulus in Bucknell, the mound of Lingen Castle and Byton Church, where the map ended. A week later, working on quite another type of evidence on the adjoining map, I was extending the straight line of the Row Ditch near Pembridge. Years ago I had personally surveyed it and found it coming down through Pitfield Farm, but there lost. I now saw that, extended south, it came through Tibhall, and finished up at the exact spot on the River Wye at Bridge Sollars where Offa's Dyke ends, and in fact lies on the Dyke for the last few hundred yards. It happens that the two maps overlapped, and looking up north I found the ley passed through Byton Church and Lingen Castle. It then dawned on my mind that the week before I had mapped out a ley from the north that came down through Lingen Castle and Byton Church. The two leys were the same ley!

On the Dorset one-inch map I found a ley over tumuli between the eastern edges of Chalbury Camp and Maiden Castle. Working afterwards on a six-inch map of the district north of Chalbury, I plotted out several leys from the short-distance evidence on that map. I then saw that one of them was identical with the long-distance evidence ley on the one-inch map.

Respecting the Walterstone Camp ley given in the Camp chapter, I had known it for many months, and when verifying it as a sunken road up from the Monnow Ford, I had several times looked from this point without success for some marking-point on the lofty mountain ridge it had to cross. When later up at Walterstone moat, and looking again for a marking-point, it was there in its exactly right position, a cairn or mound on the ridge, with none other anywhere right or left of it. The cairn was made to be seen from the height across the valley, but not from the bottom of the valley, the direction from this low point being given by a hollow road, probably appearing as a notch in those days.

Standing in a gap (hill notch) in the south-western corner of the vallum ditch of Sutton Walls (see Fig. 127), I noted that Marden and Wellington Church towers were

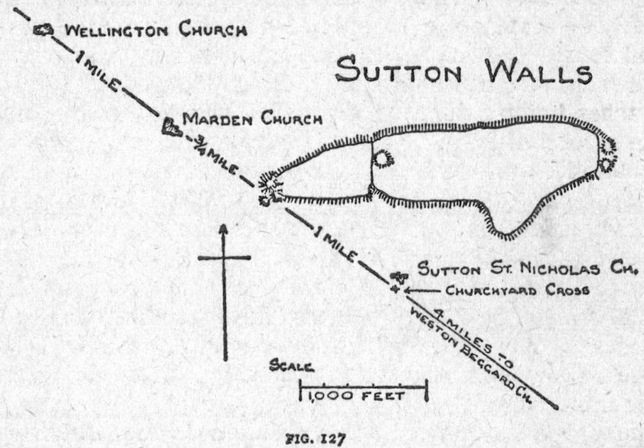

FIG. 127

in alignment to it, and continuing the ley on the spot to the south-east by sighting rods, they sighted to the highest wooded point in the Woolhope range—probably Seager Hill. I marked this on the six-inch map at the time, and found it went through Weston Beggard Church.

More than a year later the owner of Sutton Walls—Mr. Joseph Quarrel—came to me on the corn market (November 19, 1924) to say that he had just seen from the foot of the hill looking up a newly ploughed field, the ancient road as a dark mark going up towards the end mounds. I went the next morning, and Mr. Quarrel sent with me a lad who had seen it with him, and who pointed out how it went exactly to the above-named gap, and also that it came down to a certain oak tree on the road. By this time the harrow had obliterated three parts of the indication, but the dark mark, still to be seen at the top, confirmed the accuracy of the information, and the ploughman at work harrowing on the field had also noticed the dark line. The track thus seen by these three, not knowing anything of my work, was precisely on the ley which I had previously marked on the map from sighting over the two churches. It was a vivid confirmation, and another instance of a track coming to the edge of a camp. The mound terminating the camp and adjoining this gap or notch was evidently in this case more recent than the trackway, for it had encroached upon and altered the shape of the gap.

It would be tedious to give more of this type of evidence, and similar instances will be found in other chapters.

Confirmation in other districts by other persons is much to the point, and here again such evidence is condensed, with no attempt to give all procurable:

Mr. W. A. Dutt, author of "Highways and Byways of East Anglia," and an experienced investigator, writes: "I have spent much time in testing the ley system discovered by Mr. Watkins, by applying it to the earthworks and burgh sites of Norfolk and Suffolk, and I must say that the results arrived at have surprised me. For instance, taking the Tasburgh hill-fort as a high sighting point, at least fourteen leys connecting it with ancient earthworks at Attleborough, Ovington, Wormegay, Wymondham, Mileham, North Elmham, South Creake, Smallburgh, Ilketshall St. John, Bungay, Denton, Rumburgh, Eye, Kenninghall, Garboldisham, Lidgate, Bunwell, New Buckenham, Burwell and perhaps Ringland. . . . I have almost daily found evidence in support of the ley theory. . . . A study of the inch to the mile maps of Norfolk and Suffolk reveals innumerable place-names supporting the ley theory." In another letter Mr. Dutt says: "It would take a long time to tell of all the tests I have applied—and it would take much longer to relate the interesting discoveries resulting therefrom. I found after tracing some leys on the Suffolk maps that I had ruled my lines through several earthworks not marked, and of which I had no knowledge until I read of them in the Victoria History of the County *after* aligning the leys."

From Mr. Harold A. Barnes, Farnworth: "I am quite sure we have a host of leys. Within a few yards of my garden is one which from Worsley Old Hall runs through Great Lever Hall, Hall i' th' Wood, and a Druïdical Circle. Another has Wardley Hall (moated), Kenyon Peel Hall, Hulton Park, conical hill in Haigh Hall Park, Writington Hall, and a tumulus on the straight line. A third through Blackrod Church, Leyland Park, Hindley Church, a tumulus, Myddleton Hall, and Latchford Church."

Mr. C. L. Davies, writing in the "Westminster Gazette," says: "I am no antiquarian but sufficiently interested to see whether support for Mr. Watkins' contentions can be obtained from my local map. The results are rather remarkable. I find that a line from St. Albans to Pulpit Hill, on the Chilterns, touches the following points (from east to west): A ford over the Ver; a 'camp' in the centre of a wood; church and cross-roads at Leverstock Green; Hawridge (mound and other ancient remains); high ground at Leigh Gate; church at Dunsmore, and finally the Camp on Pulpit Hill. Near St. Albans my son and I discovered a grass-covered sunken pathway leading from the direction of St. Albans to the Camp in a wood on the above ley; it was quite clearly marked, but evidently had not been used for many a long day." Mr. Davies also describes four other leys in this district.

Mr. M. Paul Darr, of Leicester, writes: "I was frankly sceptical concerning the conclusions you arrive at, so I set about testing your remarkable theory to see if it could be substantiated here in Leicestershire. You will be pleased to hear that my own investigations entirely support your results, and the trackway lines I have obtained even so far are amazing."

Mr. and Mrs. Quennell in their "Everyday Life in the New Stone, Bronze and Early Iron Ages" find the ley confirmed in the Chilterns: "We found that from where the Ridgeway and Fair-mile descend the Berkshire Downs and come down to the Thames by the Ferry at South Stoke, if a straight line be drawn on the map, from the trigonometrical station of the Ordnance Survey on White Hill 293 above the Ferry, to the camp at Ravensburgh Castle in the parish of Hexton in N. Herts., about 40 miles away, it picks up many interesting points. There is another trigonometrical station on Harcourt Hill 610, then Whiteleaf Cross cut in the chalk near Monk's Risborough, and the mound on Pulpit Hill. From Beacon Hill above Aston Clinton you look down on the moat at Pilstone as a reflection point at a lower level; and to the N.E. can see Icknield Way coming over the shoulder of Beacon Hill at Ivinghoe. Then again the Five Knolls tumuli by Dunstable point the way to Ravensburgh Castle, and Icknield Way meanders along the escarpment of the Chilterns, sometimes on the line, and sometimes a little below it. It can hardly be coincidence."

Mr. A. B. Watkins, of Fritchley, Derby, writes: "I have found here sufficient confirmation of your work round Hereford. It can hardly be mere coincidence that your rules for 'ley' finding should apply equally well round here. My map work is backed by a good walking knowledge of the district, so I am well satisfied with several undoubted 'leys.' Matlock district—a line from Masson Hill through the Cuckoo Stone and the Wire Stone comes out under the Castle Hill at Chesterfield. Cromford, Tansley, Ashover, and Wingerworth Churches align, the last being a high point on the Derby-Chesterfield Roman Road, and also in a line with Clay Cross and Shirland Churches which lie south down the Derby road."

A Chelmsford correspondent (E. M. Slader), writes: "This is a country with very ancient earthworks, innumerable moats, mark stones, stocks, mounds, camps, etc., and working out results in my own county has proved a perfect mine of discovery and verification. Practically all the Essex churches lie in absolutely straight lines with outstanding sighting points at each end of the line; and almost every suggestive name such as Merk-stones, Mark's Ley, Stock, Cross Leys, etc., lies along these lines."

Mr. F. N. Gossling (of the Surveyor's Dept., G.P.O., Cardiff, whom I met at Llanthony, and who got ley-bitten there) has made and sent to me an exhaustive report on the theoretic alignments which he found on the Popular One-inch Ordnance Map Sheet 79 of Builth district, which is a mountainous one, especially rich in mark-points. He "ringed up" 146 cairns, tumuli, mounds, camps, castles, standing stones, all these marked on the map with antique type.

In these he found 33 instances of four-point alignment,

10 of five-point alignment, and one with eight points aligning, 44 alignments in all. Twenty-nine churches lie on these alignments, "the prevalence of three church lines being a curious feature." The alignments frequently go through modern Survey Triangulation points on hill-tops.

There are a number of instances of three or more alignments crossing at one point, suggesting a sighting mark there, although not now on the map, and in one such case the six-inch map did reveal at the point a *Groes Wen* (White Cross) not on the one-inch map. At least two Roman stations align with the other points. The alignments touch the edges of camp earthworks in some cases, in others going through their enclosures. There are several instances of close parallel lines, one alignment due north and south, another due east and west, three at the angle of sunrise (horizon) at summer solstice, and two for sunset (horizon) at the same season.

A full list of place-names and interpretations is a valuable feature of Mr. Gossling's report. Of the colour names 22 are white (*wen* or *gwyn*), 2 black (*du* or *ddu*), 14 red (*goch* or *coch*), and 2 yellow (*felen* or *melyn*), but this last in place-names often denotes a mill. Of the 24 church names, 12 have the prefix *Llan-*, which has much the same history and origin in Welsh as the English suffix -ley.

Mr. Gossling noticed that when alignments made on the one-inch map were tested on the six-inch map there was still precise accuracy in passing through the mark-points. At least two of his alignments I found to be identical when extended with alignments I had previously marked quite independently on an adjoining map.

Major F. C. Tyler has kindly supplied me with details of some 20 alignments to be found on the map of Dartmoor. On each of these are at least 3 stone crosses, or crosses, menhirs, or old stones. In one instance there are 5 (or possibly 6), and in two instances 4 of these ancient remains on the line.

At Blackaton Cross at least 4 lines intersect; 5 crosses lie at the intersections of 3 lines; 9 crosses and 2 menhirs at the intersections of pairs of lines.

On each of 4 lines lies a stone row, which follows the direction of the line.

These alignments of crosses, etc., in nearly every case are

supported by one or more other points, such as parish churches, tumuli, or camps, which bring them into the category of four-point alignments.

Several of these alignments, when extended on to adjoining map sheets, are corroborated by passing through similar points. For instance, one line passes through the old cross known as Mid Moor Post, on Middle Moor (St. Breward, Cornwall). Another passes through the ancient cross on Perran Sands (Perranzabuloe, Cornwall), which stands in the sand-dunes beside the ruined site of the old church, and then directly through the ancient oratory of St. Piran, which lay buried beneath the sand for so many centuries. Another alignment finishes at the promontory of Land's End. Major Tyler contributes full details of the above to "Devon and Cornwall Notes and Queries" for October, 1925.

CHAPTER XXVII

OBSCURITIES AND OBJECTIONS

Speak on, sir; I dare your worst objections.
—"Henry VIII"

THE framework of this book makes it imperfect. It expounds a geometric aspect of topography which in itself gives little information on historic sequence, unless there is brought in the aid of separate branches of research, such as archæology, folk-lore, documentary record, anthropology, and etymology. I have brought in such limited evidence in these branches as was within my resources. But there are many gaps, and chronology in particular, which I have dealt with in another chapter, is of necessity deplorably vague.

A perplexing obscurity, which is certain to be raised as an argument against the ley hypothesis, is the enormous number of burial mounds to be found in certain districts, as the Dorset Downs and on Salisbury Plain—the number, and their close proximity in many cases, appearing to be far in excess of what is necessary as sighting points on leys. Now the barrows on Salisbury Plain do align in a most remarkable manner, although I have not attempted to give these alignments in this book. The diagram of Stonehenge shows that (especially in the north-west line) certain barrows do align with sighting stones and with the centre of the temple of Stonehenge in a way which cannot possibly be accidental. But (for example in the three adjacent barrows in this north-west line) some are there which do not seem necessary to the mechanism of ley sighting. (Not having the local knowledge I can only surmise this.) We know that burial under mounds is persistent down the ages, and in fact is not yet extinct. Is it not probable as well as possible that the alignment of burial mounds continued beyond their necessity as sighting points in a ley? The proved cases of continuity of burial custom are very fully expounded in Mr. Walter Johnson's thoughtful book on "Folk Memory."

Our earliest epic, "Beowulf," in its account of the burial of its hero in "a barrow tall," "by wave-farers widely seen," while it had forgotten the reason for the site, adopts it as an honourable position. A sturdy old railway engineer I knew selected his grave on a hill, over the shaft of a tunnel he had made. Was it not the mountain-top in South Africa that Cecil Rhodes selected?

Robert Louis Stevenson, looking out from his study window at Vailima to the Vaca Mountain above, chose that height for the spot to rest his wasted body; and his Samoan friends cut through the forest the track from his home to his grave on the mountain-top.

The old primitive instinct came out again when two years ago the Earl of Carnarvon was carried up the Beacon Hill for his rest amid prehistoric earth-mounds. If this is so thousands of years after the early use of mounds, and if we still pile a mound over our dead, we can scarcely wonder if numbers continued to be added in alignment for burial only, hundreds of years after sighting methods ceased.

Thus the great number of mounds in such districts as Dorset, Wilts., and the Yorkshire Wolds seem to have obscured their real origin to those who investigate mounds in such areas. It is much as if, when investigating footprint evidence after a burglary, the police find that the whole village have been there since in nail-boots, and all chance of good evidence is gone. It has been my luck to investigate mounds in a district where they are few and far between, and where apparently none has been added to the original ones made for sighting purposes.

The question of the relation of the Druids to the sighted track is an obscurity. I have no doubt that their knowledge and the power derived from it came down from the early ley makers, but proof is wanting, and it being one of their rules that nothing was to be committed to writing, this knowledge died with them when the remnant of their body were driven by the victorious Roman invaders into Mona, the Isle of Anglesea. It was the policy of the Romans to exterminate them for political reasons, and deprived, as they appear to be, of their great power and position, it seems to have been early policy to treat them with contempt, which somehow clings to them even down to the time of twentieth-century archæologists. But still, as Sir Norman Lockyer points out, there has been in Wales a continuity in tradition and even in record of the best of the later phases of their work, that of the bards, and in the modern Eisteddfod the gorsedd or bardic circle is identical with the ancient stone circles. The Welsh Triads, quoted in other chapters, indicate this identity.

Sir Norman Lockyer concludes his book on Stonehenge with these words: "The Druids of Cæsar's time were undoubtedly the descendants of the astronomer-priests, some of whose daily work has now perhaps at last been revealed."

Siret, a Belgian archæologist says: "We are now obliged to go back to the theory of the archæologists of a hundred years ago, who attributed the megalithic monuments to the Druids."

The modern Druids' gorsedd or bardic circle is by tradition formed of unhewn stones. Lockyer thinks that "between the years 2300 B.C. and 1600 B.C. we pass from unhewn to worked stones."

An objection urged by many is that barrows cannot have been built as sighting mounds because it is abundantly proved that they are burial mounds. But the two purposes are not incompatible.

To make heaps of stones over dead bodies and to make them as mark-points for tracks were both the earliest of primitive practices, and it might easily come about that the two should become blended.

Migeod, in "Earliest Man," records that even the higher apes make a "kind of tumulus" of sticks over one of their dead, and two instances of man in the hunter stage making stone cairns as mark-points on tracks are given in Chapter XXIV. Why, therefore, in the very early leys, if the stones were collected in a heap as a sighting point, should it not be natural to rearrange them to cover a body? The earth covering would come later.

Sir Norman Lockyer has also given an answer to a similar objection, which although relating to stone circles and chambered mounds, is sound as far as it goes: "I protest against the logic of those who hold that because graves have been found in them (stone circles) they were constituted wholly for the purpose of burial, and that no other consideration was in the minds of those who set up the stones. It is the same thing as to say that because graves are found in our churches, the churches themselves were not built for the worship of God."

In any case, the whole theme of Sir Norman Lockyer's "Stonehenge" is a reply to the crude objection, "Barrows can't align except by accident because they were built as burial mounds."

It being a proved fact that barrows do align, it follows that the purpose of alignment of the ley in question must be at least as early as the burial use for those particular mounds. But the exact way in which a primary object of sighting and another of burial was combined in one mound remains an obscurity.

A stock objection to the fact of long sighted tracks in Britain is that of England at the Roman invasion being too thickly wooded for sighting methods as here outlined to be practicable. It certainly does strike all who have done field work on leys that trees are the chief obstacles to sighting if as thick as they are to-day. But there is this curious weakness in the objection: that long stretches of straight ancient roads (whether called Watling, Ermine, or Stane Streets or Foss Way) are left as facts, and, as Belloc and others have pointed out, sighting methods must have been used in their construction. So the objectors, who reject the idea of their being pre-Roman, are left assuming that the Romans made these sighted roads when the country was so wooded that sighting was impossible.

But on what evidence can it be proved that the densely wooded condition prevailed as far back as the days when sighted tracks were first made? The Scotch pine—a tree of northern climes—hangs on as a strange survival in south-midland counties, in single state, small groups or lines, but never as a wood. But its fossil remains in the south show that it once existed as a forest in places, that is, when a much colder climate prevailed. Man would be there at the time—perhaps he had commenced sighting? It is a question which our geological friends might perhaps throw light upon; the periods of glacial action in Britain were not so far removed from the presence of man but what he may have arrived at the stage of sighting trackways long before the "dense woodland" period came. It is an obscurity.

My own instinctive feeling is that the sighted tracks were as old (or much older) when the Romans came, as a genuine bit of Roman road is to us, and that it was then in partial decay, possibly on account of the increase of trees. Would not those who raised the earthworks of a Maiden Castle be also capable of a "drive" through a wood in places where such was needed?

Another objection is that moats are mostly Saxon or mediæval, and therefore cannot be prehistoric sighting points. The reply to this is that it is *sites* that a ley system divulges, and continues to divulge even if a mark stone has become a church or a cross, a mound has been enlarged and added to to provide a castle, or (in this case), a sighting pond with small island has been enlarged and altered to provide a residential moat.

The next objection is that early roads went the easy way —along the sides of the hills—did not cross the thickly wooded valleys, and certainly did not go straight up the steep sides of the hills, as man would always take the easy course. The reply to this (given in other chapters) is that man in an early stage of civilization is doing to-day exactly what these objectors say man would never do. Also that not only do such steep tracks straight up the side of a mountain exist in England to-day as evidence (see Fig. 77), but that in many cases they are still used—Figs. 49 and 50.

Many of those who write about early trackways do not seem to realize that the mentality of a man who had not got beyond the hunter stage, who had no villages, no cultivated crops, and no metal tools, would lead him to act in an entirely different way even from man of A.D. 1.

The preferences urged by objectors—for ridgeways, and tracks high up on the dry side of valleys—did prevail as civilization advanced, and the old straight track went gradually out of use.

I have mentioned the difficulties caused by the continuation of the habit of mound burial beyond the necessity of their use as mark-points. I have not worked in districts where this occurs. A paper by Mr. E. Kitson Clark (" Proc. Soc. Antiquaries," Vol. XXIII, 1911, p. 309) gives a number of maps of such districts, both in Yorkshire and in Jutland, the latter from the investigations of Dr. Muller of Copenhagen. Both investigators conclude that the barrows by their grouping and general position indicate the direction of prehistoric routes, but the routes sketched, evidently deduced not merely by the mounds, but by the author's own assumptions on other evidence, are not straight alignments. Nor is it easy to prove such with such a multiplicity of mounds. But in the illustrations and data I find very much evidence that straight leys did exist, and that the later routes sketched are—like the Roman roads in Britain—on a basis of a number of straight fragments of such leys. Map 1, for example, has this note: " Fabjerg—The remarkable direct alignment of 9 mounds extending over 1,900 metres in the portion above the centre of the map involves a relationship which can only be explained by connecting them with a route line."

Much obscurity is caused by the prior assumption made by almost every writer that there were a few main routes across a district and that their primary task is to discover them. The fact of a multiplicity of tracks upsets this basis, although it may be that there were a few chief ones for special traffic.

Cæsar records (" De Bello Gallico ") that in Britain in his time " the population is immense, homesteads closely resembling those of the Gaul, are met with at every turn." With such a population it is natural that tracks should be thick on the ground.

It might be rightly urged that the framework of this book appears to assume one race in Britain throughout early history, and that the successive influx of Iberians, Goidels, Brythons, and Belgæ are ignored. But if, as I think is the case, primitive man in the districts from which these tribes came all followed the one early instinctive method of sighting from hill-top, and marking the way with mound, stone, or notch, each of these invading tribes would have become familiar with the sighted track, whether in an earlier or a later stage of development than their predecessors practised. There may have been a halt, a leap forward, or a change in detail, but not, I think, a total

FIG. 101. SACRIFICIAL STONE. ALIGNING WITH GIANT'S CAVE ABOVE IT

FIG. 102. GIANT'S CAVE ON RIDGE OF MALVERN HILLS

FIG. 103. HOLME LACY CHURCH, ON AND ORIENTED TO ABOVE LEY, HERE CROSSING THE WYE AT MILL FARM

CHURCHES ON MARK POINTS

FIG. 106. CASCOB CHURCH, RADNORSHIRE, TOWER ON A TUMULUS

FIG. 107. WIGMORE CHURCH, ON BANK ABOVE VILLAGE

BRISTOL CHURCH LEY

FIG. 109. DOWN BROAD STREET, UNDER ST. JOHN'S CHURCH, ST. MICHAEL'S ON BANK BEYOND

FIG. 110. THE REVERSE WAY, THROUGH ST. JOHN'S GATE, UP BROAD STREET, TO CHRISTCHURCH

OFFA ST. LEY, HEREFORD

FIG. 111. FROM ST. PETER'S, SIGHTED ON CATHEDRAL

FIG. 112. FROM CATHEDRAL, SIGHTED ON ST. PETER'S

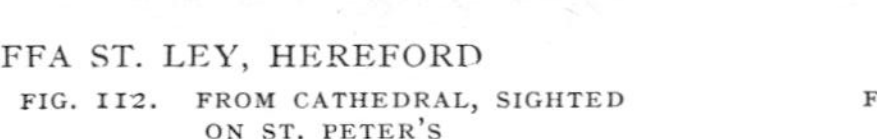

FIG. 113. ST. PETER'S, CATHEDRAL AND BEECHWOOD KNOWL, DIAGONAL. FROM AYLESTONE HILL

FIG. 114. AS ABOVE, BUT ALIGNED

CASTLES

FIG. 119. SAXON WINDOWS, EXETER CASTLE

FIG. 120. SKENFRITH

FIG. 121. WIGMORE

FIG. 122. EWYAS HAROLD

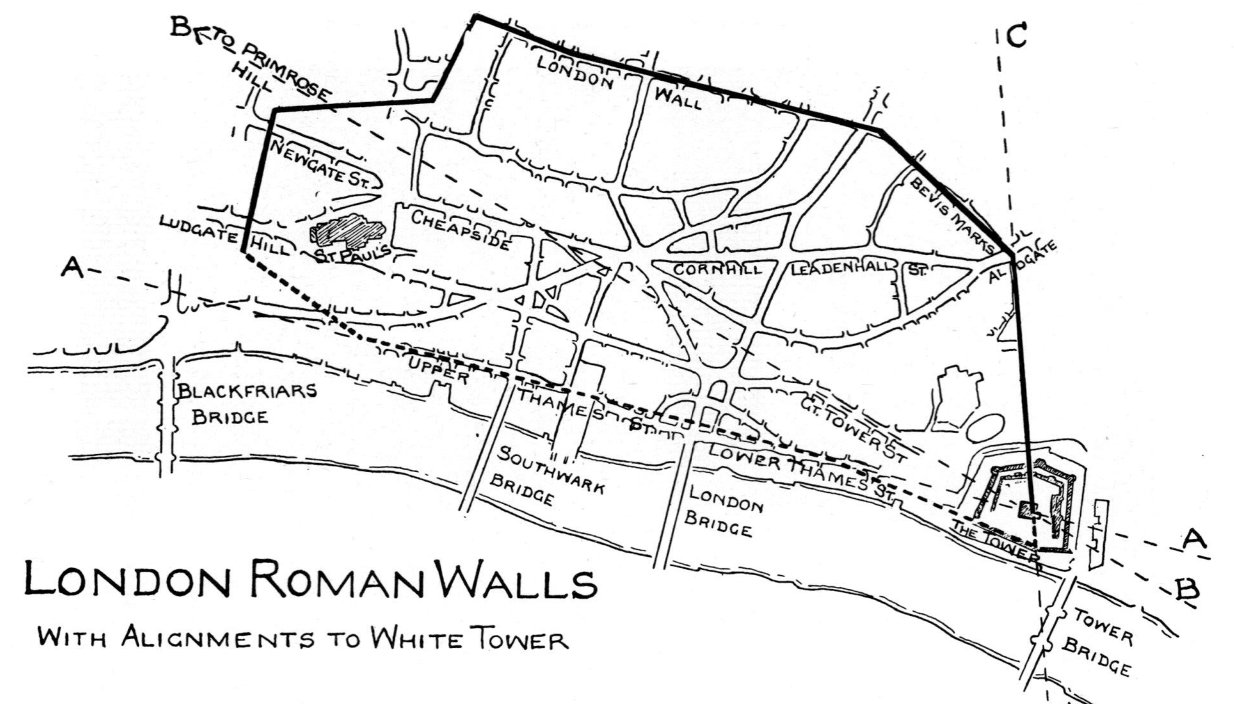

LONDON ROMAN WALLS

WITH ALIGNMENTS TO WHITE TOWER

FIG. 123

FIG. 124. CRUGER CASTLE, RADNOR FOREST. A MOUND AND BAILEY

CASTLE FARM, MADLEY

FIG. 125. CAUSEWAY TO HOUSE ON

FIG. 126. CAUSEWAY ALIGNING TO ACONBURY CAMP,

upset. It is an obscurity on which those well equipped in anthropological and archæological detail will throw light, but not a fundamental objection.

An obscurity inevitably results from the remote date of the ley, and the consequent disappearance of most of the mark-points. Even in the most clearly proved examples there are numerous gaps, in which it is now impracticable to sight from point to point. Perhaps high ground will intervene with no trace of a mark-point now on it, and if the land is cultivated such a result is almost inevitable.

Consequently, it must not be expected that a map ley will be confirmed on the ground at selected points, and intermittent confirmation is all that will be found.

For example, I give leys through Stonehenge, but have no local knowledge; and it has been objected that Sidbury Hill (which I mention as the next sighting point along the avenue and main axis) cannot be seen from Stonehenge. If so, this means that in the 7½ miles intervening there was at one time at least another sighting mark on high ground. It may be there now, but if not, it is quite in the nature of things, especially if the ground has been cultivated, that it has disappeared. As the ley is amply proved by other evidence, it is a good one all the same.

An objection which has a partial foundation in fact is that alignments cannot be assumed to be designed, but result from accidental coincidence. Without fully probing the laws of probability which govern this, I give one actual test indicating a method of investigation, and showing that four-point alignments are seldom accidental.

This is in the Andover map (sheet 283), which contains 51 churches, and there are on it no less than 8 separate instances of 4 churches falling on a straight line, in addition to the example of 5 churches in alignment already mentioned. To test the argument that this might be accidental I took a similar sized sheet of paper and marked 51 crosses in haphazard distribution over it. Only one instance could be found on this of 4 points aligning, and none of 5.

It is an interesting illustration of the law of probability that in the haphazard map there were in all 34 cases of 3 or more aligning, and in the real map where each point represented a site 38 cases of 3 or more aligning.

This indicates that with 50 sites in an area, three-point alignment is valueless as proof. But that four-point alignment is exceedingly strong evidence that such is design, not accident.

CHAPTER XXVIII

CHRONOLOGY

The dust on antique time would lie unswept.
—"Coriolanus"

THE first broad indication in chronology as taken from written records is that the sighted track is scarcely alluded to in writings concerning Britain, and it looks as if it had been forgotten before writing commenced.

One apparent reference I have seen is in "Beowulf," lines 1,408–1,416, which in the free translation of Captain Scott Moncrieff, reads:

The son of the athelings/then went over
Steep stone-cliffs,/strait passages,
Single tracks,/a road untrodden,
Beetling nesses,/nicor-houses many;
He went first,/with him a few
Prudent men,/the plain to espy
Until in a trice/the mountain trees
He found o'erhanging/a hoary stone
That joyless wood;/the water stood under,
Drumling, blood dreary.

Here the "few prudent men" taken as guides to espy the "single track" are "wisra" in the original, wise men who guide Beowulf to a hoar stone which marks the dragons' water lair.

This slight reference is merely folk-memory of long-past methods.

It is not easy to say when man began to plan systematic straight tracks. The use of the ley spread over a very long period—many thousands of years. I deduce this from their multiplicity, varied character, and duplication, seemingly of different dates. The fully developed track with its really extensive engineering of huge mounds, sighting notches, moats, causeways, and beacon points, must (judging by the same type of evidence) have been a final stage; it is impossible that it sprang into being all at once. The instance I quote of Indians in North America makes it quite probable that when marking-points were found desirable on high points and ridges they were simple cairns of loose stones, and that these preceded the more efficient earthen mounds.

This must be kept quite clear in the mind, because the most definite points on a ley are mounds; these are dateable by their burial contents, and it seems evident that the date of these is the date of their being placed in alignment for a ley. But what is not certain is that the ley, sighted by less efficient marks, might have been in existence before.

Lockyer comes to a similar conclusion when with regard to the outlying stones and mounds which he found to indicate sighting lines from Stenness Circle in the Orkneys ("Stonehenge," p. 132), "that under certain conditions and possibly in later times tumuli in some cases replaced stones as collimation marks."

Therefore when experts decide that most of the burial mounds of the round-topped variety are of the Bronze Age (not earlier), and if it is found that such mounds are the keynote of leys in a particular district, it yet does not prove that leys only date back to the Bronze Age, that is, not earlier than 2000 B.C.

There are a few broad facts which—very roughly—give some idea of ley chronology.

The ley system must have practically died out before a period of historic record (written language or symbols) commenced in Britain, for it is not recorded.

It had not completely died out when the Romans invaded Britain in the first century.

It was well known in Palestine, but also in a state of decay when many of the books of the Old Testament were written.

The above facts indicate its being in a state of decay for many centuries B.C.

Perhaps the mark stones are most significant for dating purposes. They are almost all unworked, and the Biblical tradition is for unworked stones. Now, worked stones came in with the Bronze Age, and even a little before, for stone axes and tools were used for working other stones. Stonehenge (the later portions of it) is built with worked stones, and this, if in the Bronze Age, is very early in that period, and it is doubtful whether it is not earlier, for no bronze tools have been found in the extensive excavations there. Lockyer estimates that "between the years 2300 B.C. and 1600 B.C. we pass from unhewn stones to worked stones."

The ley over unworked mark stones was in all probability far earlier than Stonehenge.

I think that the general trend of the evidence makes it likely that the ley system was brought to efficiency by Neolithic man, even if later additions and refinements were made in the Bronze Age.

As regards sun alignment, a surmised date for its introduction is provided by Lockyer's conclusion that "From about 3600 B.C. at latest Britain was inhabited by a race connected by blood with the Babylonians or Egyptians, and in close contact until at least 1300 B.C. with Egyptian culture and priestcraft." There are indications that ley planning preceded this. Stonehenge has hewn stones. The Giant's Cave described under Sun Alignment, was hewn out of the solid rock by tools, and the "sacrificial stone" below it had one worked surface. Was it a "pecked" stone?

Then the grooved stones described in the Mark Stone chapter, which, with marks of fire on them, I cannot help associating with sun ritual or sacrifice, must also have been worked by tools.

The evidence concerning beacons tends to show that they are consequent on sun alignment, being used at Stonehenge to stabilize a sunrise observation.

If, as I have suggested, the Greek god Hermes evolved from a tradition of the ley-man, it sets back the "old straight track" to very early times indeed. It belongs to a nomad life and civilization destroyed it.

As regards the date of camps, I think that the evidence which I have given shows that almost all of them—even the early ones—are later than the mounds which settled their site. This is on the evidence of experienced spade archæologists like Pitt-Rivers and Mortimer, and the leys to these mounds were therefore earlier than the camps. This points to the bulk of the leys having been made in peaceful times, and (to take another type of evidence) the long-distance leys could not well have been made over the hunting grounds of tribes at war with one another. As M. and C. H. B. Quennell point out ("Everyday Life, Old Stone Age," p. 46), "War is a civilized institution based as a rule on a desire to obtain some other nation's property," and early man in the hunting stage had nothing to gain by war.

How early it was that the beginnings of the ley system came must be a surmise, and is discussed in the next chapter; but if it came as soon as man began to import flint or flint implements, it could not well be (according to the Quennells' chronology in the little book just mentioned) less than 25000 B.C., that is, long before the Neolithic period commenced in Britain.

CHAPTER XXIX

ALPHA AND OMEGA

Look before thee, dost thou see this narrow way . . . it is as straight as a rule can make it. This is the way thou must go.

—BUNYAN'S "Pilgrim's Progress"

The rolling English drunkard made the rolling English road,
A reeling road, a rolling road that rambles round the shire.

—G. K. CHESTERTON

TO deal with the dawn of the sighted track is to make bricks without straw. I have elsewhere had to criticize those who tried to gauge by their own civilized mentality what uncivilized man would have done. Now I am doing the same thing, and must therefore point out that it is a surmise.

A highly organized and skilfully executed system like the ley system did not suddenly spring into being. There are indications that some of its component parts—the sight notches, the round barrows, and the stone causeways for example—came fairly late as improvements on more primitive mark-points. Lockyer ("Stonehenge," p. 41), speaking of indicating a sight line from a stone circle by a menhir (mark stone) says, "Later on tumuli replaced menhirs."

Pitt-Rivers (Vol. IV, p. 80) describes a stone found within Wor Barrow ("a long barrow of the Stone Age") as a "sarsen stone or sandstone, the only large one found in the barrow, and marking apparently the angle of the entrance to the enclosure." The photograph he gives shows it very clearly to be of mark stone type, with its sharp indicating edge upwards and in the right position to indicate a ley. It seems not unlikely to have been the simple mark stone on a ley which decided the site of the barrow; that is, assuming what I feel was the case, that sighted tracks came earlier than mound burial.

Just as mark stones might have preceded mounds, so probably would a simple cairn of stones, such as to this day the Ordnance surveyors use on high points, preceded the sighting—and burial—mounds on the heights.

The keynote of the ley system was utility—man's earliest need.

All the remains found of early man in Britain have been accompanied by flint implements. This was so with the Piltdown man, the first of the series, who belonged to a very early period of the Paleolithic or "Old Stone" Age. Now the suitable flints for this are only to be found in limited areas decided by geology. For example, when I picked up two humanly worked flints on an old straight track on Worsell (Hereford-Radnor border line) I knew that the flint nodules from which they were made could not have come from anywhere but the nearest chalk district, which is Wiltshire, quite 70 miles away. And how did this get to Radnorshire? I am reminded of a tale of a primitive race—the natives of South Africa—told to me by Mr. J. C. Mackay. He was short of labour out there, and spoke to one of the brightest of his own "boys" about it. "Yes, boss, I know where can get plenty boys! See great mountain" (a far-distant peak perhaps fifty miles away); "over beyond there plenty boys can get." He knew by that mysterious native telegraph communication which beat our own in the Boer War, and which our civilized mentality has not yet grasped. But that is another tale. Where this touches our present subject is that the native's way of getting to the land where the "boys" were to be found was to make a bee-line for the mountain peak which he pointed out.

This is the natural way by which earliest man—even as far back as the Early Stone Age—must have found his way to get his flints or special stones. Then when special spots for flints were noted, and later, regular factories established—as was the case at Grimes Graves and Cissbury, where all the implements are earlier than the Bronze Age—it is natural that a regular track should have been established on the bee-line between the mountains which were the initial points, and that this regular track should be marked, on the ridges by cairns of stones, and on lower ground by mark stones. All this probably while man was in the hunter stage, before food production began, and certainly before the existence of villages and towns.

For the end of the ley system, and that gradual decay which led to the end, there is more evidence, and most of this is dealt with in the Chronology chapter.

The Bible record is unmistakable in its references to the old straight track as having partly or wholly gone out of use; "the ancient high places" are in possession of the enemy; "my people have forgotten me, they stumble in their ways from the ancient paths." Here the call is to resume the abandoned straight tracks.

As civilization advanced, as people began to congregate in villages and towns, as they settled down to cultivate the land, and had to find short-distance tracks to dispose of the produce, as the pastoral life no longer provided the peculiar physique suited to a mountain-side climb that an outdoor hunter life provided, the suitability of the old straight track to the needs of the community becomes less and less.

The objection of modern critics, that man would not select a route straight up a steep mountain-side, which is quite unsound as applied to man of the Stone Age, began to be felt as the Christian era drew near. It may be that a gradual change of climate and consequent increase of trees was a factor in the decay of the ley system.

The need for walking with a sight mark always straight ahead was passing away; the old tracks were not suddenly abandoned, but divergencies made, here to go aside to a homestead, there to avoid a wet bottom, again to get round a rocky climb. New tracks were made from homestead to village, and they had to wind round the edges of the enclosures which had come into being. These same enclosures would certainly be bounded by the old straight tracks, and the old mark stones thus became boundary stones. In this way evolved the "reeling road," or sometimes the broken or serpentine road based on the old straight track, but constantly getting away from it, and again back to it.

I know of a mountain valley (the Grwyne in the Black Mountains) where a road from one farm to another was all the road system when I first went there—no public road up the valley; and this arrangement of mere homestead need seems to have come as a revulsion to the straight track. Our present highways and district roads are a patchwork using up these bits of local expediency in efforts to get from one town to another, with fortunately a few fragments of the old ley system incorporated. It is this patchwork which so many writers have wasted time over in efforts to trace primitive origins.

We have seen how, with the decay of the old straight track, its mounds and mark stones became in many cases sites of castles and churches. No student of the ley, seeing how on the map ancient homesteads with ancient names seem drawn to the line like iron filings to a line of magnetic influence, can doubt that these also were planted on mark-points of the disused track. Sometimes it was at a stone, sometimes at a sighting pond, as at Ingestone, where a cobbled causeway, successor to the old straight track, goes straight for the pond, the ley continuing through the house. Indeed, at Massington, Eastnor, a public track, until recently at least, did actually go as a passage through the house.

A striking instance of four adjacent homesteads, where houses are not thick together, aligning on the track, is three miles out of Hereford on the ancient road to Ross, where the Raven, the Upper Raven, the Blue Bowl, and the Upper Bowl houses exactly align in half a mile, and the ley continues on convincing paths, and through Aconbury Church. Three of these are on knuckles of land, high points on the ley, the fourth on a pond ; two are farms, the others cottage holdings.

Homesteads are so many in our land, and it is so evident that any chance line drawn on a map must of necessity pass through some of them, that I have not taken them as proof.

Somewhere in the notes of a London correspondent I have read how Sir William Harcourt in late Victorian days had long admired a favoured spot in the New Forest. A forester's cottage was perched on an ancient earthwork commanding delightful vistas through the woodland in all directions. It was called Castle Malwood, and he at last bought it and built on it a modest residence ; round it on the slopes and ditches of old entrenchment he developed the lawns and garden of the cultivated Englishman, preserving with loving care the charming woodland peeps.

Over this point of vantage the seer of prehistoric days, when houses were not, had sighted his track and cast his hillock as a mark-point. Its old need had passed; modern man coveted the site, and put it to new use.

CHAPTER XXX

AN OUTLINE

Trackway and Camp and City lost,
Salt Marsh where now is corn ;
Old Wars, old Peace, old Arts that cease,
And so was England born.
—KIPLING : " Puck of Pooks Hill "

A LONG series of facts have been examined and certain logical deductions made. Such deductions all relate to the old straight track, which links up many stages in the history of early man in Britain. To bring these deductions into the sequence of evolution which must have taken place involves surmises, with probable errors in chronology. But I attempt it.

Picture, then, very early man of the Old Stone Age, his brainpan almost as large as our own, a hunter and a nomad. A tool-using animal at our first records of him, his tools (flints) were often only to be had from a far-distant spot. The mountain peaks, perhaps 50 or 60 miles apart, were the directing points for such spots, and a bee-line between them formed the track. Such supply spots being always the same, it was worth while to leave heaps of stones on hill ridges to mark the way for next time; or large stones served the same purpose on lower ground.

The need for larger heaps and larger stones, unworked, but of a size to be seen from a distance, soon became apparent, and to place these in position required not one or two men, but a gang. Skilled leaders or foremen evolved, not merely to direct the labour but to fix exact sites for the marking-points. Implements—the sighting staves—were used, and the surveyor was the first professional man, with that primitive instinct for power which keeps skilled methods secret.

Where a new ley crossed an old one, a mound, or more often a stone, would be set there, or a previous mark stone moved along the older track to the new crossing point.

The straight track became an organized possession of the community for all to use, but mystery and reverence for a superior knowledge grew round its making and its mark-points. In the history of these mark-points human needs, human superstitions and beliefs gathered round them. The straight track was wanted to go long distances to the salt supply spots. Utility was the primary object. Later on, magic, religion, and superstition blended with the system. 3600 B.C. is the approximate date at which Lockyer thinks Semitic methods of sun alignment came to Britain. It may be that a crude form of it was here previously. The astronomer-priests became a power in the community, and their utility—to give seasonal information to tillers of the soil, for the hunting phase was giving way to the pastoral stage of man's history—made them a necessity. Whether the sun alignments were originally distinct from utility (trackway) alignments I cannot say, but they certainly became linked together in Britain. The beacon light—used in the first place to be a fixed point substitute after taking the line of sunrise on a particular day—became a means of laying out the trackways. Mark-points on the trackways—stones and cairns—became fire points for utility and religion, or both.

The astronomer-priests had the Druids as successors, and all the learning, religion, poetry, and science of the community centred round them.

Metals became known and used, and the need for tracks to transport them and to carry on the trade which resulted from the new knowledge, increased.

Mark stones were no longer untouched by tools, and from them and round them there developed temples at the cross-roads.

Thus far tracks were not wanted to connect towns, for none existed. Tracks were almost all long-distance ones, but the hut-circle villages were planted alongside, and as a pastoral life (which had succeeded a hunter life) demanded the occasional gathering in of flocks and herds for security, enclosed camps evolved on spaces and sites defined by the tracks and their sighting points.

It is certain that from the first the superstition and awe connected with the mark-points, whether stone, cairn, or hill point, led to a craving to be buried at them, and it may be that this was only conceded to people of position. Cairns became burial mounds, and their number increased beyond those needed for ley sighting.

The first coming of the sighted track was assuredly much nearer to a glacial period than was, for instance, the beginning of the Christian era, and trees not being plentiful, they were not in the way of sighting methods.

All down the ages the mark-points of the tracks were assembly points for the people, for law, administration, religion, trade, and recreation.

The mounds became larger, often enlarged from a smaller one. The use of the beacon made the natural trench round a mound of importance as reflecting light from a distance when filled with water. In later times it served as a ring of defence.

Ponds were dug as sighting points by reflection on the track, and through them a stone causeway sometimes ran.

With the "advance of civilization" came wars and invasions, and camps were used for defence.

The mark stones of the old straight track naturally became the points where the trader or pedlar—whether the knapper or "chip" man, who brought flints, the "white" or salt man, or the crock or "red" man who carried pots—called at on his way, and here the people knew where to find him, and markets evolved from mark stones. At the mounds, as well as at the stones and the mark trees, the courts of the land met, whether for administration or for law enactment, for all such were in the open air, even to the election of a king.

With the coming of Christianity the sites of many mark stones, "temples," and pagan altars became the sites of Christian churches or churchyard crosses, and almost all these, if of ancient foundation, align on the straight tracks, as do crosses on the wayside.

The Romans enormously raised the standard of dwelling-houses in Britain; the old hut circles had become a thing of the past; round the churches clustered in most cases the new villages, and the camps were abandoned, or, if not too large, appropriated by a great lord for his stronghold. Round the mark stones the markets expanded—the nucleus of the new towns which sprang into existence.

In the churches there lingered evidence of the old fact that they occupied mark sites, in the steeple which was still a landmark, the beacon tower which still in some cases sent forth a light to guide the traveller "o'er moor and fen, o'er crag and torrent till the night is gone." Popular legend and reverence still played round the old stone, tree, or mound.

But the sites could not be put to new uses and still retain their old one. Homesteads were planted on the mark stones and round the sighting ponds. The day of the old straight track was passing.

Almost level contour tracks, along the valley, but high on the side of the hill, in round the cwms, and out round the headlands, were engineered; and ridgeway tracks (no longer straight) along the mountain-tops evolved.

Mound burial continued after the track decayed, and new mounds not needed for sighting points were probably added—clustering on or round the old tracks.

The increase of woodland growth with an altered climate might have been a factor in this decay, for although a sighted ley was perhaps kept efficient by the clearing of trees in the line (and the earliest dictionary meaning of ley or lea confirms this), it was a heavy task for the community.

The need for short-distance expediency tracks from homestead to homestead and from town to town began, and finally destroyed the value of the old straight track.

The mark-points remained sites of interest, reverence, or assembly, and were coveted and used for defensive castles, utilizing and enlarging the mound and moat as a defence.

The seer, the ley-man, the astronomer-priest, the Druid were practically wiped out at the Roman invasion, but some branches of their work survived in the bard, the magician, the hermit, and the pilgrim; and down the ages their implement of work and of authority—the sighting staff—survived in the rod or sceptre of power, the wand of office, the pilgrim's staff, and the magician's wand.

The Romans were probably the last to practise in Britain the laying down of the sighted track. They came equipped in the method, but equipped in a different school; and although immeasurably superior to the native tradition in road surface and width, most of their work in Britain appears to be more or less planted on the old British tracks.

The post-Roman dykes, such as Offa's, were sinuous, not

straight, in their general course, but here and there they were planted on fragments of the old tracks.

In its full development, the old track was no mean achievement in surveying and engineering. Road-making was not part of its scheme, for the attitude seems to have been: "Mother earth is good enough for you to walk or ride on, and we will pave a way through the streams, soft places, and ponds; our chief job is to point out the way." This the old ley-men did magnificently.

To realize how, imagine a fairy chain stretched from mountain peak to mountain peak, as far as the eye could reach, and paid out until it touched the "high places" of the earth at a number of ridges, banks, and knowls. Then visualize a mound, circular earthwork, or clump of trees, planted on these high points, and in low points in the valley other mounds ringed round with water to be seen from a distance. Then great standing stones brought to mark the way at intervals, and on a bank leading up to a mountain ridge or down to a ford the track cut deep so as to form a guiding notch on the skyline as you come up. In a bwlch or mountain pass the road cut deeply at the highest place straight through the ridge to show as a notch afar off. Here and there and at two ends of the way, a beacon fire used to lay out the track. With ponds dug on the line, or streams banked up into "flashes" to form reflecting points on the beacon track so that it might be checked when at least once a year the beacon was fired on the traditional day. All these works exactly on the sighting line. The wayfarer's instructions are still deeply rooted in the peasant mind to-day, when he tells you—quite wrongly now—"You just keep straight on."

• • • • •

Out from the soil we wrench a new knowledge, of old, old human skill and effort, that came to the making of this England of ours.

For as Puck, in Rudyard Kipling's tale sings:

She is not any common Earth
Water or wood or air,
But Merlin's Isle of Gramarye,
Where you and I will fare.

APPENDIX A

LEY HUNTING

All the country is lay'd for me.
—" 2 Henry VI "

BOTH indoor map and outdoor field exploration are necessary. Field work is essential. It is surprising how many mounds, ancient stones, and earthworks are to be found which are not marked, even on the large scale maps. I often feel sure from small indications—such as the knowl marked by a tuft of trees, the two or three Scotch firs in straggling line, the conformation of a road with a footpath and then a hedgerow, the general " lay of the land "—that a ley exists in a certain direction. But nothing can be done without the map, and for working directions I repeat those given in my earlier book with little alteration.

You must use Government Ordnance maps. One mile to the inch is the working scale. Other maps of two or four miles to the inch are quite useless, save for checking long leys.

The (B) " Popular edition, mounted and folded in covers for the pocket," is the most convenient for field work and is the cheapest, as it contains over double the area of the older (C) 18 by 12 edition; but I have found the latter (uncoloured, in flat sheets) necessary for transferring leys from one map to the next on drawing boards in the office.

Maps cut in sections are useless for this exact work.

Two drawing boards, a light 24-inch straight edge, a T-square for pinning down the maps accurately to line with the boards, a movable head T-square to adjust to the angle of the ley, so as to transfer to the next map, a transparent circular protractor for taking orientations, and a box of the glass-headed pins used by photographers (in addition to the usual drawing-pins) are the minimum essentials for real work. A sighting or prismatic compass for field work used in conjunction with the movable head of the square are aids I have found valuable.

Pin down the map, square on a drawing board with the T-square passing through identical degree marks on the edges, latitude for leys running east and west, but longitude for leys north and south. The edges of the maps are not truly in line with the degree lines, and must not be the guide.

Look out on the map all named points on it of the following classes:

(1) Ancient mounds, whether called tumulus, tump, barrow, cairn, or other name.
(2) Ancient unworked stones—not those marked "boundary stone."
(3) Moats, and islands in ponds or lakelets.
(4) Traditional or holy wells.
(5) Beacon points.
(6) Cross-roads with place-names, and ancient wayside crosses.
(7) Churches of ancient foundation, and hermitages.
(8) Ancient castles, and old "castle" place-names.

With a "bow pen" make an ink ring about ⅜-inch diameter round each of these points, the pivot leg of the instrument being stuck into the exact point.

Stick a pin into an undoubted mark-point (as a mound or traditional stone), place a straight edge against this and move to see if three other ringed points (or two and a piece of existing straight road or track) can be found to align. If so, rule a pencil line (provisionally) through the points. You may then find on that line fragments here and there of ancient roads and footpaths; also bits of modern roads conforming to it. Extend the line into adjoining maps, and you may find new sighting points on it, and it will usually terminate at both ends in a natural hill or mountain peak.

When you get a good ley on the map, go over it in the field, and fragments and traces of the trackways may be found, always in straight lines, once seen recognized with greater ease in future.

Make a rule to work on sighting points, and not, tempting as it sometimes is, to take a straight bit of road or track as evidence. Such a straight stretch should be treated as a suggestion for a trial. If supported by three or four points, it becomes corroborative evidence. Three points alone do not prove a ley, four being the minimum. But three-point evidence—or one point and straight road—might find support in an adjoining map.

Where close detail is required, as in villages and towns, the one-inch scale is far too small, and the six-inch scale is necessary. The angle of the ley is transferred to it from the one-inch map with the aid of the movable head square.

If you travel along the actual sighting line you may find fragments of the road showing as a straight trench in untilled land, although these are few and far between, as the plough obliterates it all. The line usually crosses a river at a known ford or ferry.

In field work remember that if the evidence were plentiful and easy to find the ley system would have been discovered long ago, that ancient tracks and roads (and most of the barrows and mark stones) have disappeared wherever the plough touches, and that bits to be found are few and far between. Also that if you get on the " high place " of a proved ley, it is very seldom that you can see parts of the track from the height, or even any ponds or moats " on the ley "—trees almost always prevent.

It is detective rather than surveying work in the field. But there are plenty of unrecorded finds to be made by following a ley.

In map work certain characteristics constantly occur. The ley seeks out ancient camps, and often borders them, or passes through a mound in the earthwork. But it is impracticable to " ring " camps, as they are not points. A bit of zigzag in a road is almost invariably at the point where an ancient track crossed " at the zig." Such a point on the Hereford-Peterchurch road was known by the ancient place-name (not supported by any other " ches "- name near) of the Cheshire Turn, and a ley was found on it.

Keep your eyes open when cycling or motoring on a bit of straight road for any hill point or mound, church or castle on a bank, which is not only straight in front, but keeps fixed in the same position as you travel; for such an observation almost certainly leads to the discovery of a ley through the point and on the road.

A genuine ley hits the cross-roads or road junctions as if by magic. And it treats them as points, because mark stones once (if not now) existed at them, for it seldom lies on the present roads which cross there.

Where two or three field paths converge at a point, such a point is often on a ley, for such points and cross track points remain unchanged down the ages, when the tracks have perhaps all changed in position. It is almost laughable to find where a ley crosses a road, even if diagonally, how often there is a field gate on each side for it to go through. Field entrances remain unchanged for centuries, and at the first enclosure no doubt the entrance would be at an old track.

Faint traces of ancient track or earthwork are most easily seen when the sun is low on one side—in late evening. For this reason, and for the absence of leaves on trees, winter is by far the best time of year for a certain type of exploration, camp earthworks for example. Sun shining on one side and very low down is an ideal condition.

The method in the future is an aeroplane flight along the ley.

Faint tracks are to be seen from the air (as Mr. O. G. S. Crawford has pointed out) which are invisible on the ground. It is one of many war-time discoveries.

Remember when investigating leys round structures of ancient importance—such as Tintern Abbey or Stonehenge—that the simple stone which settled its site was probably of no more importance than scores of others all round it, and you will often find an important long-distance ley come within a hundred yards of what seems to you the all-important site, and take not the slightest notice of it.

The great multiplicity of leys in a small area will surprise and perplex you, but you will have to accept it as a fact.

APPENDIX B

BUCKINGHAMSHIRE LEYS

THESE are taken from the folding map in "Place-names of Buckinghamshire" issued (1925) by the English Place-name Society, whose members can verify the alignments with aid of a straight-edge on the map. Field investigation would probably add unmarked stones and earthworks on these leys. The proofs of ancient roads (such as the Icknield Way) being continued as leys beyond their present use, and of the alignment of churches, are here very complete:

I. The eight mile length of Watling Street, which comes down through Stony Stratford, aligns through Shenley, Great Brickhill, and Ilsworth Churches, and the centre of Maiden Castle earthwork near Dunstable.

II. The five mile straight length of Akeman Street, east of Aylesbury, extended in alignment westward, coincides with three short lengths of Akeman Street, and eastward to Berkhamstead Castle, thus stretching across the map.

III. Several miles of the Lower Icknield Way (north of Princes Risborough), although in broken fragments, are on a ley through Aston Rowant and Marsworth Churches.

IV. The three miles of the Icknield Way through Dunstable (diverted to go round the church) align through Dunstable, Toternhoe, Hulcot, and Chilton Churches.

V. A five mile straight length of Akeman Street (on the left side of the map) aligns through confirming points to Ivinghoe Church.

VI. An alignment comes down through Berkhamstead Castle, through a "moat" and then a "camp" west of Chesham, the "camp" (with church or chapel on) at West Wickham, Fingest Church, and an ancient church east of Nettlebed.

VII. Horn Hill Church, "Camp" near Lee, Beaconhill Farm, Alton Church, two moats east of Aylesbury, and a moat near Elmdon (N.W. corner of map) all align.

VIII. Six churches—Hartwell, Grafton Regis, Lillingstone Lovel, Lillingstone Dayrell, Tingewick, and Barton Hartshorn—are on one alignment.

IX. Five churches—Pyrton, Lewknor, Kingston Blount, Crowell, and Monks Risborough—align to a 811 feet hill near Ivinghoe.

X. Through the above 811 feet hill five other churches—Kensworth, Whipsnade, Halton, Sydenham, and Chalgrove—also align.

XI. A white or salt ley runs from White Hill (E. of Moulsford), over White Hill (E. of Cholsey), and through Ewelme, Cuxham, Wheatfield, and Whitchurch Churches.

XII. To the great mound of Windsor (the centre of the castle ground-plan on the map) comes an alignment which lies on the length of Stowe Avenue, 45 miles away, and it passes through Stowe, Fleet Marston, and Little Kimble Churches.

XIII. To Windsor Castle Mound is also aligned Queen Anne's Ride in Windsor Great Park.

XIV. The Long Walk in Windsor Park, although not sighted on the mound, but through the residential part of the Castle, continues as a ley through Stoke Poges Church and Stoke Court to Berkhamstead Castle, a centre for at least five alignments.

XV. An exactly N. and S. alignment (at left-hand edge of the map) runs up from Lollington Hill (316 ft. Ord. mark) through left edge of Sinodun Camp, Dyke Hills, cross road marked Joseph's Stone, left vallum of Alchester Camp (the supposed ÆLIA CASTRUM), and a "Camp" near Evenley. This ley lies on five miles of a present-day track.

APPENDIX C

OXFORD CITY LEYS

THESE two leys are specified on page 121, but crossing as they do at Carfax, which was the centre of early municipal life, they are so interesting to all lovers of Oxford that a sketch map (Fig. 128) is here added. The northern

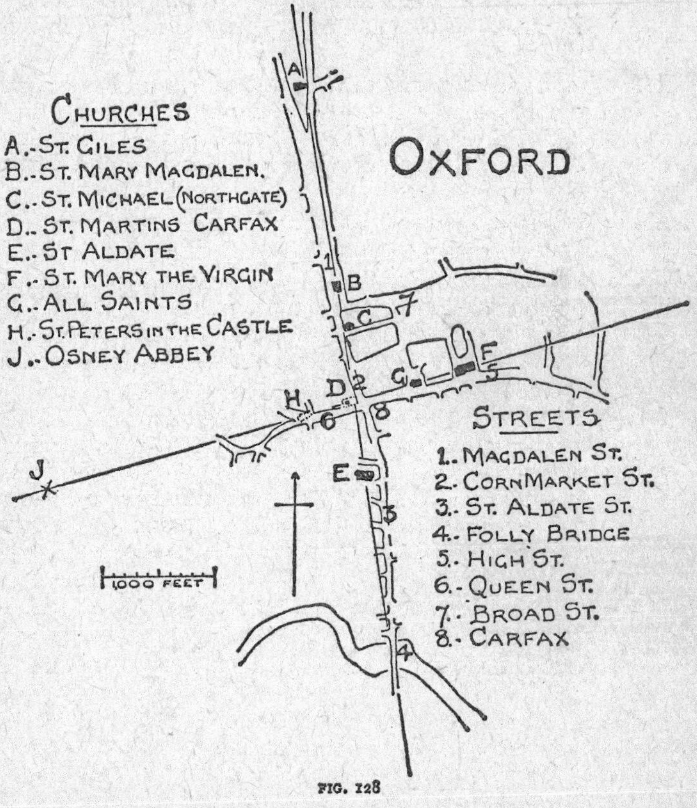

FIG. 128

ley so closely touches St. Michael's tower that it is doubtful whether this and not the Northgate was not on the original mark-point. And the western ley goes through the site of Osney Abbey, a fact not at first noted.

APPENDIX D

BRECON CAMPS

THE Gaer Camp (at which skilled excavations on the site of the Roman settlement are now proceeding), and three earlier camps near it, afford such clear evidence of alignment, deciding the sites of both types of camps, that a sketch map (Fig. 129) is deemed necessary.

This evidence is remarkably complete in the case of the three early camps—Twyn-y-Gaer Camp, Camp in Fenni Wood, and Pen-y-Crug Camp (all within three miles)—for two alignments

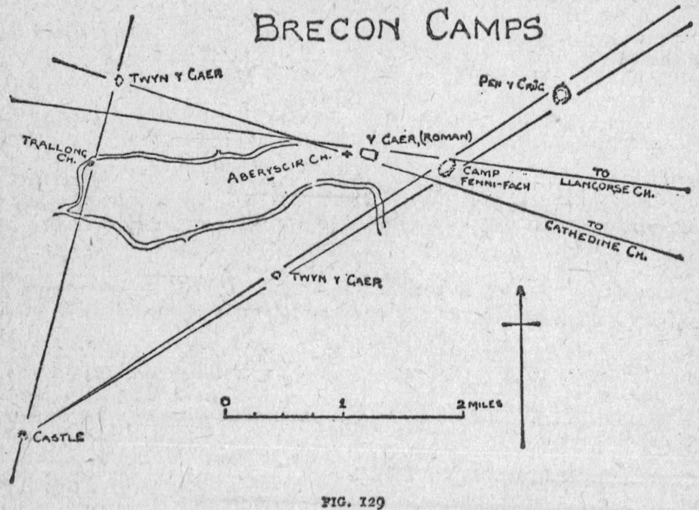

FIG. 129

radiating from a large mound marked "Castle" exactly touch the northern and southern entrenchments of all three, which are, however, entirely of contour outline.

In the case of the Roman settlement, both north vallum and south vallum (not influenced by contour lines) appear to me to be entirely decided by pre-existing track alignments.

The ley on the south vallum is the one with most corroborative points; besides Twyn-y-Gaer Camp and Aberscir Church to the west, on the east when approaching the Black Mountains it lies on several lengths of present road, through a tumulus near Treberfedd and Catherdine Church.

INDEX

Contractions: Cas. = Castle.
Ch. = Church.
Cp. = Camp.
Md. = Mound.